True Tales *of the*
Mojave Desert

CENTER BOOKS ON THE AMERICAN WEST

GEORGE F. THOMPSON, SERIES FOUNDER AND DIRECTOR

Thousands of petroglyphs such as these of bighorn sheep dot the Mojave Desert. No one knows for sure what they mean or who carved them into boulders and cliff faces, but the strange figures serve as modern links to the dream world of the Mojave's original inhabitants.

True Tales *of the*

Mojave Desert:

From Talking Rocks

to Yucca Man

EDITED BY PETER WILD

THE CENTER FOR AMERICAN PLACES
SANTA FE, NEW MEXICO, AND
STAUNTON, VIRGINIA

PUBLISHER'S NOTES: *True Tales of the Mojave Desert: From Talking Rocks to Yucca Man* is the inaugural volume in a new series entitled *Center Books on the American West.* This book was issued in an edition of 400 hardcover and 2,100 paperback copies with the generous support of the Friends of the Center for American Places, for which the publisher is most grateful. The publisher also thanks *Popular Science* and all others who waived their fees in order to make this book possible. Original sources and specially requested credits, permissions, and/or copyright information appear at the end of individual chapters in the text. For more information about the Center for American Places and the publication of *True Tales of the Mojave Desert,* please see page 214.

The Center for American Places, Inc.
P.O. Box 23225
Santa Fe, New Mexico 87502, U.S.A.
www.americanplaces.org

Distributed by the University of Chicago Press
www.press.uchicago.edu

9 8 7 6 5 4 3 2 1

ISBN 1-930066-19-8 (hc)
ISBN 1-930066-20-1 (pbk)

Library of Congress Cataloging-in-Publication Data is available from the publisher upon request.

Contents

Introduction

LYING BETWEEN THE GAMBLING EMPIRE of Las Vegas to the east and the megalopolis of Los Angeles on the Pacific Coast, the Mojave Desert, one of today's busiest transportation corridors, is the best-known arid region in the nation. Reflecting that beyond a surface familiarity this harsh land is all but unknown by the general public, the book you hold is unique, the first gathering of material exploring the rich intricacies of the incredibly varied story of the Mojave Desert.

In parallel fashion and more personally, the book also is an exploration of the human spirit, the often unfulfilled but sustaining yearnings of us all. That is, I would argue, a central element with ramifications into the surprising worlds of the Mojave ranging from its little-known but brutal slave trade to the sometimes violent white settlement to today's more beneficent aesthetic approaches to what in total is the treasure of our desert heritage. To grasp such things in their full dramatic sharpness, however, requires some brief comment on the much larger context of American culture from which it arises.

In their ecstatic moments the New England transcendentalists sat watching their gentle woods shimmer before their very eyes into spiritual intimations corresponding with the earnest longings of their own souls. Since at least the mid–nineteenth century, the buoyant airiness has been a strong and persistent aspect of romanticism, and of American nature writing in particular, through the decades and into our own times, as the writings of Frederick Law Olmsted, John Muir, Joseph Wood Krutch, and Annie Dillard readily bear out. Nature succors, even reflects, our deepest, beneficent selves. The impulse in great part helped engender a delicacy of prose informing our culture, a vibrating electric thread running through the main strain of American writing.

This would not apply directly, however, to the early Anglo experience of nature in the brutal land of the Mojave Desert. As Irene Brennan says of military assignments there, "Being ordered to Fort Mojave in the 1860s was like banishment to hell" (vi). Just about everyone of the day, soldier or not, reflected the revulsion. This vast, gaping, dry, Dantean landscape of rock and sand overwhelmed the beholder. And it wasn't only Anglos from the green and well-watered East who trembled at that grim prospect. The few Indians who lived in the midst of nature's hostility did so by default. They had been pushed out into this great no man's land by stronger tribes who had given them the sharp choice of death or the constant rigors of staying alive in a place so barren, so destitute of food and water that no sane person would willingly choose it for a home. As to the arrival of the somewhat more fortunate Spanish and Anglos, the Mojave Desert was a bewildering phenomenon in ways beyond concerns for survival as they staggered across it. That a supposedly benevolent Providence would create a useless expanse in the Great Plan for a good earth presented an unfathomable reality shaking travelers' deepest foundations. Could God have made a mistake? Whatever the theological churnings, people facing this wasteland had a more immediate purpose: To cross the wide evil as quickly as possible and arrive at some other, better place, as embodied in the wonders of palm trees, fruiting gardens, and the soothing sea breezes of coastal California.

In contrast there was little, indeed, gentle about the Mojave, and in consequence early writings about it reflect no such impulse toward belles-lettres as flowered from the Apollonian New England mind, metaphysically secure among amiable green hills. When somewhat past the mid–nineteenth century, people of European background began coming to the Mojave to stay, they were driven into the desert by economics. Railroad tracks needed to be laid and forts established to protect transportation routes. A few adventurers wandered about picking out the little gold and silver to be found there. People came to the desert to make a living as best they could, not to write literature for future generations.

Yet cultures undergo strange, unpredictable mutations. When in the 1880s some of the greatest strikes of precious metals on record lured men by the thousands in a mad, greedy rush into the sandy stretches, attitudes went through a marvelous change. The Mojave wasn't a waste-land after all! Overnight a person could become fabulously rich (so went the common enthusiasm), and in that interplay of fantasy and reality, of economics coloring hopes and in turn influencing views of the land, sud-denly the Mojave was a beautiful place. The very site of the greatest sil-ver strike, in the past unnamed because useless places need no names, now became the Calico Hills—for the lovely bands of colors glowing there in the sunsets.

The flood had started. Along with the discovery of the "new" Mojave came other benefits, some real, some imagined, but all compelling to the fevered American mind. Strange fruits, known only in Sinbad tales, would spring out of the soils of the former wasteland. Yet if oranges, withered by the Mojave's winter cold, didn't quickly line one's pockets, other things would. The get-rich-quick schemes became an exciting emollient ranging from plans for vast eucalyptus groves to grandiose real-estate dreams promising cities soon to rival Boston and Pittsburgh in wealth and culture. Supporting all this would be alfalfa fields waxing acrylic-green from horizon to horizon, great steel mills, and (fantastic as it sounds today) hydroelectric plants tapping imagined subterranean reservoirs to infuse all with unlimited energy. The genie of hope, once released, went through amazing transmogrifications. Of course, in all this frenzy, in all this reinventing of reality, there was some truth—small kernels, at least—enough to keep the fantasies bubbling; some people *did* get rich, often from one scam or another, then scurried off to build man-sions in San Francisco, while, more democratically, others discovered the desert's dry air was a balm for the nagging and sometimes deadly respi-ratory problems then plaguing America in the age before antibiotics. All these things coming together in no way abrogated the realities, only dis-guised them; but in terms of the culture they effectively turned the Mojave into a dreamland of wealth and health for many people follow-ing the old lure, the old longing in the process of America's westering toward the chimera of a Promised Land.

Other factors came into play here, injecting further eupeptic elements into the vision of the Mojave. They arose from the old strain of romanti-cism, transplanted thousands of miles. As forests fell and prairies turned into suburbs, America was running out of wilderness. Where could one go to peer into pristine Nature and see the face of God conjoined with the soul's desires? Loudly bannering the appeal of the exotic, then much in vogue—after all, the desert was the nation's weirdest landscape—John C. Van Dyke had the answer. Flee out there to the long-ignored desert! So he shouted in 1901—out there where the wolves run free, the heel of man has not yet sullied the land, and each evening in a Wagnerian performance the sun crashes down through the dramatic rock spires. As it happened, there were no wolves on the Mojave Desert, but the fact of the matter hardly staunched Van Dyke's frothing enthusiasm as it worked on the Mojave's landscape. That took some change of mindset, of course; yet, so fueled by romance, the ugly had become the beautiful, the desolate the sublime—at least for those writers who could afford the luxury of such notions and for readers in Connecticut and Ohio enjoying them vicariously in the comfort of their homes. Settlers on the Mojave might continue to ditch and grub as they always had in their endless and often futile struggle to get enough water to grow corn and beans. Significantly, however, Van Dyke was an outsider—certainly not a grubber in the earth—a man of considerable means, a rarefied art critic from New Jersey's prestigious Rutgers College (now University). He whizzed across the Mojave in plush Pullman cars, spinning the delicate prose fantasies awing the late Victorians as well as inspiring us today. Yet, as we'll see in the following pages, he was but among the first of many fortunate Ausländer turning oneiric in the land of little rain and much suffering.

All of which is to say that, no matter how lofty literature may become, its underpinnings are the nuts and bolts of reality, in the case of the Mojave a harsh and insistent reality eventually breaking through dreams and demanding its due. For this, in this sometimes beautiful confusion, the literature of the Mojave is no one thing. As reflected ahead, it is instead a sometimes boisterous, sometimes richly enameled, panoply, a blend, sometimes even a turmoil, involving economic forces, aesthetics, thrill-seeking, political conflicts, hard times, and just plain hooliganism. We'll find a shocking slave trade, the whim-whams of desert "character" Death Valley Scotty as he charms a nation clamoring for a desert Disneyland, and the early (and extremely dangerous) flying that turned the first goggled, scarf-arrayed, pistol-packing aviators into Mojave heroes.

At first glance, little of this will be evident to modern Mojave visitors. They stop to gaze out from some designated traveler's vista on a scene more sea-like than of the land—on an endless undulation of lava-black peaks washed by white sand climbing up their sides in a strange new version of waves forever frozen. All is still. The impression is of repose and peace in a great space, is redolent of a profundity we feel but cannot define. This is the calm beyond understanding. What can be said about such a place when the impression itself, perhaps in a realm outside meaning, is so moving?

Given this, in compiling a representative selection of writings about the Mojave Desert caution is in order against the temptation to pick and choose, to come up with the most colorful events—the lynchings, flouncing prostitutes, and barroom brawls—Hollywood has schooled us to expect and which we in turn accept as familiar and hence valid. As indicated earlier, anything approaching the truth of the Mojave is much more subtle and complex than that; yet the crux of the matter, letting us off the hook, is that the story of the Mojave is so colorful in itself that angling for effect hardly is necessary. The slave trade stands for itself and needs no dandifying; the facts of Death Valley Scotty's life are so bizarre they need no colorful daubing. This is so, I'd at least suggest, because of a basic irony lying at the Mojave's heart.

Deserts always have been places for visions; and barren as the Mojave is, yet forced into the nation's consciousness by the necessity of crossing it, this particular desert has always been a fantasyland, first of the bewitching mirages torturing fainting travelers, then the locus of sometimes extravagant aspirations, as if human hope grows huge when most challenged, as if the most sandy ground will yield the most flamboyant flowers. Flowers often found, we might add, more in the mind than erupting out of the cracks in the Mojave's rocks and alkaline soils. Yet, still, as we'll see, out there, while some see spaceships whispering down at night, citizens nonetheless have dreamed and made their dreams real, witness not only the astonishing yet mundane fact of ordinary people today actually living on the Mojave, but the crenelated castles here and there dotting the Mojave's stretches.

Which is to say that in few other landscapes do fantasy and reality live on such familiar terms, sometimes overlapping until the two lose their identities as they blend into their own reality—gauzy, semilegendary. This in the trickery of yearning also is a valid aspect of history, of the human experience on the Mojave. On the one hand, much to the good in my way of thinking, the Mojave today, as was even more evident in the past, is so sparsely settled that each person, each individual, brilliant or not, rich or poor, assumes an iconographic importance in the larger society. Yet typical of the strangeness of the Mojave, that appealing stability is no guarantee of solid psychic ground, for coexisting with it is another trembling reality challenging our grasp of everyday life. Because of this, at times in my wanderings over this desert I have returned a troubled writer. Did I really have that surreal conversation in the ramshackle mountaintop lair of a man called Crazy Rob? On yet another occasion, I could not possibly have entered an old barn standing abandoned in a field and seen there, before my eyes, whirring computers and men in neckties gazing at banks of monitors, while secretaries in beehive hairdos teetered on high heels earnestly up and down the halls. Surely such must have been Dickensian, caused by a bit of undigested pickle; yet for all that, I know what I saw. Or so I think. We need to dream, no matter how troubling the dreams may be. Many of us would have it no other way.

Today, as we've outlined in rough geographical dimensions, the Mojave Desert is that great space lying between the pulsing neon empire of Las Vegas to the east and the nearly incomprehensible urban hodgepodge of the Los Angeles area, over the mountains on the Pacific Coast. Parsing the Mojave's characteristics and boundaries more closely certainly can be done comfortably enough for most of us, but it will bring frustration to perfectionists. As with many a definition, that of the Mojave starts blurring around the edges. Even scientists sometimes disagree about the exact extent of this and other deserts. However, specialists Gary Hulett and Amanda Charles give a helpful, if somewhat clinical, outline of the Mojave:

> Smallest of the North American deserts, found mainly in south-eastern California, southern Nevada, northwestern Arizona, and extreme southwestern Utah and blending biotically with the Great

Basin Desert to the north and the Sonoran Desert to the south; generally thought to be transitional between these two larger North American deserts. . . . The Mojave Desert exhibits a typical basin and range physiography with several north-south mountain ranges, extensive bajadas, and numerous undrained basins (368).

This, however, hardly captures the emotion, the aura of the Mojave, for in whatever terms we consider this land of sand and rock, with its bare mountains towering over empty lakes, the Mojave is a strange place, an anomaly in modern America. The landscape seems an apparent emptiness, yet one rich in undiscovered history—a refuge for armed lunatics, seekers of ashrams, and government schemers carrying out Big Plans beyond the public's view—but most importantly a domain, for all its lack of people, roiled by battles over a future which soon will tell what kind of accommodation we want to make with the land and thus what we ourselves as a nation wish to become.

The story of a particular landscape can be a threatening pursuit because it challenges our present comfort. People commonly see the Mojave, with its graceful lines and subtle colors, as a restful place, a place of profound, inenarrable peace. That view is entirely valid; but behind it lie disturbing complexities, conflicts, and ironies. For all its apparent ageless stability and impressive repose, the Mojave has been a land of flux, and not only because of the earthquakes that periodically turn the land into a moving liquid. In a larger sense, it is a flux speeding into turmoil the closer one comes to modern times. The Indians who roamed there before recorded history, perhaps counterbalancing somewhat their hard lives, were supreme dreamers, as may be seen in their rock art and myths. The slave trade their neighbors started, continued by the Spaniards, only contributed to the harshness. Then in the Anglo period came the disruptions of mining crazes, ranches, military clashes, and the laying of railroad tracks in the 1880s. Thus began the era of technology, followed by Barney Oldfield, the Human Comet, blasting across the Mojave in his Stutz, the beginnings of mass agriculture dependent on pumps, and from all this the growth of cities and military bases—a growth in more recent times deeply pondered and met by urges to reverse such intrusions on nature by strong movements to counter modern forces and preserve the desert as it once was.

Yet in many ways the Mojave continues to reflect what it was to the wandering bands of Chemehuevis; as escapees from the cities such as Crazy Rob reinvent their lives in mountaintop aeries appropriately fortified against civilization to match their bizarre imaginings; as society's disaffected flock to communes in hopes that the desert will yield them spiritual balm; and as strange craft zoom out of secret airfields to bewitch the night. That is, whatever the changes, the Mojave remains a dreamland, perhaps more so, and more ominously, than ever before.

The following, drawing on my many years of research in the Mojave and several resulting books, is taken from letters, novels, newspaper articles, and personal reminiscences—all echoing the above hopes and shifts over the years. I've kept the introductions to selections relatively short, giving mainly information required to understand the context and out of respect for the material chosen, because each offers a richness requiring little more than minimum background to grasp its many implications. Those reverberations, however, certainly go on and on. For readers interested in the pleasure of pursuing them further, a suggested booklist might be nearly endless. That aside, a very fine start would be W. Storrs Lee's *The Great California Deserts*. Lee gracefully shows the cultural, economic, and demographic forces coming together to shape both our attitudes toward deserts and the deserts themselves. More formally, Clifford Walker's *Back Door to California: The Story of the Mojave River Trail* traces the history of the region from the age of giant sloths and lush forests of palm trees through the era of conquistadors and cowboys to the present. My own anthology *The Desert Reader: Descriptions of America's Arid Regions* gives the wider perspective, offering selections from classic writings over the years about the wide heritage of our arid lands. After that, the dessert: Dix Van Dyke's *Daggett: Life in a Mojave Frontier Town*, a sometimes rollicking account by rancher Dix of a frontier town dragged kicking and screaming into the modern world. The extensive bibliographies in these books will lead readers to many hours, possibly years, of enjoyable study.

As to other matters, my hope is that, as they explore the following, readers will find themselves entering the "other" world of the Mojave—that unknown world uniquely waiting to be discovered in any landscape—through authentic and sometimes chromatic documents, and will find through these that they are becoming adventurers on their own. Perhaps one thing needs mention. The word "Mojave" sometimes appears as "Mohave." The etymology of the word, going earlier through such weird stages as Jamajabs, Amaguagua, and even Hamoekháve, would make a book on its own. However, for present purposes all that's needed is to know that the more frequent "Mojave" most often is found in the California portion of that desert, while "Mohave" has more narrow geographical application. It usually is associated with the Indian tribe living along the banks of the Colorado River and with the nearby geographical features along that watery border separating California and Arizona. The edition of Erwin G. Gudde's *California Place Names: The Origin and Etymology of Current Geographical Names*, revised by William Bright, does neat scholarly work in setting forth the complexities of a word reflecting the intrigue, even the mysteries, of the whole region.

As to the texts of the following, a few obvious cases offer the prose as is, to preserve the homey flavor. Otherwise, in the main the following presents the texts of the original writings with only minor revisions, these particularly in cases of clearly unintended mistakes, such as obvious misspellings, whose retention would be of no value to the reader.

References

Brennan, Irene J., ed. *Fort Mojave, 1859–1890: Letters of the Commanding Officers.* Manhattan, Kansas: MA/AH Publishing, 1980.

Gudde, Erwin G. *California Place Names: The Origin and Etymology of Current Geographical Names.* 1949. Revised by William Bright. Berkeley: University of California Press, 1998.

Hulett, Gary K., and Amanda Renner Charles. "Mojave Desert." *Encyclopedia of Deserts.* Ed. Michael A. Mares. Norman: University of Oklahoma Press, 1999.

Lee, W. Storrs. *The Great California Deserts.* New York: G. P. Putnam's, 1963.

Van Dyke, Dix. *Daggett: Life in a Mojave Frontier Town.* Introd. Peter Wild. Baltimore: The Johns Hopkins University Press, 1997.

Van Dyke, John C. *The Desert: Further Studies in Natural Appearances.* 1901. Ed. Peter Wild. Baltimore: The Johns Hopkins University Press, 1999.

Walker, Clifford. *Back Door to California: The Story of the Mojave River Trail.* Ed. Patricia Jernigan Keeling. Barstow, California: Mojave River Valley Museum Association, 1986.

Wild, Peter, ed. *The Desert Reader: Descriptions of America's Arid Regions.* Salt Lake City: University of Utah Press, 1991.

GALLERY

Chemehuevi Indians. A small and weak tribe, the Chemehuevi were driven into the wasteland of the Mojave Desert by more powerful neighbors. Wandering the expanses of sand and rock, the Chemehuevi survived by eating lizards, roots, and rats.

Mohave Indians. Tall, powerful, and well fed, the Mohaves fished the Colorado River and farmed its rich bottomlands. The Mohaves also traveled widely, both out of curiosity and to make war, and were proud of their position as a dominant force in the Mojave region.

Olive Oatman. Taken captive as a girl, she was tattooed by the Indians who turned her into their white slave. Photograph (AHS 1927) reproduced by permision of the Arizona Historical Society, Tucson.

Conquest of the Mojave by camels. A U.S. soldier sits atop one of Lt. Beale's famous camels, conquering the Mojave's distances. Eventually turned loose, some of the camels survived into modern times, their weird, surprise appearances as they gawked over sand dunes giving lonely prospectors the jimjams.

Another monster on the Mojave. Lt. Ives's steamboat, *Explorer*, chugs up the Colorado River, astounding the Indians. They mocked the adventurers, however, when the belching craft repeatedly became stuck on sand bars.

Top: A rough Mojave town. Daggett, California, here about 1906, periodically boomed and busted through waves of silver strikes and land speculation. A smiling Death Valley Scotty stands center, arms akimbo. Today, the little town looks much as it does in this photo.

Bottom right: Daggett's justice of the peace. Representing the law in a wild place, the local "Judge" either matched the town's toughness or quit. This one, T. S. Van Dyke, stayed, filling the position for more than twenty years. He was not a man to trifle with. Photograph reproduced by permission of The Huntington Library, San Marino, California (Theodore P. Lukens Papers, Box 7, Album 4).

A settler's cabin on the Mojave, early twentieth century. Despite the Spartan aspects, this was an upscale dwelling as compared to the caves, tents, and holes in the ground often occupied by early settlers.

A prospector sets forth. Despite the hardscrabble life offered by the Mojave, new-comers were a hopeful lot, buoyed by the fabulous riches rumored to be waiting them in the hills. Here in the central Mojave, a prospector strides out into the wild country, pursuing his dreams into the gold fields of the Ord Mountains.

Fred Harvey's hotels and restaurants dotted the railroad at strategic locations. This is Casa del Desierto, the Fred Harvey House in Barstow, California. The lavish establishment rising out of the bleak desert was a visual wonder in the Mojave. Not only that, as a forerunner of civilization it offered stately rooms and gracious meals. This particular building, under restoration, may be visited by today's travelers.

Barney Oldfield blasts through Barstow on the Los Angeles-to-Phoenix Road Race of 1914. Roaring in his Stutz across the sandy roads of the Mojave, the Human Comet heralded rapid changes to the desert as technology rang down the curtain on the frontier. By the way, Barney, a crowd favorite, won the race, but he was so covered with mud his fans didn't recognize him and burst into cheers as he zoomed toward the finish line only after they recognized him by the stub of a signature cigar in his mouth.

For the most part technology was a welcome change on the Mojave, bringing excitement and comfort to hard lives. In this 1925 photo, Lenora T. Helsom, the daughter of the deputy sheriff in the mining town of Silver Lake, glows with the thrill of her ride after coming down from a flight with a barnstorming pilot. Photograph reproduced by permission of Lenora T. Helson.

Change did not happen overnight. The prospector with his pick and burros persisted well into the twentieth century. This is F. M. "Shady" Myrick, the Mojave's foremost gem collector, in a portrait shortly before his death in 1925. Besides finding opals and jasper, affable Shady rescued lost tenderfeet addled by stories of gold, had two huge pet lizards, and lived in a cave.

Hard times for Shady. Prospecting could be a cruel mistress, brightly luring men on but often betraying their dreams. In this penciled letter Shady Myrick contacts relatives on the California coast. "All of my deals has fallen down," he writes, then asks "for enough [money] to pay all debts and enough to run for a while."

Fifty years of scouring the Mojave for gems had brought Shady fame as a desert character but left him broke. A depressed and aging Shady determines to "quit California. I will go back to Colorado and stay there. I am out of luck here." A few months later he died in Leadville, Colorado, where as a youth he had been a deputy sheriff.

With the comforts of technology, the desert turned friendly, almost downright fuzzy-wuzzy, at least to those reading about it. Published south of the Mojave, in Palm Desert, for decades, *Desert Magazine*, founded in 1937, promoted the romance of the desert, giving desert folk a positive image of themselves and inviting outsiders to explore such wonders as ghost towns and Indian reservations. This sketch of the magazine's new headquarters, built in 1948 in the Santa Fe style, catches the magazine's airy, almost transcendental, outlook. Today, the lovely building, surrounded by the boutiques and other modern glitz of fashionable Palm Desert, retains its charm at 74225 State Highway 111.

NEW HOME OF DESERT MAGAZINE, PALM DESERT, CALIFORNIA

Despite modern times and a growing population, in some ways the Mojave becomes ever more mysterious and unknowable. An airliner with no identifying marks takes off from Las Vegas's McCarran International Airport, passing the Luxor Casino on its way to the infamous Area 51.

Right: A flying saucer over the Mojave. Well, not exactly. This build-it-yourself model, put out by the Testor Corporation, incorporates the features of strange craft that hundreds of desert aficionados swear they have seen hovering over the cactus flats, then mysteriously disappearing. Reproduced by permission of the Testor Corporation.

Bottom: The heart of the Mojave. A few miles east of Barstow, the Calico Hills, famed for a fabulous silver strike in the late nineteenth century, rise to the left, while also to the left the sandy bed of the Mojave River meanders eastward into the desert distances. The Mojave, the nation's smallest desert, is nonetheless a place of vast spaces.

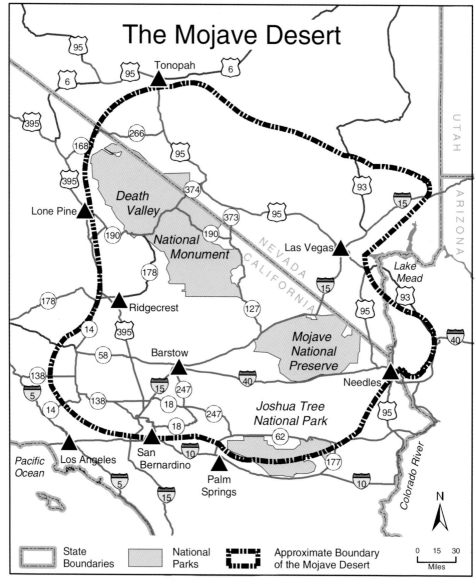

The Mojave Desert

The Mojave Desert. Located at the southern end of the Great Basin, the Mojave Desert (ca. 15,000 square miles) is an arid landscape of partially buried mountains (2,000 to 5,000 feet elevation) separating small drainage basins. Once part of an ancient interior sea, the desert was formed by volcanic action and material deposited by the Colorado River. Near its center, 100 miles west of Las Vegas, lies Death Valley, the lowest elevation in the United States. Annual rainfall in the Mojave, on average, is five inches, mostly in winter. (Sources: John C. Hudson, *Across This Land: A Regional Geography of the United States and Canada*, Johns Hopkins, 2002, and *The Columbia Encyclopedia, Fifth Edition*, Columbia, 1993.)

True Tales *of the*
Mojave Desert

The Talking Rocks
and the Chemehuevi Origin Myth
(Prehistory)

Thousands of charging warriors, leaping bighorn sheep, and a few Spanish conquistadors inhabit the Mojave. They may be seen on the boulders and the faces of cliffs across the desert where the figures were chipped hundreds, even thousands of years ago. No one knows for sure what the petroglyphs mean. Perhaps they depict spiritual visions, record everyday events, or simply are the doodling of bored travelers. Likely, they arise from a variety of impulses.

Who did them also is problematic, since the population of the Mojave hardly has been static through the centuries but a flux of peoples moving back and forth over this inhospitable land. However, although this strange rock art is but an example of the Mojave's intriguing mysteries, one thing is certain. Whatever their meaning, the images serve as a link to a psychic world totally different than our own, a link to a magical world in which animals and humans shift roles in a nonlinear series of events which nonetheless often have the convincing "rightness" of dreams.

Recorded by anthropologist A. L. Kroeber, of Ishi fame, the following is the origin myth of the Chemehuevi. A tiny Paiute tribe driven out of better lands by more powerful neighbors, they were consigned to wander the desert, surviving on lizards, roots, rats, and whatever else fortune brought their way.

THE HEROES ARE COYOTE and his elder brother Puma—the Chemehuevi equivalent of the Wolf of the northern Plateau—who build a house on Charleston Peak while the world is still covered with water. When the earth has become dry through the instrumentality of an old woman in the west, Hawichyepam Maapuch, Coyote, failing to find men, marries a louse, from whose eggs spring many tribes. The Chemehuevi themselves, however, the Mohave, and other southerners come from Coyote's own voidings. They are taught to eat game by being given parts of a person, a human example of animal food. Puma is killed by eastern enemies, who, unwinding a powerful object that he has made, bring on the first and an unbroken night. Coyote mourns, but wishes daylight to burn his brother's belongings. He restores it when he shoots the yellow-hammer. After the completion of the funerary rites— the instituting ones for the world—Coyote recovers his brother's scalp from the foes who are dancing before it and escapes their pursuit.

* From A. L. Kroeber. *Handbook of the Indians of California.* 1925. New York: Dover, 1976. 598.

4

What the Sky and Earth Did:
The Mohave Origin Myth
(Prehistory)

In contrast to the Chemehuevi and other desert wanderers, the Mohaves, of the Yuman group, were a powerful and numerous tribe well aware of their role as the area's foremost presence. Tall, well-fed, and athletic, they fished along the Colorado River and farmed its rich bottomlands, enjoying the luxury of taking breaks to travel widely. On trips of hundreds of miles, they trotted along, to trade as well as to make war. Their journeys also arose out of sheer curiosity to see what lay beyond the endless succession of desert mountain ranges.

The Mohaves' belief in dreams was especially intense, to such an extent that individuals' very identities were creations of what they dreamed their identities should be, explorations, as it were, even into their "shadow lives" before conception. Nonetheless, the Mohaves had their more traditional stories, bizarre and dreamlike as they might seem from our perspective. Here, making an interesting contrast with the Chemehuevi tale of the preceding selection, is the Mohave origin myth.

THE FIRST WERE SKY AND EARTH, male and female, who touched far in the west across the sea. Then were born from them Matavilya, the oldest; Frog, his daughter, who was to cause his death; his younger brother or son Mastambo, his successor and greater than he; and all men and beings. In four strides Matavilya led them upward to Aha'-av'ulypo, "house-post water," in Eldorado Canyon on the Colorado, above Mohave land; the center of the earth, as he found by stretching his arms. There he made his "dark round," the first house. With unwitting indecency he offended his daughter, and plotting against him, she swallowed his voidings, and he knew that he should die, and told the people. Coyote, always suspected, was sent away for fire, and then Fly, a woman, rubbed it on her thigh. Coyote raced back, leaped over Badger, the short man in the ring of people, snatched the god's heart from the pyre, and escaped with it. Mastambo directed the mourning, and Han'ava, the cicada, first taught how to wail. Korokorapa, also called Hiko or Haiko, "white man," alone had sat unmoved as Matavilya lay dying, now sank into the ground with noise, and returned westward to Pi'in, the place of universal origin.

Matavilya's ashes offended, and wind, hail, and rain failed to obliterate them. In four steps Mastambo strode far north, plunged his cane of breath and spittle into the earth, and the river flowed out. Entering a boat, Mastambo journeyed with mankind to the sea, twisting and tilting the boat or letting it run straight as he wished wide bottom lands or sharp canyons to frame the river. He returned with the people on his arms, surmounted the rising waters to the mountain Akokahumi, trod the water down, and took his followers upstream to the northern end of what was to be the Mohave country. Here he heaped up the great pointed peak Avikwame—more exactly Avikwa'ame—Newberry or Dead Mountain as the Americans call it, where he, too, built himself a house. It is of this house that shamans dream, for here their shadows were as little boys in the face of Mastambo, and received from him their ordained powers, confirmed by tests on the spot. Here, too, Mastambo made the people shout, and the fourth time day and sun and moon appeared.

Then he plotted the death of "sky rattlesnake," Kammay-aveta, also called Umas-ereha, a great power far south to the sea. Message after message was sent him; he knew that the sickness which he was summoned to cure was pretended; but at last he came, amid rain and thunder, stretching his vast length from ocean to mountain. As his head entered the great house it was cut off. It rolled back to the sea in the hope of reconstituting its living body, but became only an ocean monster; while from his blood and sweat and juices came rattlesnakes and noxious insects whose powers some shamans combat. This was the first shaman killed in the world.

Now Mastambo's work was nearly done. To Walpai, Yavapai, Chemehuevi, Yuma, and Kamia he gave each their land and mountains, their foods, and their speech, and sent them off. The youngest, the Mohave, he taught to farm, to cook in pottery, to speak and count as was best fit for them, and to stay in the country. Then meditating as to his own end, he stretched his arms, grew into saksak the fish eagle, and flew off, without power or recollection, ignorant and infested with vermin.

* From A. L. Kroeber. *Handbook of the Indians of California.* 1925. New York: Dover, 1976. 770–71.

❦

The Mojave Slave Trade

(Prehistory to ca. the 1860s)

Whatever fantasies we might enjoy from the natives' dream world, today's freeways, often following old Indian trails while speeding travelers across the Mojave, belie a more enduring if discomforting truth. Since ancient times this desert, barren as it is, has been a major transportation corridor between greener lands to the east and west. Much of the traffic of centuries past would shock us: droves of stolen horses and mules and, stumbling in their dust, distraught men, women, and children taken as slaves by warring parties and trekking for days through sands along routes we now cross in a few air-conditioned hours.

❦

Tᴴᴱ Iɴsᴛɪᴛᴜᴛɪᴏɴ ᴏғ sʟᴀᴠᴇʀʏ has had wide distribution in time and geography and in technique. It has existed throughout the world, involving all races over a period of many thousands of years. This inhuman, yet human, institution existed in North America before the continent was discovered by the Spanish-speaking people in the fifteenth century. The American Southwest had a history of slavery (and had some unique features of human bondage) during the Indian, Spanish, Mexican, and American periods. An important area and link in the slave trading in the southwest was the Mojave Desert with its ancient Mojave Indian Trail—a route that actually stretched beyond the confines of the Mojave Desert itself. It went from east of the Colorado River to the Mojave River and across the San Bernardino Mountains to the Pacific Ocean.

The Mohave Indians at one time occupied the land along both the Mojave River and the Colorado River, but later resettled in several villages along the Colorado River.[1] Here they became adept at raising muskmelons, watermelons, corn, beans, crude wheat, and even cotton.

8

They became middlemen in a trade that extended from the Hopi pueblos in Arizona and New Mexico to the coastal Indians around the present cities of Santa Barbara, Ventura, and San Gabriel. The network of routes had a branch that went as far north as Bakersfield, where the enterprising Mojave went to trade.[2] A branch of the Mojave Indian Trail later became part of the Old Spanish Trail and still later part of the Salt Lake City–Los Angeles road of "Forty-niner" fame.

In order to visualize the ancient trade system of the Mohave, one must read the accounts of the Spaniards who entered the Mojave Desert. The first Spaniard who entered the Mojave Desert in 1772 was Pedro Fages, looking for runaway soldiers and unhappy neophytes, who were not slaves per se, but were sometimes used for involuntary colonization and service.[3] Little is known of Fages's experiences in the Mojave Desert, but the second Spaniard who entered this desert fortunately recorded his observations in his diary. Fray Francisco Hermenegildo Garces in 1776 traveled up the Colorado River to the Needles area; and then with Mohave Indian guides, he continued on the Mojave Trail over to the Mojave River and across the San Bernardino Mountains to the San Gabriel Mission. Father Garces was credited with alerting California and Spanish authorities to the importance of the Mojave Indian Trail.

Even before reaching the Needles area, Garces recorded the Mohave Indians' practice of obtaining captive slaves.[4] In fact, the good padre's first encounter with the Mohave resulted in the purchase of two captive women slaves whom he later released and sent back to their own village. This purchase occurred while Garces was traveling up the Colorado River from the Yuma villages toward the Mohave villages. The Mohave had received word of the Spanish visitors among the Yuma, and being an inquisitive people, they were approaching the country of their southern friends to satisfy their innate curiosity. Garces shared his provisions with the Mohave party and discovered they had with them two captive Jalchedun (Halchidhoma) women.[5] It took some insistent bargaining before Garces succeeded in purchasing the two captive Indian women slaves with what he termed "a poor horse and some other small presents." After five more days of travel up the river toward the Mohave villages, Garces sent the two women slaves home with an old interpreter who had been instructed to assure the Halchidhoma of the missionary's friendship. Father Garces had principles of humanity not frequently encountered among mankind throughout the world during the eighteenth century.

The origin of slavery among the Mohave Indians was undoubtedly connected with their warlike operations. The practice evolved from simply killing their enemies to that of using those captured for work and trade. During a long prehistoric period, they had captured or traded for women and children whom they took back to their villages along the Colorado River. There the captured slaves were used to assist with the cultivation of crops planted in the rich soils of the overflow of the river. Sometimes the captured children were permitted to grow up and live with the Mohave. Slave women were sometimes adopted, tattooed at puberty, and even married. In some instances the slaves were traded to other tribes, killed, or even tortured until death resulted. Olive Oatman, whom the Mohave purchased from the Apache, was a white slave of the Mohave for approximately five years during the mid–nineteenth century. She related not only her own experiences, including being tattooed, but also the tribe's custom of killing a slave as a sacrifice should any member of the tribe be killed in battle.[6] Slaves were often tortured and killed if they attempted to escape and were recaptured. Lieutenant A. W. Whipple noted when he was traveling through the Mohave villages in 1854 that "several sad looking fellows in the crowd are slaves." An Indian war captive was considered a disgrace. Even if he were to be returned to his tribe, his family would discard him as unworthy.

*From Gerald A. Smith and Clifford Walker. *Indian Slave Trade along the Mojave Trail.* Redlands, California: San Bernardino County Museum, 1965. 1–2, 4. Reprinted by permission of the San Bernardino County Museum Association.

ORIGINAL NOTES

1. The accepted spelling of the Indian tribe is *Mohave,* singular and plural, whereas the river and desert have assumed the Spanish spelling of *Mojave.*

2. The Indians around Bakersfield on 6 August 1806 told Lieutenant Francisco Maria Ruiz and Father Jose Maria Zalvidea of Santa Barbara Mission and the presidio that the Majagua

(Mohave) Indians came to this spot to trade. Details were even added as to the scarcity of water during the ten-day journey. Other Spanish documents show them as far north as Mission San Miguel and San Luis Obispo.

3. Jesse D. Stockton, *Spanish Trailblazers in the South San Joaquin, 1772–1816* (Bakersfield: Kern County Historical Society, 1957), p. 1. George William Beattie and Helen Pruitt Beattie, *Heritage of the Valley, San Bernardino's First Century* (Pasadena: San Pasqual Press, 1939), p. 2.

4. Elliot Coues, *On the Trail of a Spanish Pioneer, the Diary and Itinerary of Francisco Garces (Missionary Priest) in his travels through Sonora, Arizona, and California, 1775–1776, Translated from an Official Contemporaneous Copy of the Original Spanish Manuscript, and Edited with Copious Critical Notes in Two Volumes* (New York: Francis P. Harper, 1900), I, 216–17, 248.

5. The Halchidhoma were one of the weaker Colorado River tribes of Yuman linguistic stock living near the present town of Parker. Garces referred to them as the Jalcheduns.

6. R. B. Stratton, *Captivity of the Oatman Girls* (Salem: Oregon Teachers Monthly, 1909), Chapter XVI. Although this source has been proven to be weak in historical facts and overly romantic, it does give insight to Mohave life and customs. Grant Foreman, ed. *A Pathfinder in the Southwest: The Itinerary of Lieutenant A. W. Whipple during his explorations for a railway route from Fort Smith to Los Angeles in the years 1853 and 1854* (Norman: University of Oklahoma Press, 1941), p. 237. See also Whipple, p. 127, for another example of Mexican slavery in central New Mexico.

✿

First Crossing by a White Man

(1776)

In 1776, the year of our nation's birth, a priest, Francisco Garcés, accompanied by Mohave Indians (called Jamajabs below), became the first white man of record to cross the Mojave Desert. Garcés was a good man for the job. An eighteenth-century hippie, the missionary, sometimes under the scowls of his fellow Spaniards, went native—eating, dressing, and otherwise taking on many ways of the Indians. For that, Garcés's account is unique, for the Spaniards, clinging to the far more amenable California coast, avoided the desert and, hence, rarely wrote about those feared lands.

Especially valuable for the notes by eminent nineteenth-century historian Elliott Coues, the brief excerpt touches on the confusion of naming, sometimes making the Mojave Desert seem a foggy land of shifting mysteries. This perplexing, if sometimes intriguing, aspect of the Mojave has gone on into fairly recent times. For instance, the river Garcés, dubbed the *Arroyo de los Martires*, or the River of the Martyrs, we now know as the Mojave; and the area called the Caves in Coues's note 13 now is known as Afton Canyon.

More practically, anyone idealizing the lives of desert Indians might consider the abject condition of the band that Garcés encountered.

✿

MAR. 9. I WENT 5 LEAGUES [west] 1/4 westsouthwest, and arrived at a gap in the sierra that I named (Sierra) Pinta for the veins that run in it of various colors. Here I encountered an arroyo of saltish water that I named (Arroyo) de los Martires.[12] There is good grass.

Mar. 10. I went 6 leagues up the arroyo on a course westsouthwest, and with various windings I halted in the same arroyo, at a place where it has cottonwoods, much grass, and lagunas.[13]

Mar. 11. Having gone one league eastsoutheast I arrived at some rancherias so poor that they had to eat no other thing than the roots of rushes (*rayzes de tule*); they are of the Beñemé nation and there were about 25 souls. I gave them of my little store (*los regalé con mi pobreza*), and they did the same with their tule-roots, which my companions the Jamajabs ate with repugnance. The poor people manifested much concern at their inability to go hunting in order to supply me, inasmuch as it was raining and very cold, and they were entirely naked.

*From Francisco Garcés. *On the Trail of a Spanish Pioneer*. Trans. and ed. Elliott Coues. New York: Francis P. Harper, 1900. 238–40.

ORIGINAL NOTES

12. Mar. 9 is the memorable day on which Garcés discovers Mojave river, never before seen by a white man. He has reached the sink of the river, modern Soda lake, and names it *Arroyo de los Martires* [River of the Martyrs]—a term appearing as "*R. de los Martires*" on Font's map of 1777, but "*R. de los Martinez*" by misprint on the reduced copy in Bancroft, and *Rio de los Martires* having originally been Kino's name of the Colorado in 1699. Hence arose some confusion; but there is not the slightest doubt of Garcés's discovery and present position. Mojave river has no outlet, but sinks in the sand at Soda lake or marsh, a place which varies much in appearance at different seasons or conditions of water supply. The sink has an extent of about twenty miles from N. to S., but is narrow in the opposite direction, and the main road takes directly across the middle of it from E. to W. when the water is low. When I crossed it was nearly dry except in some reedy patches, and most of the surface was whitened with alkaline efflorescence; the water was bad, as Garcés says, the grass was poor, there was no wood, and myriads of mosquitos tormented us, though water had frozen half an inch thick in our buckets on the night of 31 Oct. On the W. side of the sink a road goes northward; the road to follow is the left-hand one, which runs about W. S. W. and strikes the river a few miles higher up, as the river comes into the extreme S. end of the sink. This is Garcés's course for to-morrow, "*arroyo arriba con rumbo al Oestsudoeste* [upriver toward west-southwest]."

13. The distance given should set Garcés in the vicinity of a place on the river called the Caves [now Afton Canyon]—a usual first stopping place in going up the Mojave from Soda Lake.

Jedediah Smith Gets His Nose Bloodied:
A Massacre of Mountain Men

(1827)

In the 1820s, Anglo trappers from the Rocky Mountains began crossing the Mojave to the California coast. It's curious how laconic their accounts are about the desert part of the journey, which must have been pretty horrific. But then, these were hardened men, and the desert likely seemed just another hardship, just a bad place they needed to get across as quickly as possible in their eagerness to trap, trade, and woo the sloe-eyed señoritas on the other side.

However, Jedediah Smith, the first American we know of to make the trip, got badly mauled by the Mohave Indians on his second crossing in 1827, a sign of worsening relations to come. The event makes this account especially notable. Also of interest, reflecting the political complexities then beginning to swirl around the Mojave, is the chary reception awaiting the survivors of arrows and days of slogging through sand, for the Mexican officials on the California coast were suspicious that their unannounced visitors were heralds of American expansionism, which, of course, unintentionally, they were.

They followed the same route which Smith had pursued the previous year. He

Proceeded on S. and S.E. until he passed the Utaw Indians with whom he had concluded a treaty the year before; he also passed the Sampatch and Piules [*sic*], living on the west border of the sand plains and in the vicinity of the Colleredo. His course was S. and S.W., leading down the Colleredo until he came to the Muchabas Indians, whom he found apparently friendly as usual; he remained with them three days, trading of them occasionally some articles of their country produce such as beaver, wheat, corn, dried pump-kins, and melons. After the trade and intercourse with the Indians was over, Mr. Smith and his party, in attempting to cross the river on a raft, was attacked by those Indians and completely defeated with a loss of ten men and two women (taken prisoners), the prop-erty all taken or destroyed.[461]

Smith had undertaken to ferry his men across the river on rafts, but, as soon as the party was divided, some of them on either bank and some of them still on the rafts, the Indians, "who in large numbers and with most perfect semblance of peace and friendship were aiding the party to cross the river, suddenly rose upon them and surrounding the party in a most unexpected moment and manner," began the attack.[462] The party, being divided, was taken at a great disadvantage. Those already across, includ-ing Smith, seem to have suffered least. Those on the river were very likely all killed as were also most, at least, of those on the eastern bank.

The official narrative continues:

The loss of all papers and journals prevents Mr. Smith from giving precise dates; it happened in August, 1827. Then, as no other alter-native was left, and in a country destitute of provisions and water, he was obliged to make for the Spanish settlements in California in the vicinity of San Gabriel, which he accomplished in nine and a half days, including nights, across the sand plains and destitute of almost every necessary of life. Here he procured some few neces-saries to enable him to proceed to his party before mentioned, made his report by letter to the nearest place of civil intercourse, left two men, one, by his request,[463] and the other on account of a wound which he had received in the attack.[464] Then, with the remaining seven, he pushed on northwardly, joined his party but in a very unpleasant situation; their supplies were almost entirely exhausted and he without any to assist them.

During Smith's absence the men had been in difficulties with the Mexican authorities. Even before his departure, in May, the head of the

Mission of San José, Padre Duran, had accused the men of enticing his neophytes to desert. Although this charge had been dismissed by the commandant at San Francisco, orders were issued, 18 May, to find out who the strangers were, what their business was, and to demand their passports, in short, to detain them till further orders.[465] It was too late, however, to secure Smith, for, on the twentieth, he had set out for Great Salt Lake, having the previous day written Padre Duran as follows:

Reverend Father: I understand through the medium of one of your Christian Indians that you are anxious to know who we are, as some of the Indians have been at the Mission and informed you that there were certain white people in the country. We are Americans, on our journey to the river Columbia. We were in at the Mission of San Gabriel, January last. I went to San Diego and saw the general and got a passport from him to pass on to that place. I have made several efforts to pass the mountains, but the snow being so deep, I could not succeed in getting over. I returned to this place, it being the only point to kill meat, to wait a few weeks until the snow melts so that I can go on. The Indians here, also, being friendly, I consider it the most safe point for me to remain until such time as I can cross the mountains with my horses, having lost a great many in attempting to cross ten or fifteen days since. I am a long ways from home and am anxious to get there as soon as the nature of the case will admit. Our situation is quite unpleasant, being destitute of clothing and most necessaries of life, wild meat being our principal subsistence.
I am, Reverend Father, your strange but real friend and Christian,
J. S. Smith,
May 19, 1827[466]

Far from satisfying the authorities, this letter only roused them to greater exertions. By 23 May, Echeandía [the governor], having learned of the situation, sent word to Smith, not knowing that he had already departed, ordering him to start homeward at once or else to come to San José, or to sail on the first vessel that would convey him north of the forty-second parallel.[467] After it was discovered that the leader of the expedition had gone, however, less interest seems to have been taken in the Americans.

*From Harrison Clifford Dale. *The Ashley-Smith Explorations and Discovery of a Central Route to the Pacific, 1822–1929.* Cleveland: The Arthur H. Clark Company, 1918. 23–33.

ORIGINAL NOTES

461. *Brief Sketch of Accidents, Misfortunes, and Depredations Committed by Indians on the Firm of Smith, Jackson, and Sublette, since July 1, 1826, to the Present, 1829*, Kansas Historical Society Mss.

462. Warner, J. J. "Reminiscences of Early California," in Southern California Historical Society, *Publications*, vol. vii, 181. The Indians had probably been warned by the Mexican government not to allow Americans to cross the river and enter California. News of the disaster did not reach St. Louis till a year later, "I have recently heard of the loss of eight men," etc. Draft of a letter of Ashley to Benton (?), December 24, 1828, Missouri Historical Society, Ashley Mss.

463. Isaac Galbraith. "On October 8, Galbraith asked for an interview with Echeandía wishing a license to remain in the country or to rejoin his leader. He also corrects an impression that Smith is a captain of troops, stating that he is but a hunter of the company of Smith, Jackson, and Sublette." Bancroft, *California*, vol. iii, 158, footnote, citing *Department of State Papers*, Mss., vol. ii, 36, 37. Galbraith was not dismissed at this time but accompanied Smith north and did not withdraw from his service till December 17, 1827. Sublette Mss., carton 10, Missouri Historical Society.

464. Thomas Virgin. He was sent to San Diego where he was placed in prison but afterwards released to rejoin Smith. Warner states that Smith, himself, was conducted to San Diego but this is unsupported and seems improbable. Warner, J. J. "Reminiscences of Early California," in Southern California Historical Society, *Publications*, vol. vii, 181 ff.

465. *Archivo del Arzobispado*, Mss., vol. v, part i, 27 and *Departmental Records*, Mss., vol. v, 45, cited by Bancroft in *California*, vol. iii, 156, footnote.

466. In Guinn, "Captain Jedediah S. Smith," in Southern California Historical Society, *Publications*, vol. iii, part 4, 48 ff.; also in Cronise, *The Natural Wealth of California*, 44–45. Padre Duran was in charge of the Mission at San José and president of the Alta California missions, 1825–1827.

467. Echeandía to Martinez (acting commandant at San Francisco), *Departmental Records*, Mss., vol. v, 48, cited by Bancroft, *California*, vol. iii, 158, footnote.

𝖜

A War Whoop:
Incident on the Frémont Expedition
(1844)

Testifying to his fame, many a city has a street with his name. Known as The Pathfinder, John C. Frémont—explorer, soldier, politician— was a controversial figure in American history. At once headstrong and meticulous, he often delivered more than his (sometimes cha-grined) superiors expected.

Contributing immensely to Americans' understanding of the shape of the West, Frémont made five trips across the Mississippi River. On his second exploration, from which I present this passage, he names the Mojave River, delivering it from a welter of confused nomenclature. Traveling along the river's length during April, the explorer stands amazed as the "naked sand" blooms before his eyes into flowers—an excitement shared by today's tourists at the desert's spring display.

But, as we shall see, all was not floral appreciation on such trips.

𝖜

B
UT, THROUGHOUT THIS NAKEDNESS OF SAND AND GRAVEL, were many beautiful plants and flowering shrubs, which occurred in many new species, and with greater variety than we had been accus-tomed to see in the most luxuriant prairie countries; this was a peculiar-ity of this desert. Even where no grass would take root, the naked sand would bloom with some rich and rare flower, which found its appropri-ate home in the arid and barren spot. . . .

In the afternoon of the next day, a war-whoop was heard, such as Indians make when returning from a victorious enterprise; and soon Carson and Godey appeared, driving before them a band of horses, rec-ognized by Fuentes to be part of those they had lost. Two bloody scalps, dangling from the end of Godey's gun, announced that they had over-taken the Indians as well as the horses. They informed us, that after

Fuentes left them, from the failure of his horse, they continued the pursuit alone, and towards nightfall entered the mountains, into which the trail led. After sunset the moon gave light, and they followed the trail by moonshine until late in the night, when it entered a narrow defile, and was difficult to follow. Afraid of losing it in the darkness of the defile, they tied up their horses, struck no fire, and lay down to sleep in silence and in darkness. Here they lay from midnight till morning. At daylight they resumed the pursuit, and about sunrise discovered the horses; and, immediately dismounting and tying up their own, they crept cautiously to a rising ground which intervened, from the crest of which they perceived the encampment of four lodges close by. They proceeded quietly, and had got within thirty or forty yards of their object, when a movement among the horses discovered them to the Indians; giving the war shout, they instantly charged into the camp, regardless of the number which the *four* lodges would imply. The Indians received them with a flight of arrows shot from their long bows, one of which passed through Godey's shirt collar, barely missing the neck; our men fired their rifles upon a steady aim, and rushed in. Two Indians were stretched on the ground, fatally pierced with bullets; the rest fled, except a lad that was captured. The scalps of the fallen were instantly stripped off; but in the process, one of them, who had two balls through his body, sprung to his feet, the blood streaming from his skinned head, and uttering a hideous howl. An old squaw, possibly his mother, stopped and looked back from the mountain side she was climbing, threatening and lamenting. The frightful spectacle appalled the stout hearts of our men; but they did what humanity required, and quickly terminated the agonies of the gory savage.

*From John C. Frémont. *The Exploring Expedition to the Rocky Mountains in the Year 1842, and to Oregon and North California in the Years 1843–1844.* Washington, D.C.: Gales and Seaton, 1845. 262, 262–63.

The Mormons: Shooting an Ox

(1849)

The Mormons (properly, Latter-Day Saints) played a large role on the Mojave. Suspiciously eyed, and sometimes brutalized, by nineteenth-century Americans because of their practice of plural marriages, to escape persecution Church members plunged off into the desert wilderness and founded Salt Lake City, Utah, in 1847. From there envisioning more fertile land as well as an expanded theocracy and an outlet to the sea, some members of the Church crossed the desert to settle San Bernardino, California, beyond the western edge of the Mojave.

Hence, the Mormons were desert trailblazers, and as we'll see in the selection after this one, for this reason the Forty-niners of William L. Manly fame hired Jefferson Hunt, a Mormon familiar with the trans-Mojave route, to guide them across the sands to safety. At the outset, Captain Hunt, as he was called, cautioned his charges that the crossing would be bad enough even if they all stuck together and followed his orders. That those who did had a horrid enough time of it, recorded here by a Mormon missionary on his way to the South Pacific, only emphasizes the dire peril of those, such as the people in Manly's party, who, following a fraudulent map, foolishly took it into their heads to leave their party and strike out on their own for an imagined better route.

As a side note expanding a bit on a point of natural history made earlier, Brown's reference to wolves very likely is to coyotes, much smaller relatives of wolves.

ABOUT 2 P.M. we came to the Las Vegas, where we rested a day, then continued our journey over mountains and across dry deserts from day to day until we reached a stream of water about three rods wide. It was so strong with alkali that we dared not allow our cattle to drink of it, but put the lash to them so that they could not get a sup as we crossed it twice. Thence we traveled across a very sandy desert for twelve miles to the Salt Springs, where the train went around a point of the mountain. A. Pratt and I, with three or four others, followed on a

small trail that passed over a notch of the mountain. While going through a narrow pass, Brother A. Pratt said it looked as if there might be gold there. At that we went to looking in the crevices of the rock, and in a few minutes one of the party found a small scale, and then another. Among the rest, I saw the precious metal projecting from a streak of quartz in the granite rock. From there we went over about one and a half miles to the Salt Springs, and met with the teams. Several of the party journeyed back to look further for the gold. I took along a cold chisel and hammer, and chipped out some at the place I had found, but as our teams were weakening very fast and there was neither food nor water at that place to sustain our stock, we had to push on across the sandy desert of seventy-five miles, day and night, until we came to the Bitter Springs.

These were the springs that Captain Hunt had told the emigrant company about before they left Salt Lake City, that from thence it was "away hellward to California or some other place." It certainly began to look that way now, when our cattle began to weaken and die all along the trail. The springs would have been as properly named if they had been called Poison Springs, instead of Bitter, for it seemed that from that place our cattle began to weaken every moment, and many had to be turned loose from the yoke and then shot to get them out of their misery.

We had to shoot one of Brother Pratt's oxen to end its suffering. This act fell to my lot. Oh, how inhuman and cruel it seemed to me, to drive the patient and faithful dumb animal into a barren desert, where there is neither food nor drink, to goad him on until he falls from sheer exhaustion, so that he bears any punishment, to make him rise, that his master sees fit to inflict, without giving a single moan, then to walk around and calmly look him in the face and fire the deadly missile into his brain, then leave his carcass to the loathsome wolves and birds of prey!

In looking back over a period of fifty years since then, the writer cannot call to memory a single act in his life that seemed so cruel and ungrateful as that; and still there was no earthly means to save the poor creature from a more horrible death.

*From James S. Brown. *Life of a Pioneer: Being the Autobiography of James S. Brown.* Salt Lake City: George Q. Cannon and Sons, 1900. 138–40.

The Deserta Horribilis
(1849)

Today we are blessed. As we glide across the desert on paved roads, listening to music and turning up the air-conditioning to out-wit the sun beating ever more futilely on the tinted windows, we might remember that Death Valley was well named.

As touched on in the previous piece, in 1849, westering pioneers came across a mysterious map. It showed an easy alternative route to the much-desired gold fields of California. Dissension broke out over the course to take, and as a result some members of the wagon train ignored Captain Hunt, their hired Mormon guide, and split up. One band, following the map, found itself not among the promised green pastures and springs, but in the sandy wasteland memorialized as Death Valley National Monument (est. 1933).

Sure of a slow death unless they could find a way out of this labyrinthine hell, the leaders camped by a seep and chose two young men to strike out for the California coast, believed to be nearby, and bring back help.

Instead, the youths found themselves hopelessly lost in an end-less sea of bare mountains. Then they began to stumble across the corpses of Jayhawkers, wayward men from Kansas who also had plunged off in their own directions.

The two men, William L. Manly and John Rogers, managed to flounder out and return with food and water for their companions. Meanwhile, in this classic account of desert horrors, we see in the Mojave's teetering balance scales of life the importance of a blade of grass and a few slivers of ice. This, however, is no ancient story; almost every year several people get lost and die of thirst on the Mojave. Here is a sample of what they suffer.

"Just look at the cursed country we have come over!" said Rogers as he pointed over it. To the north was the biggest mountain we ever saw—peaks on peaks towering far above our heads, and covered with snow which was apparently everlasting.

22

This mountain seemed to have very few trees on it, and in extent, as it reached away to the north, seemed interminable. Southward was a nearly level plain, and to the west I thought I could dimly see a range of mountains that held a little snow upon their summits, but on the main range to the south there was none. It seemed to me the dim snowy mountains must be as far as two hundred miles away, but of course I could not judge accurately. After looking at this grand but worthless landscape long enough to take in its principal features we asked each other what we supposed the people we left behind would think to see mountains so far ahead. We knew that they had an idea that the coast range was not very far ahead, but we saw at once to go over all these mountains and return within the limits of fifteen days, which had been agreed upon between us, would probably be impossible. Still we must try as best we could, so down the rocky steep we clambered and hurried on our way. In places the way was so steep that we had to help each other down, and the hard work made us perspire freely so that the water was a prime necessity. In one place near here, we found a little water and filled our canteens, besides drinking a good present supply. There were two low, black rocky ranges directly ahead of us which we must cross.

When we were part way down the mountain, a valley or depression opened up in that direction, up which it seemed we could look a hundred miles. Near by and a short distance north was a lake of water and when we reached the valley we crossed a clear stream of water flowing slowly toward the lake.

Being in need of water, we rushed eagerly to it and prepared to take a big drink, but the tempting fluid was as salt as brine and made our thirst all the more intolerable. Nothing grew on the bank of this stream and the bed was of hard clay, which glistened in the sun.

We now began the ascent of the next ridge, keeping a westerly course, and walked as fast as we could up the rough mountain side. We crossed the head of a cañon near the summit about dark, and here we found a trail, which from indications we knew to be that of the Jayhawkers, who had evidently been forced to the southward of the course they intended to take. They had camped here and had dug holes in the sand in search of water, but had found none.

We stayed all night here and dug around in some other places in the bottom of the cañon, in hope of having better luck than they did, but we got no water anywhere.

The hard exercise made us perspire so freely that we seemed almost perishing for want of water. In the morning we started on, and near the summit we came to the dead body of Mr. Fish, lying in the hot sun, as there was no material near here with which his friends could cover the remains. This Mr. Fish was the man who had left camp some two weeks before in company with another and who carried the long whiplash wound about his body, in the hope that he could somewhere be able to trade it for bread. No doubt in this very place where he breathed his last his bones still lie.

As we came in sight of the next valley, we could see a lake of water some distance south of our western course.

We had followed the Jayhawkers' trail thus far; but as we found no water in small holes in the rocks, which we were likely to do where we were the first to pass, we decided to take a new route in the hope of finding a little water in this way, for we had no hope of finding it in any other. This valley we now crossed seemed to come to an end about ten miles to the north of us. To the south it widened out, inclosing the lake spoken of. This valley was very sandy and hard to walk over. When about half way across, we saw some ox tracks leading toward the lake, and hoping we might find the water drinkable we turned off at right angles to our course and went that way also. Long before we reached the water of the lake, the bottom became a thin, slimy mud which was very hard on our moccasins. When we reached the water we found it to be of a wine color, and so strongly alkaline as to feel slippery to the touch, and under our feet.

This side trip had cost us much exertion and made us feel more thirsty than ever.

We turned now west again, making for a cañon, up which we passed in the hope that we should find at some turn a little basin of rain water in some rock. We traveled in it miles and miles, and our mouths became so dry that we had to put a bullet or a small smooth stone in and chew it and turn it around with the tongue to induce a flow of saliva. If we saw a spear of green grass on the north side of a rock, it was quickly pulled and eaten to obtain the little moisture it contained.

Thus we traveled along for hours, never speaking, for we found it much better for our thirst to keep our mouths closed as much as possible, and prevent the evaporation. The dry air of that region took up water as a sponge does. We passed the summit of this ridge without finding any water, and on our way down the western side we came to a flat place where there was an Indian hut made of small brush. We now thought there surely must be some water near and we began a thorough search. The great snow mountain did not seem far off, but to the south and southwest a level or inclined plain extended for a long distance. Our thirst began to be something terrible to endure; in the warm weather and hard walking we had secured only two drinks since leaving camp.

We were so sure that there must be water near here that we laid our knapsacks down by the little hut and looked around in every possible place we could think of. Soon it became dark and then we made a little fire as a guide and looked again. Presently the moon arose and helped us some, but we shouted frequently to each other so as not to get lost.

We were so nearly worn out that we tried to eat a little meat, but after chewing a long time, the mouth would not moisten it enough so we could swallow, and we had to reject it. It seemed as if we were going to die with plenty of food in our hand, because we could not eat it.

We tried to sleep but could not. After a little rest we noticed a bright star two hours above the horizon, and from the course of the moon we saw the star must be pretty truly west of us. We talked a little, expressing fear that we could not endure the terrible thirst much longer. The thought of the women and children waiting for our return made us feel more desperate than if we were the only ones concerned. We thought we could fight to the death over a water hole if we could only secure a little of the precious fluid. No one who has never felt the extreme of thirst can imagine the distress, the despair, which it brings. I can find no words, no way, to express it so others can understand.

The moon gave us so much light that we decided we would start on our course, and get as far as we could before the hot sun came out; so we went on slowly and carefully in the partial darkness, the only hope left to us being that our strength would hold out till we could get to the shining snow on the great mountain before us. We reached the foot of the range we were descending about sunrise. There was here a wide wash from the snow mountain, down which some water had sometime run after a big storm and divided into little rivulets, only reaching out a little way before they had sunk into the sand.

We had no idea we could now find any water till we at least got very near the snow, and as the best way to reach it we turned up the wash, although the course was nearly to the north. The course was up a gentle grade and seemed quite sandy and not easy to travel. It looked as if there was an all day walk before us, and it was quite a question whether we could live long enough to make the distance. There were quite strong indications that the water had run here not so very long ago, and we could trace the course of the little streams round among little sandy islands. A small, stunted brush grew here, but it was so brittle that the stems would break as easily as an icicle.

In order not to miss a possible bit of water we separated and agreed upon a general course; if either one should find water he was to fire his gun as a signal. After I had gone about a mile or so I heard Rogers' gun and went in his direction. He had found a little ice that had frozen under the clear sky. It was not thicker than window glass. After putting a piece in our mouths we gathered all we could and put it into the little quart camp kettle to melt. We gathered just a kettleful, besides what we ate as we were gathering, and kindled a little fire and melted it.

I can but think how providential it was that we started in the night for in an hour after the sun had risen that little sheet of ice would have melted and the water would have sunk into the sand.

*From William L. Manly. *Death Valley in '49*. 1894. New York: Wallace Hebberd, 1929. 155–60.

White Slave Girls
(1851)

Stories of Indians carrying off white people had an electrifying effect on the popular imagination in the nineteenth century. This was especially true when white girls were involved, for this triggered the mind's delicious indulgence in sexual horrors.

In February of 1851, a lone pioneer family traveling across the desert of western Arizona was attacked by a band of Yavapai warriors (here mistakenly called Apache). The father, pregnant mother, and several children were clubbed to death. One brother, knocked unconscious, was left for dead and managed to stumble back to civilization. Meanwhile, two sisters, Olive, age thirteen, and Mary, age seven, were taken as slaves. Eventually the Yavapai traded them to a band of the Mohave tribe living near present-day Needles, California.

This is the brutal story of the two girls, told from the lecture notes of Olive Oatman, who, after her ransom in 1856, became a sensation on the lecture circuit. Such was the craze for her that for a while there was a rash of Olive Oatman impersonators, Olive Oatman look-alikes, and, later, at least one person claiming to be her half-Indian son. Likely, the truth of this last will never be known, for, despite other moving details, Olive Oatman maintained a Victorian decorousness when it came to the sexual aspects of her captivity. The following preserves Olive Oatman's punctuation, spelling, and grammar. However, Olive Oatman often writes in one-sentence paragraphs. In order to save space and for ease of reading, I have combined most of these into more comprehensive units.

T HE INDIANS CAME TO THE WAGON & pretended to be friendly. They asked for a *pipe* & tobacco, as they said in Spanish in token of friendship; this was given & my Father smoked with them, they asked for food & my Father told them of our scanty supply & yet divided with them they asked for more & this Father denied them, telling them that it would famish us.

They immediately went by them selves & commenced & held a consultation in the Appache language. We saw that they were offended & seem'd determined to do us injury.

Father had returned to finish realoading the waggon. Mother was on the inside, arrangeing matters. I, with my older sister, was standing on the opposite side of the waggon. *Mary Ann 7.* Years of age sat down upon a stone holding on to a rope attached to the horns of the formost teams & the rest of the children were on the opposit side of waggon—from the Indians—when suddenly these wilde savages with a *fiendish yell* & *tigers* bound fell upon us.

Concealed from our view beneath a wolfskin shirt, they carried huge clubs which they brought out & brandished in the air screaming & leaping like so many Deamons began their cruel slaughter. They struck my Father, eldest brother first, & as one of them forced me away; I turned arround opened my eyes, and—"O, my God"—what a scene met my eyes. The emotions of my heart will not allow a recital of those barbarities of that awful hour.

After the terible tragedy I remember, I became faint & I thought I was struck, & fell to the earth. I then heard my poor *bleeding, mangled Mother* utter a moan & I sprang wildly toward her. The Indian standing over me snatched me back & lifted his club and threatened me.

We staid near the spot, I should think, about one hour, when, after plundering our waggon, we were hurried down the hill by the way he had travelled. My feelings, when turning to leave my parents & brothers sisters, all murdered, cannot be imagined much less discribed.

My little sister only *seven* years of age & my self *thirteen,* driven by savages in to the thick forest gloom, to meet perhaps, a fate worse than death—was to me the extreem of earthly misery. My little sister sobbed & cried aloud & clung to me saying "sister I do not want to leave my Dear *Father* & *Mother* here" I asked them to kill me & plead with them to take my life; but my prayers were only answered, with taunts & ridicule by the two wretches into whose charge we had been committed.

We left the road before recrossing the *River* at the foot of the hills; from this we travelled through a dark crooked ravine, & then came to a place where Indians had encamped before. We here haulted; our captors killed one of the cows. They then made a daugh from water & meat taken from our waggon & baked it in the sand. Tough & stringy as was the meat they ate four times as much as an *American* could have done. We could not eat.

Oh, what an hour was that at that *camp*—to me & to my poor little sister. We expected they would burn us, for they would grin & laugh & then point us back up the *hill* as if deriding us for our sorrow. I cannot speak of the thoughts that ran through my mind at that *hour*. I thought of *home*, of the bright days when we bid our playmates *good* bye in Illinois. I thought of our present condition, young as we were; while standing by the camp fire, in the hour of our greatest agony; we breathed a silent prayer to *God*. "O *Father* we claim thy promises."

At times all seemed a dreame, & I tried to have it so; but all ended in the bitter knoweledge of a dredful reality.

Poor *sister Mary*, her sighs for Father & mother still linger in my ears. My sufferings wer forgotten in my sympathy for her. A part of the captors took the cattle in one direction while we were started off in an other direction. We were driven on during the night & if we faltered, a blow was given to quicken our pace. Near daylight *Mary* fell to the earth & gave up. She asked me to let them kill her & I go on. When I caught a glimpse of her face, I thought her sleeping or dead, I could not tell which. I can not dwell upon that first night of my captivity. My sympathies for my sister, my wearied aching body, the constant fear of the brutal *Apachee* & the awful uncertainty of the future were sufficient to make my misery most *intence*.

The next day we met the Indians who had driven the cows an other way. They had killed them & smoked the meat leaving some for an other trip as I learned long after. These brutes have regular dark places of halt well selected through this region.

The path over which we traveled the next day was rough & hilly. The Indians were much offended at being obliged to carry my little sister Mary & they frequently tried to drive her, but could not. On the second day I became nearly exhausted, my feet were bleeding, & I had nearly determined to yeald & compel them to kill me.

About noon while thus weighing matters in my own minde, we came upon a party of Indians. They met us at a short turn in the trail, around a spur of a bluff mountain. The place where we met them, was so hidden as to give us no warning of their approach. They belonged to a powerful tribe a long way at the *South East*, & were on a hunting expidition for game & for white *men*, who might pass the over land rout. They were *Commanches*. They were fierce deceitful in appearance, while with their eyes fastened upon me & busily talking with our captors; one of them suddenly sprang his bow & let fly an arrow at <u>me</u> pearcing the skirts of my tattered dress.

He was in the act of hearling an other (as was an other by his sid) when one of our captors seized him stepping between us shielding us from the exibition of their murderous hate. Neither of us cared to live & hence we did not fear their deadly weapons

Mary said frequantly afterwards, "I wish they had killed us"

Our party came near having a general fight with these Indians.

The Indian who tried to kill me, had lost a brother by *white man* on the *Santa Fe* Trail a short-time before, & I learned he had vowed to take the life of the first white person he should see to revenge the deed. This is their law in such matters. A few hurried us on while others staid to make up the difficulty.

On the *fourth* day we came suddenly in sight of *wigwams*, & soon found that our captors were near home. It was a small village of half underground huts surrounded by a rocky range of hills. From each of these holes in the ground came men women & children. Some were naked, others partly clad with bark and fur, & such creatures for human beaings, I never had even *dreamed* to see. They wer the very embodiment of filth poverty & degridation.

Could you have seen us about 4. O.C. P.M. you would have witnessed a scene never eaqualled in pandemonium it self. With bleeding feet—torn skirts—chilled with cold, we were placed upon a bundel of sticks, while these fierce, laughing, whooping wretches form a circle about us. The rang the news of arrival through the village & soon from all quarters they rushed to see & to hear. One of our captors made a short speach & then untied the bundels & exibited their spoils. Then we were made to stand up in their midst & they all danced & shouted about us, hallooing & shrieking like fiends. They would scream in our ears, spit in our faces, & by motions made us know by what death we should die, if we attempted to get away. They kept up this tumult all night & would not allow us to lie down. That night was among the most horrible of our captivity. We thought they would kill us & hoped they would do so. Towards *day break* we were taken to the chiefs family, & in the rude hut tried to rest.

Now when you remember our ages, our journey of over *two hundred* miles in four days & four nights, the scene of slaughter witnessed; our fears & the attack of the Commanches; our bleeding, aching limbs; & this introduction of two young girls to Indian life; & then you get somthing of an idea of our situation, & the Providence that sustained us.

The next day they showed how to dig roots & kept us at it. I can not dwell upon particulars;—we were kept for one year at perpetual drudgery. The parents would place their children to watch us & drive us about, & if we did not obey these filthy children, we were beaten by the parents. I do not think, during this first year we had a single day of rest.

The Apaches were a part of the *parent* band of that name, who had left the others on account of the Catholic missions formed among them & gone by them selves to live by plunder. They were filthy, lazy & ignorant. The men especially, were indolent & only when stern necessity drove them to it would they seek for *food.* We soon learned their language & we told them of the whites & their industry; this excited their rage, & they called us big liers (Hiecoes) While here we were whole days without food, yet the lazy men, might have founde plenty of game near by. They have a few superstitions, but of these & their traits I have spoken of in my book.

After we had been here about one year we saw some strange Indians in the village. We soon learned that they belonged to a tribe about 200. miles away called Mohaves. These tribes were friendly & would come once a year to trade vegetables for furs. At this visit they bargined for us, though we did not know it at the time. One day Mary & I were out gathering roots, when we saw in the distance a partie coming—an Indian riding upon his horse & a squaw walking by his side Prior to this, we heard that we were sold & it proved that the partie now coming wer sent by the *Mohave Chief* to pay for us. The Appaches came near a general fight over our sale, for our old captors were much opposed to it. But the price was paid & amid much anxiety we started for our new home which we reached the 9th day.

These Indians when excited have no sense of mercy. Our coming was expected & when with in five miles from their village *men, women* & *children* came out to dance & shout about us. The chiefs daughter showed some kindness & seemed carful of *Sister Mary*. We slept beneath her Blanket on our journey & were taken to the house of the Chief on our arrival, & she gave us some cake which was being baked in the sand. We got a little sleep that night; though the Indians had their war dance nearly all night.

We were *sad* & *gloomy,* because we now saw our selves burried more deeply in the mountains & farther from the whites than before We were slaves here as before & heardships placed upon us beyond our years to endure. In consequence of this Mary soon began to decline & I can not now trace the steps by which she went to her grave in one short year.

In the spring of *1852,* the river, on whose Banks we were located, did not over-flow as it usually did, & hence in the fall of that year there was great scarcity of food. The wife of the chief gave us some wheat & a spot of ground on which to plant it but our hopes were *blighted*, as well as the *seed*, by the drought.

Food of every description was scarce, *roots, seeds* & *burries* could [not] be found without great difficulty, & the winter with its rains winds & frosts was fast approaching. Feeble as Sister Mary was we spent whole days in search of *roots* & *seeds* with out getting as much as we could hold in our hands.

Poor Mary, she faded fast—her sad look; her dejected countenance are before me still When she was so weak that she could not accompany me, I have left her & spent whole days in search of Black-birds eggs, that her poor wasting body might be nourished & the pangs of hunger allayed. We heard of some seed away to the north & I went with some squaws over 60. miles in search of it. Two of our number died on this trip, & several children died in our absense. We gathered our Baskets full of the Othtota bury, a poor substance for food; and hastened home where we found others still dying. In fact we were in the midst of a terrible famin.

Toil, & hunger had so preyed upon *Mary*, that I now saw she must soon die.

Oh! How dark the night of my sorrow? My family dead (as I supposed) & now my only sister, a sweet little Girl of 10 summers in the pangs of hunger & Starvation & to be left alone. How ardently I prayed to God in that fearful hour. Mary used to say to me "you ought not to labor to keep me alive; I am willing to die, I shall soon be where *Father* & *Mother* have gone, to that better "world"--and then she would ask God to take care of me. She would frequently ask me to sing with her the hymn commencing "There is a happy land far, far away" & it was a favorite with her. She would sometimes ask for something to eat & I had nothing for her. At such times, how my heart would ace for her, & then she would tell me "not to weep for her."

When we sang, the Indians & their wives would gather around us withe wonder & ask what we were singing; they were solemn & some of them wept. They asked her if she wanted to die. She said yes. They asked why? She told them she should go to Heaven, where her Parents, Brothers & Sisters had gone; and thus the dying Girl taught those *rude, rough* sons of the forrest, the "*gospel* of the *grace* of *God*" The wife of the chife came & bent over her, the night she died, & appeared as did her daughter to weep bitterly. I can never forget (though I can not explain) the affect that *that* dying scene seemed to produce upon those savage bystanders. I can only say *God was there* & the wilde untutored nature of the Indians, experienced the power of the divine presence.

She was a sweet singer & after she had sung one of her Sabboth School hymns nearly through with a clear sweet voice, she quietly feel a sleep & with in ten minutes was with the Angels. And so *one* of the *Captive Girls* was set at liberty.

*From Olive Oatman. "Olive Ann Oatman's Lecture Notes and the Oatman Bibliography." Ed. Edward Pettid, S. J. *San Bernardino County Museum Association Quarterly* 16.2 (Winter 1968): 10–18. Copyright © 1968 Edward Pettid.

Fantastic Experiment with Camels

(1857)

If you happen to see a long-necked, goggly-eyed creature staring at you over a sand dune, don't reach for the Prozac.

In 1857, beset by supply problems across the West's great distances, the Army tried imported camels. Despite much joking and hoots of derision, the experiment worked. Led by Lt. Edward F. Beale, the high-stepping beasts carried huge burdens uphill, downhill, doggedly plodding on for days at a time, requiring little water on the way—and, to Lt. Beale's surprise, the weird, gangly-legged beasts could even swim!

Why this novel mode of transportation came to naught can't be exactly said. For one thing, camels tended to frighten the bejeezies out of horses and mules, upsetting whole caravans; then, too, they required special handling, and their imported Arab handlers, upon reaching California, promptly ran off to the gold fields.

The camels were turned loose, spread across the desert, and now and then, appearing in the light of a campfire, gave a poor prospector the blue jimjams. Even in my childhood I heard stories of sightings, and, although they likely were more folklore than reality, it wouldn't hurt when out in the Mojave Desert to keep an eye peeled for the possibility.

Having successfully crossed the major barrier to camels, the Colorado River, into the greater Mojave, Lt. Beale writes the Secretary of War, John B. Floyd, an enthusiastic letter.

Colorado River, California, October 18, 1857

Sir:

I have the honor to report my arrival in California, after a journey of forty-eight days. . . .

Leaving home with all the prejudice invariably attaching to untried experiments, and with many in our camp opposed to their use, and looking forward confidently to their failure, I believe at this time I may speak for every man in our party, when I say there is not one of them who would not prefer the most indifferent of our camels to four of our best mules; and I look forward, hopefully, to the time when they will be in general use in all parts of our country.

Reading the accounts of travellers who had used them a great deal in the East, and who, I presumed, were entirely acquainted with their habits and powers, I was rendered extremely anxious on the subject of their swimming; foreseeing that, however useful they might be as beasts of burden in inhabited parts of the country, their usefulness would be impaired, if not entirely lost, to those who desired to use them where ferry boats and other such conveniences did not exist.

The enterprising priest, Father Huc, whose travels have lately been published, in speaking of his detention at the Yellow River, in China, because of the impossibility of crossing the camels, concludes by saying "for this animal cannot swim"; hence my great anxiety for the entire success of this experiment with camels was very much increased on my arrival at the Colorado River. All my pleasure in looking upon this noble stream, and all the satisfaction I derived in the reflection of a successful journey accomplished, was clouded by this doubt. However, the effort was to be made, and after having resolved in my own mind what to do in the event of failure, I determined to test the truth of the statements which I had seen in relation to that fact. The first camel brought down to the river's edge refused to take the water. Anxious, but not discouraged, I ordered another one to be brought, one of our largest and finest; and only those who have felt so much anxiety for the success of an experiment can imagine my relief on seeing it take to the water, and swim boldly across the rapidly flowing river. . . .

Very respectfully, your obedient servant,

E. F. Beale
Superintendent

*From Stephen Bonsal. *Edward Fitzgerald Beale: A Pioneer in the Path of Empire, 1822–1908.* New York: G. P. Putnam's Sons, 1912. 211, 215–16, 217.

More Monsters:
A Steamboat on the Colorado
(1858)

If the Indians of the eastern Mojave stood astounded at Lt. Beale's long-necked camels, the smoking, fire-belching monster coming up the Colorado River toward their settlements along the shores shortly after must have tried their faith in reality.

In the decades following the well-run expedition of Lewis and Clark in 1804–1806, the government sent out probe after probe into the West. Almost always, their purpose was multiple: to survey routes for railroads, determine the resources of the region, and assert territorial control. Yet strong intellectual and aesthetic elements are reflected in the artists, botanists, and geologists who went along to record the wonders of the West.

Today, anyone leafing through the oversized, lavishly illustrated, and meticulously compiled reports can't help but applaud the enlightened minds of our forefathers. We join one of them, Lt. Joseph C. Ives, riding a flame-plumed beast, a little steamer called *Explorer*, into the heart of the Mojave and in his account catching both the wonder of entering an unknown land and his sympathy for the complexities of the consequences to the native peoples.

THE NAVIGATION TO-DAY has been generally good, but we struck one sunken rock, and passed several that are now visible, but that would be dangerous at a higher stage of water unless their position were accurately known. The iron put into the hull of the Explorer must have been of excellent quality or she would have been sunk long ago by some of the thumps she has experienced.

We met, in the cañon, two Chemehuevis, with their wives, children, and household effects, paddling toward the valley below, on rafts made by tying together bundles of reeds. There being no bars to interrupt us we passed them under a full head of steam, and made a great impression.

They drew their rafts into a little cave when they saw us coming, and peered out at the steamboat, as it went puffing by, with an amusing expression of bewildered awe. Having, themselves, heavy loads to carry, I imagine they appreciated, better than their friends below, the advantage of being able to stem the current without manual labor.

As Captain Robinson and myself were walking out this evening we suddenly came upon two Indians reclining on the top of the bank, in sight of the steamer. I at once knew them to be Mojaves. One of them must have been nearly six feet and a half in height, and his proportions were herculean. He was entirely naked, excepting the ordinary piece of cotton about his loins, and his chest and limbs were enormously developed. A more scowling, sinister looking face than that which surmounted this noble frame I have seldom seen; and I quite agreed with a remark of the captain, that he would be an unpleasant customer to encounter alone and unarmed. His companion was smaller, though a large man, and had a pleasant face. Neither took the slightest notice of us, but both continued looking at the steamboat, the taller man with an expression that indicated a most unamiable frame of mind. Doubtless they were sent down from the valley above to learn something in regard to our party. I am sure that the report of one of the two will be anything but complimentary to the steamboat and ourselves. I can scarcely blame him for his disgust, for he must suspect that this is the first step towards an encroachment upon the territory of his tribe.

*From Joseph C. Ives. *Report upon the Colorado River of the West.* Washington, D.C.: U.S. Government Printing Office, 1861. 59.

Military Life: As Reflected in Letters

(1859, 1860, 1861)

As revealed here, the daily concerns of life in the hellholes of military forts were not Indian attacks and pursuit of outlaws but such things as scurvy, bad food, and lack of shoes. Compounding the degenerating situation, the sorry conditions led to the constant problem of deserters—pursued, of course, by their fellow soldiers, who, however, once beyond sight of their forts, sometimes joined in the escape toward a better life beyond the punishing Mojave.

Head. Qrs. Fort Mohave
Octr. 5th 1859
Orders
N1

All dogs found running at large after 12 o'clock M. to day will be shot by the Guard.

By order of 1st Lt. L. C. Bootes

Hd Qrs. Fort Mojave
Oct 16th 1860

Captain:
I have directed Lieut. Bryant, 6th Infty, the act. asst. Commiss. of Subs to make out, and transmit estimates for Cattle (Fresh meat), some Forage for the Cattle, and for an additional supply of subsistence Stores. I send this letter as an explanation, to show you the importance of our call, and seek immediate attention to the estimates. . . .

The Cattle on hand will supply our present command with fresh meat until the Second week in January next, if no loss nor accident occurs. But the distances, between Camps having water, for cattle on this route, are too great (one march is 33 miles) for the cattle to travel without causing them to lose their flesh. They will fall away at first in flesh, and therefore they should be allowed, on reaching this Post, a little time to rest and recover the lost flesh, before being slaughtered. We must have *fresh meat* here and frequently—it is our main protection from Scurvy. Unfortunately, we have but very little grass upon the river bottom, and none at all in the higher grounds. Even such as we have is very coarse (and the greater part is an alkaline grass which the Cattle will not touch at all,) and is rapidly disappearing for want of rains, or the overflow of the Colorado. We must therefore be prepared to save all from suffering for food, and to Keep the few wanted for immediate consumption in a condition to furnish the Garrison with a wholesome quality of Fresh Beef, and not with a mass of Bones only.

Very respectfully
Your obedt servant
G. O. HALLER
Capt. 4th Inf. & Bvt. Maj.
Comdg. Post

❧

Capt. M. D. S. Simpson
Comssy of Subsistence
Hd Qrs dept of California
San Francisco

To: Surg. Charles McCormick, Chief of Medical Corps, Dept. of the Pacific, San Francisco, Cal.

Date: March 26, 1861.
I beg leave to call your attention to the fact that act. asst Surgeon, F. G. Cooper at this Post, has intimated his intention to withdraw from the

service at the expiration of his contract, on the 10th proximo. He stated that [he] has given the necessary notification, to the medical Department, heretofore, of his intention.

The scurvy has manifested itself, in this command and the sick report, from various causes, has Kept up for several weeks past to 13 and sometimes to 15 in numbers. Three cases of obstetrics are expected to occur in the month of April.

A medical Officer is absolutely necessary to this Post, hence I will feel it my duty to detain the Doctor, by any pecuniary inducement he will accept, until some medical Officer arrives to relieve him.

Very respectfully
Your obedt servant
G. O. HALLER
Capt. 4th Inf. & Bvt. Maj.
Comdg. Post

*From Irene J. Brennan, ed. *Fort Mojave, 1859–1890: Letters to the Commanding Officers.* Manhattan, Kansas: MA/AH Publishing, 1980. 1, 8–9, 9–10. Copyright © MA/AH Publishing. Reprinted by permission of Sunflower University Press, P. O. Box 1009, 1531 Yuma, Manhatten, KS 66505-1009, U.S.A.

The Mojave Outlaw Culture
(1860s)

Many of the military's nagging problems on the Mojave were "solved" in 1861. The outbreak of the Civil War caused the federal government to close forts in the desert and withdraw many troops to eastern battlefields. This created a vacuum on the Mojave, leaving its great basin in control of outlaws and Confederate sympathizers, both scorning the tenuous reach of civil authority, centered over the mountains in the county seat of San Bernardino. Also catching on to the loosening of the reins were the Indians, who threatened to bring to a halt what commerce was left across the desert. Even further compounding a tumultuous situation and showing the historical complexities behind surface events were the long-simmering resentments of some Mormon settlers. Now the disenchanted joined in the fray and started taking revenge for what they deemed past injustices.

W ITH THE ONSET OF THE CIVIL WAR, San Bernardino began to see an increase in lawlessness, elements of which extended out into the Mojave Desert. Of particular concern to the citizens of the county was the sharp rise in horse theft, which was often attributed to secessionists who wanted additional mounts for their return home to join the Confederacy. One victim of theft at the beginning of the war was young Silas Cox, who, upon returning to San Bernardino from a stay on the desert, learned from his father that his favorite horse, Chappo, had just been stolen. He then discovered the thieves were actually men he had spent some time with in the mining region of Holcomb Valley:[1]

I asked father if he had any idea who stole him. He said he thought it was a bunch of young men, mostly gamblers, who had been in Holcomb Valley and San Bernardino for some time. I asked him if they were in town. He said, "No, that they had all disappeared."

After he told me their names I knew them all myself. The most of them were Texas boys, and some of them were pretty good boys. It was just the breaking out of the Civil War, and I suppose they wanted to get back home, but I objected to them taking my Chappo along with them.

The plucky teenager chased after the thieves and came upon their camp, which consisted of eight men and 12 horses, near the Warner Ranch in San Diego County. Waiting until dark, he sneaked into the camp while the men were asleep, and not only recaptured his own mount, but also got away with all the other horses. Cox said that it was unlikely any of the thieves were able to get back to Texas, at least for some time, and that a few of them actually returned to San Bernardino County and eventually became productive citizens.

Other secessionist horse thieves also used the roads leading east and south out of San Bernardino, while some escaped north through Cajon Pass and then traveled east on their return to Texas. However, during 1861 the majority of thefts were committed by local men who were running horses into Utah, and it was speculated that profit was the motive. After several horse-stealing incidents in April of 1861, the Los Angeles *Star* commented on the increasing activity, stating, "There seems to be a great demand for horses somewhere in the adjoining Territories, and those in want of them seem to know how to procure them cheap, without cash."[2] Right in the path of the horse thieves trafficking on the upper Mojave was Lane's Crossing. Aaron Lane was in great danger, for the next several months in particular, from criminal elements all around.

In early June another theft occurred involving Don Ygnacio Palomares, a prominent Californio and owner of the north half of the Rancho San Jose (Pomona), which he called San Jose de Arriba.[3] Palomares had been tending a herd of his cattle on the Mojave, and upon leaving the desert to return to his ranch, he encountered six Americans driving more than 20 of his own cattle, horses and mules out into the desert.[4] Palomares stopped to pass the time of day and exchange pleasantries with the thieves before hurrying back to his ranch to get help. He and his vaqueros caught up with the thieves, and what was described as a "short contest" took place. One man was killed in the confrontation—an Indian whom the Americans had placed in charge of the stolen livestock. The Americans escaped with most of the animals, but several mares were recovered, along with the thieves' baggage. Included in the baggage were several daguerreotypes of men "well-known" in San Bernardino.

Several days later, four of the six men were captured while in possession of 23 horses, most of them belonging to Palomares, with the remainder having a sprinkling of different brands. The thieves were all well known, being San Bernardino "Mormons," a term which during these years had become a catch-all that referred to anyone who had ever been connected with the Mormon community, including ex-Mormons, Jack-Mormons, Reorganized Mormons, and people who associated with Mormons. This was the first of several episodes involving Mormon horse thieves to occur over the next few months. The four men who had been arrested were Roy McBride, Isaac Hawley, Robert Graham and James H. Ferry. Upon reviewing the evidence, the grand jury indicted all four for grand larceny (more than $50), and trial was set for July 6, 1861, with Justice of the Peace Moses Morse presiding.[5]

McBride was tried first, and as his defense he claimed that he had come by the horses honestly and did not know they were stolen. Aaron Lane was called as a witness, probably because he had seen the men and horses, as well as the pursuers, pass by his station. Since his testimony was not recorded, nor that of the other witnesses, the details of the case are vague. The description of the stolen stock provided by Palomares was given in great detail, listing all brands, marks, colors and distinguishing features. When the jury found McBride guilty, the other three defendants changed their pleas to guilty, and all were sentenced by Judge Morse to two years in state prison.

While the trial was underway, the two other members of the gang, Lot Huntington and William Alma (Al) Williams, who had also been indicted and bench warrants issued for their arrest, were reported as having been seen at the lower crossing of the Mojave River. It was said that the two escaped men swore "vengeance because of their failure, and threatened while at the Mojave to come in three months and get even," a threat which they would make good.[6] This had to have been an embarrassment for the respectable Mormon community. Al Williams was the brother of Thomas Williams, the merchant killed by Indians and buried at Bitter Springs the year prior. It is somewhat ironic that Al Williams had been living with Justice Morse during the previous year, which is shown by the 1860 census, and for that matter may yet have been living with him when the Palomares theft occurred. Lot Huntington's father, Dimick, was the brother of William Dresser Huntington, a prominent Mormon in San Bernardino.[7] William Huntington's son Heber, Lot's cousin, was later the owner of a way station in the 1870s, in what is now Victorville.[8]

Sheriff Anson Van Leuven assembled a posse of seventeen men to pursue the two fugitives in the desert. The posse was within a few miles of where the culprits were thought to be when trouble broke out. The men started to argue among themselves and a shoot-out began between the members of the posse. Guns blazed and bullets flew, and when it was over, four men were wounded, two "desperately" so. The group was forced to abandon the chase, and returned empty-handed to San Bernardino[9]

*From Richard D. and Kathryn L. Thompson. *Pioneer of the Mojave: The Life and Times of Aaron G. Lane*. Apple Valley, California: Desert Knolls Press, 1995. 63–66. Reprinted by permission of the authors.

ORIGINAL NOTES

1. "Silas C. Cox: Daniel Boone of the West," *San Bernardino County Museum Quarterly*, Vol. XXII, No. 1, Fall, 1974, pp. 11–12.

2. Los Angeles *Star*, April 20, 1861.

3. For biographical data on Palomares, and a history of his ranch, see Garner, Bess Adams, *Windows in an Old Adobe*, Progress-Bulletin, Pomona, 1939.

4. Los Angeles *Star*, June 8, 1861.

5. Court of Sessions Book, 1860–62, pp. 211–247, San Bernardino County Archives. See also *People v. McBride, Hawley, Graham, Ferry, Huntington and Williams*, Court of Sessions Case No. Six.

6. Los Angeles *Star*, July 13, 1861.

7. The Huntingtons were early and well-connected adherents of the Church of Jesus Christ of Latter-Day Saints. Zina Baker Huntington joined the Church in 1835, just five years after its founding by Joseph Smith (see Carter, Kate B., *Our Pioneer Heritage*, Vol. 10, Daughters of Utah Pioneers, Salt Lake City, 1967, pp. 391–2). Zina and her first husband, William Huntington, lived in Watertown, Jefferson County, New York. She later became a wife of Brigham Young (Floyd, Elizabeth, *Some Descendants of James Clark of New Haven, Connecticut, and Allied Families*, San Diego Genealogical Society, 1971, p. 2, in chapter entitled "The San Bernardino Clarks"). Precindia Huntington, daughter of Zina and William, joined the Church in 1836, and in 1841 was married in the Mormon Temple, or "sealed," to Joseph Smith. She later married Heber C. Kimball, who was one of the original Twelve Apostles of the Church, and who came to be Brigham Young's right-hand man (Carter, Vol. 10, p. 377).

One of Precindia's brothers was Dimick B. Huntington. When the Mormons moved to Utah, he became proficient in the Indian languages of that region and was one of two men officially authorized to deal in matters involving the Indians. His exploits are scattered throughout various volumes of Carter's work, but Vol. 8 (1965) is especially recommended. Dimick's son, Lot, was born in Watertown on April 29, 1834, just before the family became involved with the new religion. According to the 1860 federal census, he was living with his parents in Salt Lake City. Lot's uncle (Precindia and Dimick's brother) was William Dresser Huntington. William was a frequent traveler between San Bernardino and Salt Lake City, making the trip once a year for several seasons (Carter, Vol. 4, 1961, p. 432). He had three wives, two of whom, Caroline and Harriet Clark, were sisters. Given the prominence of the family, Lot's activities as a horse thief must have created quite a stir throughout the Mormon community.

8. Heber owned the station when a government survey was taken in the 1870s, and his station was subsequently shown on the map prepared from that survey. The map was entitled "Wheeler Atlas 73." When the property was advertised for sale in the April 25, 1877, issue of the San Bernardino *Weekly Argus*, the house was described as having eleven rooms, a large-sized structure for the time.

9. Los Angeles *Star,* July 6, 1861. The part Sheriff Anson Van Leuven played in tracking and capturing the criminals, and transporting them to Los Angeles after their conviction, is recounted in a biography entitled, "Mrs. Elizabeth F. Van Leuven," in the *History of San Bernardino and Riverside Counties* by John Brown Jr. and James Boyd (Western Historical Association, Chicago, 1922), pp. 1103–1106. Elizabeth was Anson's wife, and it was probably she who supplied the details of the incident, Anson having died in 1896. The story of the posse who fought amongst themselves was not included, but it is interesting to note that of all the crimes that took place during Van Leuven's tenure—and he served in troubled times—the episode involving the six Mormon thieves was the one chosen to be told.

The Gates Fly Open: Mojave Tourism Begins

(1885)

In later years, he would stroll about under a big black flat-brimmed hat in the outfit of a Spanish grandee, strumming a guitar. Charles F. Lummis was "Mr. Southwest," the region's greatest promoter, but preferring all things exotic, he especially warmed to being called Don Carlos.

For the nonce, we meet him, showman par excellence, beginning his lifetime of stunts. Not yet famous, the twenty-five-year-old would wrest fame from the world by walking from Chillicothe, Ohio, where he edited a small newspaper, to Los Angeles, sending dispatches on his progress to the *Los Angeles Times*—a progress followed in the national press.

And what dispatches they were! Along the way, two convicts tried to kill him, he had to shoot his dog, and, having broken his arm, he set the bone by standing on a boulder, tying the arm to a tree—then leaping off!

Dreaming of the pioneer heroics of an era recently passed, the nation loved it. One, after all, could be a hero in wild nature. This was the country's first real-time group experience of the Mojave, revealed by its plucky protagonist as a land both terrible and beautiful.

Here, a little dose of each.

T HAT NIGHT, TO MAKE A SHORT CUT, I tramped through a long, low range of the peculiar hills of the desert. As I trudged along over the white, bare sand, or the areas of black, volcanic pebbles, the moonlight gleam on some peculiar object drew me over a few hundred feet to the right of my pathless course. As I came nearer and nearer, a thrill of awe ran through me, for the strange object slowly took shape to my eyes—a shape hideously suggestive in this desolate spot. As I knelt on the barren sands and lifted that bleached and flinty skull, or looked around at the bones which had once belonged to the same frame, now wide-scattered by the snarling coyote, there rose before my eye the tragedy of that Golgotha, vivid as day. . . .

Next day the lying mirage nearly fooled me to a like end. I had camped, unable to reach a station, my water was gone, and all day I had been half dead with thirst. And down in yonder seething valley I saw a broad, blue lake, its very ripples visible as they danced in the westering sun. It was as hard an effort of the will as I ever made not to rush down the long, gentle slope and throw myself into that azure paradise and soak and drink—but I knew there was no water there, simply because so large a lake does not exist in the desert; and that even if it were water it would be poison, since there was neither inlet nor outlet to that bowl of a valley. And so with tottering legs, and blear eyes that dared not look back, and cracked lips and tongue, I ran away until out of sight behind a friendly ridge; and after two fearful hours fell exhausted under a tank by the railroad.

On over the sandy, volcanic wastes, past the barren, contorted ranges of savage ruggedness and wonderful color, I trudged rapidly as possible; and still neither too hurried nor too beset with discomfort to extract a great deal of interest and information from every cruel day. This is a country of strange things; but none stranger than the appearance of its mountains. They are the barest, barrenest, most inhospitable-looking peaks in the whole world; and they are as uncordial as they look. Many a good man has left his bones to bleach beside their cliffs or in their death-trap valleys. They are peculiar in the abrupt fashion in which they rise from the plain, and more so in their utter destitution of vegetable life in any form. But strangest of all is their color. The prevailing hue is a soft, dark, red brown, or occasionally a tender purple; but here and there upon this deep background are curious light patches, where the fine sand of the desert has been whirled aloft and swept along by the mighty winds so common there, and rained down upon the mountain slopes where it forms deposits scores of feet in depth, and acres in extent. The rock bases of the mountains are completely buried in gentle acclivities of sand, while the cream or fawn-colored patches are often to be seen many hundreds of feet above the surrounding level. These mountains are not very high—none, I should judge, over 5000 or 6000 feet—but very vigorous in outline, and, at certain stages of the daylight, very beautiful in color.

*From Charles F. Lummis. A *Tramp across the Continent*. New York: Scribner's, 1892. 260, 262–63.

❧

The Mojave as the New Araby:
"The Desert Gives Forth Perfume"
(1896)

Thanks to Lummis and other enthusiasts, a rainbow light was effusing over this land of horse thieves and travelers writhing from thirst. When in January of 1896 a reporter rode a train east over the mountains into the Mojave, he had the vision of one entering an ethereal rose garden. In his mind's eye he saw not skulls and scattered bones or the grim landscape threatening William L. Manly a few decades before but a beneficent land of flowers, of hyperactive agriculture, and mountains arrayed before him like some grand confection, in edible colors. Blessed by the discovery of gold and the ease of travel provided by technology, the Mojave had become a land of "fantasticalities."

In the course of things, early on the reporter below offers a somewhat scrambled, if imaginative, description of the Joshua tree, signature plant of the Mojave. Yet, in general, the writer is not too far off the mark in picturing this impressive mass of crazed vegetable matter, wild arms thrashing as it rears above the desert.

❧

January 11, 1896, 8 a.m., we leave the mountain-rimmed city of Redlands on a Santa Fe train, bound for Florida.

After a stay of one hour in the shire town of great San Bernardino county, we climb up through Cajon Pass into the wonderful Yucca Gardens of Hesperia—gardens of brevifolia that God has nourished and guarded lo, these many years.

Unbranched yuccas, with trunks five to seven inches in diameter and three feet in height.

Their green tops look like stiff-standing boas; wire seems to have entered into their manufacture, so very stiff are the leaves. Last June we saw each club-like, boa-extended tree with a huge, handsome blossom at its terminus—four to six inches across, and as fragrant as a water lily or a

48

magnolia. Some of these yucca brevifolias have two, some three, some five and some hundreds of branches, and many make weird-looking trees from five to fifty feet in height, with spreading top in apple-tree fashion. But each boa-like branch is from one to five feet in length and each has the trace of last year's blossom at its end.

A now-and-then recurring village of bee-hives reminds us that in leaving California we are leaving the Land of Flowers, where even the desert gives forth perfume more delicious, more delicate than the odors of Araby.

We pass Victor, where a dam is to be thrown across the Narrows of the Mojave river for the irrigation of two hundred thousand acres of land. When this comes to pass the iron horse will betake him to higher ground.

Oro Grande heaves in sight—a mining town with quartz mills and lime kilns and their invariable accessories. Now and then a school-house greets our gaze—and baled hay piled up in the form of a dwelling. Buildings of all styles, from thatched hut to bay-windowed and conservatory adorned home diversity the scene.

At Barstow a luncheon is taken and watches are turned ahead one hour. The train reaches Barstow at 12:30, stays twenty minutes and leaves for The Needles at 1:50!

We have left Pacific time and taken up Mountain time.

We are in the Calico district, where all the greys and all the purples, all the greens and all the browns—and yellows, with all the varying shades of red, meet and commingle in the mountains. All the fantasticalities of a volcanic region with all the splendors of oriental coloring are before us.

"Roll along, roll along"—soon we make Minneola and its submerged dam, by which the waters of the Mojave are to be diverted from their river bed for the watering of "countless" acres. Here, in the summertime of ninety-five, Mrs. Minnie Robinson, for whom the dam and place were named, entertained us right royally. . . .

This is the Atlantic and Pacific road, connecting Barstow with The Needles. The ground is scattered with black-looking stuff like charcoal and soot and tufa. It is lava, and great lava beds lie beyond us.

Here is the "City of Lavic," with craters of Stygian darkness near it—blackest lava in small pieces and large are scattered all about. "The city was great and large; but the houses were not builded and the inhabitants were few."

So quotes from the Good Book a passenger in a white neck-cloth and a close buttoned waist-coat. And from the opposite section a dapper fellow, who may be a traveling man, pipes up—"p. d. few."

We strike a curve, and the graph wires follow our course, leaning away from the convexity of the curve—some of them as much as 25 degrees. Riding as we do in the observation car, under a canopy of blue, an opportunity is offered us to study history as written in the rocks.

The train stops at Ludlow, California, the entrance to Death Valley, about which sentimentalists have been privileged to overdraw pictures at their pleasure—to tell of volcano-guarded passes and death-dealing waters;—while those not seeking a sensation have reported an entirely different state of affairs.

Meeting a water-train, we realize that for a hundred miles in this Mojave Desert water is now brought in tanks and stored in concrete cisterns under ground.

We make the Horse-Shoe Bend, and on a bridge read 1174. This is the 1174th railway bridge—numbering from Albuquerque.

Making a halt at Siberia, we look in vain for Russian exiles—and for snow. This little town on the A. and P. road, this namesake of an Asiatic country, has a warm climate and a clear sky. It has dwellings curiously made of railroad ties. One is laid up of ties lengthwise—and one, endwise; each has a flat roof of gravel—and each is a comfortable retreat in a hot day on this desert. Three or four dark-skinned children emerge from one to see the train; while in the other there appears to be neither woman nor child.

The railway station has a double roof; the upper roof, two feet above the lower one, is suggestive of hot weather. January 11, we ride outside, with neither wrap nor parasol for protection.

At Bagdad we mind us of Aaron the Just and of the simple shoemaker who, happily hammering his last, never even desired to go outside the walls of his native city till that same going out was forbidden by law.

Then he was attacked by such a desperate desire to do what he had been forbidden to do that he went out—and lost his life for the going.

And we mind us, too, of the lovely Scheherizade, who tactfully evolved the thousand stories, and so saved her own life.

At Bagdad is a freight car rigged with a double roof. In it the engineer lives. His sweet-faced little daughter stands in the door, and his dog lies on the doorstep. No tree, no shade—coal bunker, water train—a Mexican village of a hundred inhabitants.

*From "From Redlands to Bagdad." *The Citrograph*. [Redlands, California] February 15, 1896.

Greed Civilizes the Mojave:
"Scarlet Women," Horn Spoons, and Wizards
(1897)

Despite the pleasant words and happy imaginings of the previous piece, in realistic terms greed settled the Mojave. With the discovery of bonanzas—gold, silver, and other precious minerals—in the late nineteenth and early twentieth centuries, thousands of men (and a few women) came pouring into the desert, for the lure of gold instantly brought in droves of fortune hunters to a once despised land. The resulting topsy-turvy camps of shacks and tents were indeed wild, sometimes more bizarre than the movies depict, as music blared all night in the makeshift dance halls and addled rejects from society wandered the streets. Although some of the settlements grew into substantial affairs, with posh hotels and opera houses, after a few years of hyperactive glory most of them "busted" as the precious veins ran out and the hopeful moved on. This has left the Mojave dotted with its present shambles of ghost towns. Nonetheless a few settlements hung on, for, supporting the wild frenzy up in the hills, outside capital flowed into the desert to build railroads, furnish equipment to process ore, and establish supply centers, with all their merchants, doctors, and lawyers. Some of these became the Mojave's present-day Barstow, Needles, and Victorville.

Along these lines of a coalescing society, people who believe that the late Victorians were a prissy lot and their women confined to home and church will be disabused by this frank and admirably written portrait of a wild mining camp drawn by a woman journalist traveling on her own. Despite the 250 "sporting women," the ribald saloons turning out a supine parade of corpses, and a local wizard prowling about in "sockless majesty," Lou V. Chapin emerged unscathed to give us a witty and accurate portrait of boom-town dynamics. Soon after the time of this piece, Randsburg "ghosted," leaving today's shanty-like buildings staggering along its gulch. Today they're occupied by a strange assortment of dreamers, self-proclaimed movie stars and other exiles from cities, who, despite the lack of the gold validating castles in Spain, continue to dream on in their isolated desert community.

M Y FIRST VIEW OF RANDSBURG was under a ghostly night sky, after a thirty-mile stage ride across the wind-swept level of the desert. Sentimentalists may declare that the romance of travel has been destroyed by the railway, but after such a ride on the Colorado desert with the thermometer somewhere near the freezing point and the wind blowing a forty-mile gale, one is inclined to believe that reality in a Pullman is preferable to romance in a stagecoach.

To be sure the railway journey from San Bernardino to Barstow, at which point the road diverges to Kramer, the nearest station to Randsburg, is far short of comfort, even though the traveler to the Rand have a first-class ticket, unless, indeed, he travel by night, when he is permitted to ride in the Pullman. Should he travel by day, however, he is assigned, in spite of all his protests, to the smoking car. A newspaper correspondent, even though a woman, soon learns to conquer over-squeamishness, but a ride in a car occupied by Chinamen, negroes and emigrants is hardly pleasant. In this special instance the brakeman seemed to be of such violent Calvinistic tendencies that he could not refrain from giving the passengers a foretaste of the future of the wicked. The stoves were heated until what there was of atmosphere fairly quivered, but deaf to all pleadings to desist he heaped on more coal. Two drunken miners enlivened the weary stages of the journey by offering their bottles to each and every passenger in turn, and the ubiquitous news agent related his love affairs in a high falsetto voice to two Randsburg-bound females.

After the monotonous desert landscape the hills of Randsburg, even though seen under a night sky, have a charm of their own, and in the light of the sun they form a most picturesque setting for the town which is situated in a gulch and on the slopes of the adjacent ridges. The main street, and the only one which is all "right with the compass," is Butte Avenue, and houses are scattered over a wide area, seemingly without rhyme of reason. Every known variety of domicile, and some hitherto unknown, make up the town, the majority being "pinto" board shacks and ordinary tents.

Joaquin Miller and Bret Harte have created the belief that a mining camp is the scene of a perpetual blood-and-thunder melodrama, but American manhood, even in the rough, can be relied upon to vindicate its reputation, and it was, therefore, with the utmost confidence that I, a "lone and solitary woman," alighted at the one hotel of the place and made my way into the "office." The crowd of men about the stove smoking, chewing, and exhibiting specimens of ore to one another, made way respectfully, and then paid no further attention to me, which was a rude form of delicacy much appreciated. Through the adjoining walls came the sounds of revelry and the rattle of dice boxes, while the tinkle of a piano and the shuffling of dancers could be heard in the lulls of conversation.

The hotel was formerly 20 feet wide by 100 feet long. The office was the congregating place of all who could get in and stand about between the tables, for it was also the dining-room of the place, and when the meals were disposed of was utilized for a bedroom, cots and blankets, and even the bare ground serving for a couch to the weary. There was the adjunct of a small tent in which were eleven cots, and this was called "Room 2." Facetious traveling men who had been in Randsburg advised the unsophisticated of their kind to telegraph ahead for "Room 2," when visiting the place, extolling the accommodations, airiness and space of that choice apartment.

It was decided to enlarge the hotel, but with a large daily influx of guests it was somewhat difficult to accomplish without closing business. It was done, however, by building the new structure over the old. The floors were laid while the office was thronged with guests, and bedrooms were taken and cheerfully occupied by as many as could get in, when there was no roof upon the building. A side addition was made and the walls completed before the floor was placed. It was then found that it would be impossible to sink a large boulder that was on the ground in the middle of the room, and, incredible as it may seem, it was blown up with dynamite without any damage to the building.

In this hotel office, mining men from South Africa, Cripple Creek, Oregon, and Mexico compare notes and exchange opinions. There are among them men of education and ability, who have studied chemistry and assaying in the most famous universities of the world, and have visited all of the great gold fields on the globe, as well as grizzled miners from northern camps, who "know ore," and are experts not to be despised. All are enthusiastic over the Rand district, and predict a great future for it. "If this proposition were in Colorado, where the ore lies deep and mining is all a venture of luck," said one of these men to me, "there would be a shaft on every claim, and millions of money would be invested, but here, where from the very surface down it is pay dirt, and men can plow the ground and turn up wealth, they hang on to their claims like grim death, refusing all offers to sell, and they `coyote,' instead of sinking shafts. Most of the claim-holders are `alfalfa miners,' and while they know placer-mining, know nothing about ore. What we want here is capital to buy those fellows out and develop their holdings."

I had always supposed "the great horn spoon," by which the irreverent emphasize their declarations was an empty figure of speech and substitute for more sulphurous profanity, until I visited Randsburg. There I found it the titular deity, and the only one in general reverence. It is consulted with all the gravity and more success than with which the Greeks sought the Delphic oracle, and its decisions are given in a manner to convince the wise and simple.

The "great horn spoon" has neither "handle nor bowl," but it is the horn of a cow, sawed longitudinally and smoothed on the inside. Its natural accompaniment is an iron mortar and pestle, and to these the prospector submits his ore, pounding it to fine dust. He then places this "pulp," as it is called, in the horn and rocks it back and forth in water, eliminating in this way the ground quartz. The gold dust, should there be any, sinks to the bottom of the horn and adheres in shining grains, while the lighter material flows off with the water. "Horning ore" is a most absorbing employment, and it has a tragic side, too, for the decisions of the oracle of the "great horn spoon" have meant defeat and despair to many a seeker after fortune.

There is a fascination about this whole business of wresting wealth from the primitive elements that charms the "tenderfoot," and gives him some understanding of the life of a miner. His daily occupation is a species of gambling, with nature as the stakeholder, and there is little wonder that in his scant leisure he becomes a passionate devotee of the green table. He drinks to relieve mental strain, and gambling and drunkenness are the common vices of miners.

Every gambling house in Randsburg, and there are probably a dozen, is filled nightly, and eager crowds stand about the tables waiting their chance for a smile of fickle fortune. The bar runs wide open and at many of the gambling houses the scarlet woman is a prominent feature. She sells beer, shakes dice, sings, dances, and drinks with the miner and is the lure for his "dust." Quarrels and shooting scrapes are frequent, and it is safe to say that the single newspaper of the town leaves out of its columns every week enough sensational matter to make the fortune of a great city daily. There are 250 "sporting women" at Randsburg who keep close within the walls of the resorts and who ply their trade without let or hindrance, "a necessary evil," the residents say.

A photographic view of one of the gambling halls would furnish a representation of the various types of the region. There is the rough miner just in from the outlying camp, dressed in blouse, overalls, and hob-nailed shoes, explaining with drunken gravity some "proposition" to one of his kind, who, equally maudlin, is talking at the same time, neither heeding what the other is saying. Tilted back on a chair against the wall is a prospector "down on his luck," fast asleep under the combined influence of his potations and the heat of the stove. The mining expert, the capitalist, the tenderfoot all are here "picking up pointers," and sprinkled about are the flotsam and jetsam of humanity that naturally drifts to a mining camp. Crowds of men stand about "talking ore" and interlarding their conversation with profanity. Half way down the hall a sodden-faced boy saws away at a fiddle with the expression of a sleep-walker, and by his side a murderous-looking Mexican toys with a guitar. If they make any sound it is audible only a few feet away, so great is the general hubub. At many of the tables professional gamblers, cool, calm and silent, handle the chips; and roulette, faro and every other known game of chance is in full swing. From its platform in the rear of the hall comes now and then the notes of a piano, played by a muscular, black-eyed woman with puffy eyelids and unnatural complexion, and then a bedizened creature, with a voice like a fish-wife's, leers at her audience and sings some concert-hall ditty which they appreciate and greet with more or less enthusiastic applause. She comes down and moves among the men, drinking and exchanging ribald jests. The barkeeper, with his sleeves rolled up above his elbows, serves liquid refreshments, and day and night these places are never closed, although they are seen at their busiest from nightfall till daylight.

It is stated in the various accounts given of the discoveries in the Rand that F. M. Moores and others were the original finders of the Rand group, which led to other great discoveries in the district. This story is emphatically denied by William Langdon, who states that in 1894, while engaged in mining at Summit, eighty-five miles distant, he made up his mind to go out prospecting for ore. Some time before he had become acquainted with a man named Golor, who had crossed the desert in an early day and found gold ore. From his description of the place Langdon believed it to be in what is now known as the Randsburg hills. He had befriended Moores and grub-staked him upon this expedition, and together they went to the hills and discovered the Rand group. They made a location, but, as no district was yet formed, no record was made of it. Langdon states that he left Moores to attend to his interest while he went to Oregon and Colorado, but when he returned several months later, he found that Moores had, with others, re-located, and he was left out. Langdon has begun suit under the Federal laws to recover his interest, and he is said to have good prospects of success.

Langdon is, by the way, one of the most interesting characters of the district, and has been a miner all his life. His experiences on the desert and in the mountains would fill volumes, and he has a most interesting manner of relating them. It was he who sometime ago found an old-fashioned Indian bottle half-full of gold-dust thirteen feet beneath the ground while prospecting in the desert.

One of the characters greatly in evidence in Randsburg is the local wizard, who claims to have the power of locating gold, silver, water, gas or oil, and to tell how far they lie beneath the surface. He is long-bearded and long-winded, affecting scientific terms and profound wisdom. He carries in his pocket a black wooden knob with a brass star in the end of it, and in the sides of this knob are two small holes to receive a couple of whale-bone rods tapering at one end, and wrapped with common copper wire. When he is practicing his "magic," which he does for a consideration of $20, cash in hand, he removes his shoes from his feet and strides across the hill in sockless majesty, the wind waving his long whiskers, mystery and speculation in his gaze, holding, of course, his divining rod in his hands. When he comes to a place where there is ore, he declares that the rod will rotate of its own accord, and by the number and character of the rotations he is able to discern, by applying a magic oil to the brass star on the end of the handle, just the depth of the ore below the surface, and its character. Fifty claims have been "located" by the wizard, but, unfortunately for the "magic," nothing has been discovered so far on any of them but sand and boulders, although some of the credulous have dug twelve or twenty feet instead of two or three, advised by him, and several of his dupes have sunk wells but found no water. In spite of these failures, the wizard solemnly assures the stranger that his wand is infallible. When I suggested to him that it would be far more profitable for him to locate mines for himself instead of others, when he had an unfailing guide to wealth, he declared that his love for mankind was so great that he would rather be its benefactor than the owner of the wealth of Ind. and pleaded the simplicity of the needs of a man of science.

I was the first woman to enter the St. Elmo mine, which lies upon the desert six miles from both Randsburg and Johannesburg. The shaft goes almost sheer down, and I confess to a thrill of terror as the bucket swung off and I began the descent into the nether darkness. There is nothing specially startling in the sight of the tunnel, running a hundred feet along the course of the vein at the depth of fifty-five feet, but when you are told that the first shipment of the common-looking rock netted $800 for 800 pounds, you have more respect for it. This, of course, was picked ore, but thousands of dollars have been taken out of this shaft in the form of ore in the past few weeks, and a company has been organized to carry a shaft 500 feet down, cross-drift, and fully develop the mine.

The cooking tent at the St. Elmo, presided over by a versatile genius yclept "Scotty," is a model of masculine housekeeping. Everything is neat and handy, and in the smallest space, and the viands are cooked in granite ware, and served in granite-ware plates and cups. Water is hauled a distance of twelve miles, and the edibles all come from Los Angeles to Mojave or Kramer, and thence by team to the mine, but the table did not lack in good cheer. Three kinds of canned vegetables, delicious coffee and condensed cream, cabbage, frijoles, pumpkin pie and oranges comprised the dinner served to me, and the company boards all of its men. In spite of the isolation of the life, men who can earn $3 a day by the labor of their hands, where the climate is healthful, have nothing to complain of when they have such sustaining food, and adequate accommodations for sleeping.

The new town of Johannesburg, a mile and a half from Randsburg, will probably be the permanent center of the Rand District, for it has an ample supply of water for all present needs, and prospects for supplying all that will be needed in the future. About three hundred lots have been sold so far, and building is brisk, a hotel of forty rooms just finished, and a bank building in process of construction being the most pretentious structure in the place. This embryonic desert city lies on an ideal site on a level plain 3500 feet above sea level, and all about it are the lovely hills.

How these hills would look on a near view I will not undertake to assert, although they are doubtless utterly devoid of verdure, but at a distance they are touched with the softest and most radiant colors of the artist's pallette. Chrome green, red and gray are the predominating tones, given to them by the mineral sulphites and other "ites," and under the blue skies and in the pellucid air of the desert they possess an ethereal beauty.

From every point of view the outlook from Johannesburg is alluring, from an aesthetic as well as financial plane. It is true that at Johannesburg, as well as at Randsburg, the saloon, the gambling hall and the courtesan are social features not to be overlooked, but there are reasons to believe that it may be a center of homes in the future, and that here will grow up a city which will have a permanent life, and which will attract a railroad.

The sampler works recently located at Randsburg buys the ore in small or large quantities from the miner, giving him 95 per cent. of the assay value, and it is shipped to Denver to the smelter, the producer paying the shipping charges. The ore of any lot is divided into four parts and each of the four parts again divided into four, and four or five hundred pounds are taken out at random for the assay. This is crushed by two different machines and a small quantity of the pulverized material is rubbed in a mortar to a powder and then further "pulped" on a zinc metate. It is then equally divided between the assayist and the owner, so in case any fault should be found with the result another assay could be made. The assayist weighs and measures, notes and records everything as he proceeds. He weighs his sample of the "pulp," then mixes it with a chemical which causes the metal to sink to the bottom in a mass. This small mass is placed in a bone-ash tray and set at the mouth of a white-hot furnace, and all of the minerals remaining except gold and silver are either oxydized and pass off in fumes or are absorbed by the bone ash, leaving the gold and silver in shape like a small button. This is placed in a retort and subjected to nitric acid, which dissolves the silver and precipitates the gold in the form of a fine powder. From the weight of the sample of gold the yield of a ton of ore can then be accurately computed. The stamp mills yield but 60 per cent. of the assay value of the ore, and when the milling charges have been paid there is but a small margin of profit for the miner. There are those who declare that the tailing pits of the stamp mills will be worth a fabulous sum in a few years, when they have had deposited within them 40 per cent. of the rich ore of the Rand that will be milled by them. After a while, when these tailings have so largely accumulated that nobody can compute to whom they belong, the mill owner will work them over and realize more than he could were he the owner of the richest single mine in the district. This is one of the features of the business that makes the miners long for the establishment of a smelter at Barstow, or some near-by point where there is plenty of water, and they declare that capital so invested would bring enormous returns, for tributary to such smelters would be the largest and richest gold field of the world.

The return journey from Randsburg is usually made by way of Mojave, a distance of something more than fifty miles. Three relays of horses are required for this trip, and in many places along the way are witnessed instances of humble desert tragedies. The worn-out horses from freighters and stage coaches are cut loose in the waste, far from food or water, to die by the roadside, and at one place along the road are strewn bones of 400 sheep that perished from thirst one day last summer when they were being driven to Mojave. Human skeletons have been found, too, in this desolate, waterless region, and many a stout-hearted prospector has met a most horrible death in this arid region, which the Indians believed to have been created by the devil.

The Rand is well worth visiting by philosopher, capitalist, tourist and student of mineralogy. Its social aspects are full of interest, its opportunities for investment vast, its scenery grand and unique, and its mineral wealth unrivaled. The picturesque and the primitive disappear before the invading railway, and should there arise no new Bret Harte to immortalize the Rand, in a few years its romance will have become but a fading tradition and a memory.

*From Lou V. Chapin. "A Woman's Impressions of the Randsburg District." *Los Angeles Times*, March 14, 1897: 22.

McTeague: The Mojave as Grim Novel
(1899)

Due in large part to publicity over gold strikes, by the late nineteenth century the Mojave was becoming fixed in the national consciousness. Way off there in the distances of the West was a wondrous, if dangerous, place, a land increasingly on the minds of entrepreneurs as well as writers—in other words, a region waiting for the dramatic pen. However, in contrast to Lou Chapin, novelist Frank Norris was wont to emphasize the grim, deterministic aspects of human existence, and, following his doomsday bent, he seized on the desert for one of his most gruesome scenes.

McTeague is about a San Francisco dentist so oafish he pulls teeth with his bare fingers. What better way to show the downward spiral of his sorry life than to end it with a horrifying fate met in Death Valley?—thus matching a barren life with the nation's bleakest landscape.

In 1923, Erich von Stroheim turned *McTeague* into a movie, *Greed*, released a year later by MGM.

"HANDS UP!" shouted Marcus a second time. "I'll give you three to do it in. One, two—"

Instinctively McTeague put his hands above his head.

Marcus rose and came towards him over the break.

"Keep 'em up," he cried. "If you move 'em once I'll kill you, sure."

He came up to McTeague and searched him, going through his pockets; but McTeague had no revolver; not even a hunting knife.

"What did you do with that money, with that five thousand dollars?"

"It's on the mule," answered Mcteague, sullenly.

Marcus grunted, and cast a glance at the mule, who was standing some distance away, snorting nervously, and from time to time flattening his long ears.

"Is that it there on the horn of the saddle, there in that canvas sack?" Marcus demanded.

"Yes, that's it."

A gleam of satisfaction came into Marcus's eyes, and under his breath he muttered:

"Got it at last."

He was singularly puzzled to know what next to do. He had got McTeague. There he stood at length, with his big hands over his head, scowling at him sullenly. Marcus had caught his enemy, had run down the man for whom every officer in the State had been looking. What should he do with him now? He couldn't keep him standing there forever with his hands over his head.

"Got any water?" he demanded.

"There's a canteen of water on the mule."

Marcus moved toward the mule and made as if to reach the bridle-rein. The mule squealed, threw up his head, and galloped to a little distance, rolling his eyes and flattening his ears.

Marcus swore wrathfully.

"He acted that way once before," explained McTeague, his hands still in the air. "He ate some loco-weed back in the hills before I started."

For a moment Marcus hesitated. While he was catching the mule McTeague might get away. But where to, in heaven's name? A rat could not hide on the surface of that glistening alkali, and besides, all McTeague's store of provisions and his priceless supply of water were on the mule. Marcus ran after the mule, revolver in hand, shouting and cursing. But the mule would not be caught. He acted as if possessed, squealing, lashing out, and galloping in wide circles, his head high in the air.

"Come on," shouted Marcus, furious, turning back to McTeague. "Come on, help me catch him. We got to catch him. All the water we got is on the saddle."

McTeague came up.

"He's eatun some loco-weed," he repeated. "He went kinda crazy once before."

"If he should take it into his head to bolt and keep on running—"

Marcus did not finish. A sudden great fear seemed to widen around and inclose the two men. Once their water gone, the end would not be long.

"We can catch him all right," said the dentist. "I caught him once before."

"Oh, I guess we can catch him," answered Marcus, reassuringly.

Already the sense of enmity between the two had weakened in the face of a common peril. Marcus let down the hammer of his revolver and slid it back into the holster.

The mule was trotting on ahead, snorting and throwing up great clouds of alkali dust. At every step the canvas sack jingled, and McTeague's bird cage, still wrapped in the flour-bags, bumped against the saddle-pads. By and by the mule stopped, blowing out his nostrils excitedly.

"He's clean crazy," fumed Marcus, panting and swearing.

"We ought to come up on him quiet," observed McTeague.

"I'll try and sneak up," said Marcus; "two of us would scare him again. You stay here."

Marcus went forward a step at a time. He was almost within arm's length of the bridle when the mule shied from him abruptly and galloped away.

Marcus danced with rage, shaking his fists, and swearing horribly. Some hundred yards away the mule paused and began blowing and snuffing in the alkali as though in search of feed. Then, for no reason, he shied again, and started off on a jog trot toward the east.

"We've *got* to follow him," exclaimed Marcus as McTeague came up. "There's no water within seventy miles of here."

Then began an interminable pursuit. Mile after mile, under the terrible heat of the desert sun, the two men followed the mule, racked with a thirst that grew fiercer every hour. A dozen times they could almost touch the canteen of water, and as often the distraught animal shied away and fled before them. At length Marcus cried:

"It's no use, we can't catch him, and we're killing ourselves with thirst. We got to take our chances." He drew his revolver from its holster, cocked it, and crept forward.

"Steady, now," said McTeague; "it won' do to shoot through the canteen."

Within twenty yards Marcus paused, made a rest of his left forearm and fired.

"You *got* him," cried McTeague. "No, he's up again. Shoot him again. He's going to bolt."

Marcus ran on, firing as he ran. The mule, one foreleg trailing, scrambled along, squealing and snorting. Marcus fired his last shot. The mule pitched forward upon his head, then, rolling sideways, fell upon the canteen, bursting it open and spilling its entire contents into the sand.

Marcus and McTeague ran up, and Marcus snatched the battered canteen from under the reeking, bloody hide. There was no water left. Marcus flung the canteen from him and stood up, facing McTeague. There was a pause.

"We're dead men," said Marcus.

McTeague looked from him out over the desert. Chaotic desolation stretched from them on either hand, flaming and glaring with the afternoon heat. There was the brazen sky and the leagues upon leagues of alkali, leper white. There was nothing more. They were in the heart of Death Valley.

"Not a drop of water," muttered McTeague; "not a drop of water."

"We can drink the mule's blood," said Marcus. "It's been done before. But—but—" he looked down at the quivering, gory body—"but I ain't thirsty enough for that yet."

"Where's the nearest water?"

"Well, it's about a hundred miles or more back of us in the Panamint hills," returned Marcus, doggedly. "We'd be crazy long before we reached it. I tell you, we're done for, by damn, we're *done* for. We ain't ever going to get outa here."

"Done for?" murmured the other, looking about stupidly. "Done for, that's the word. Done for? Yes, I guess we're done for."

"What are we going to do *now*?" exclaimed Marcus, sharply, after a while.

"Well, let's—let's be moving along—somewhere."

"*Where*, I'd like to know? What's the good of moving on?"

"What's the good of stopping here?"

There was a silence.

"Lord, it's hot," said the dentist, finally, wiping his forehead with the back of his hand. Marcus ground his teeth.

"Done for," he muttered; "done for."

"I never *was* so thirsty," continued McTeague. "I'm that dry I can hear my tongue rubbing against the roof of my mouth."

"Well, we can't stop here," said Marcus, finally; "we got to go somewhere. We'll try and get back, but it ain't no manner of use. Anything we want to take along with us from the mule? We can—"

Suddenly he paused. In an instant the eyes of the two doomed men had met as the same thought simultaneously rose in their minds. The canvas sack with its five thousand dollars was still tied to the horn of the saddle.

Marcus had emptied his revolver at the mule, and though he still wore his cartridge belt, he was for the moment as unarmed as McTeague.

"I guess," began McTeague coming forward a step, "I guess, even if we are done for, I'll take—some of my truck along."

"Hold on," exclaimed Marcus, with rising aggressiveness. "Let's talk about that. I ain't so sure about who that—who that money belongs to."

"Well, I *am*, you see," growled the dentist.

The old enmity between the two men, their ancient hate, was flaming up again.

"Don't try an' load that gun either," cried McTeague, fixing Marcus with his little eyes.

"Then don't lay your finger on that sack," shouted the other. "You're my prisoner, do you understand? You'll do as I say." Marcus had drawn the handcuffs from his pocket, and stood ready with his revolver held as a club. "You soldiered me out of that money once, and played me for a sucker, an' it's *my* turn now. Don't you lay your finger on that sack."

Marcus barred McTeague's way, white with passion. McTeague did not answer. His eyes drew to two fine, twinkling points, and his enormous hands knotted themselves into fists, hard as wooden mallets. He moved a step nearer to Marcus, then another.

Suddenly the men grappled, and in another instant were rolling and struggling upon the hot white ground. McTeague thrust Marcus backward until he tripped and fell over the body of the dead mule. The little bird cage broke from the saddle with the violence of their fall, and rolled out upon the ground, the flour-bags slipping from it. McTeague tore the revolver from Marcus's grip and struck out with it blindly. Clouds of alkali dust, fine and pungent, enveloped the two fighting men, all but strangling them.

McTeague did not know how he killed his enemy, but all at once Marcus grew still beneath his blows. Then there was a sudden last return of energy. McTeague's right wrist was caught, something clicked upon it, then the struggling body fell limp and motionless with a long breath.

As McTeague rose to his feet, he felt a pull at his right wrist; something held it fast. Looking down, he saw that Marcus in that last struggle had found strength to handcuff their wrists together. Marcus was dead now; McTeague was locked to the body. All about him, vast, interminable, stretched the measureless leagues of Death Valley.

McTeague remained stupidly looking around him, now at the distant horizon, now at the ground, now at the half-dead canary chittering feebly in its little gilt prison.

*From Frank Norris. *McTeague: A Story of San Francisco.* 1899. Garden City, New York: Doubleday, Page, 1914. 435–42.

The Mojave as Colorful Reminiscences

(early 1900s)

One of the joys of reminiscing is remembering the past as it pleases us, and that the process may well distort the hard facts of history into pleasantries in a sense matters little if the story delights us. I doubt very much that the childhood town Carita Selvas creates here was in reality anywhere near as fetching as she presents it. Miles from civilization and full of saloons, Daggett was a tough, skull-cracking place—hard enough on whites and likely even less tolerant of wandering Indians. Yet the picture of Mohaves with painted and tattooed faces clinging to the tops of boxcars as they arrive certainly is appealing in a way typical of much Mojave lore.

A S A CHILD I lived for a short time at Daggett, a little railroad and mining center on the Mojave desert. From Daggett were shipped, by the Santa Fe railroad, all the vast mineral riches of the nearby Calico Mountains and Death Valley. It was then miles from civilization.

Barstow, then a tiny railroad junction, was about nine miles west. Two or three miles east was the station, section house, and railroad water tank of Newberry. The roaring mining camp of Calico lay a few miles to the north. This was our world—a happy, contented world, though a strange one.

The sights I was wont to behold at Daggett never lost interest to me. There were huge mines and rough miners, and great roaring silver stamp mills, where the ore was crushed and made into bullion for shipment. There were the 20-mule team borax wagons and their trailers, driven with a single jerk line by extremely rough and ready teamsters. And there were heavily laden pack trains of little mouse colored, long-eared burros to excite my wonder. Many of these half wild little creatures wandered freely about the town. They had been set free by their former owners who had deserted this dry country. Happy the child who was able to corral one for a slow, and usually short ride! Never shall I forget the rude awakening I had and the stars I saw when I tried to ride one. He objected!

But best of all, were the fine people, kind hearts, and sincere friendships to be found in Daggett.

On the other side of the tracks was the business section—grocery stores, many saloons, and a dance hall open all night. There, too, was all the vice which usually went with a wide open western town. Out the far corner of my eye I often caught glimpses of painted, flashily dressed women, who seemed apart from the desert town. But my straight-laced New England mother, not long from her Boston home, always hurried me on with averted eyes.

Among all these strange new sights, nothing filled me with greater wonder than the bands of Mojave Indians who roamed at will over the desert. Their home was on the Fort Mojave Indian reservation, just over the border in Arizona. I never failed to welcome the arrival of these strange roving people—unusually tall handsome men, with long black hair and flashing eyes, and their fat, squatty women with their painted and tattooed faces, and the little greasy, beady-eyed papooses strapped upon their backs. The young Mojave girls were quite trim and pretty but, when older, they grew fat and unkempt.

Although I had been taught both to fear their anger and respect the rights of the Mojaves, I liked to observe them from a safe distance. They were so unconscious of their surroundings, so delightfully unconventional in dress and manner. They bore themselves with such a proudly superior air that the little town looked upon them with mingled respect and fear.

The Mojaves enjoyed almost unlimited freedom among us. No one dared to tamper with them or excite their revengeful anger. One look from those fiery, eagle eyes was enough to overawe one of only ordinary courage. Even the Santa Fe Railroad officials, fearing their treachery, made friends of these "children of the desert" by allowing them to ride free at their own sweet will on top of or inside the empty freight cars. And they were not slow about using this privilege, but kept up an almost constant journeying back and forth between the little desert towns scattered along the railroad. Sometimes, when the mesquite beans were plentiful there, they camped in the dry river bed near Daggett for weeks at a time, building rude shelters of brush and sticks.

My family lived in a large comfortable old adobe house, with a wide veranda along its two sides. It was bordered by a row of tall shiny green cottonwood trees. These were kept alive in summer by a stream of water from the faucet.

This cozy desert home had been built by an old time saloon keeper who had grown affluent, and had sought fairer fields of endeavor. It was located on the right side of the tracks, for the railroad ran through the middle of the town, with a very wide sandy street on either side. Its former owner had surrounded the place with a tight foundation, topped with a high white picket fence. This was to keep out rattlesnakes and sidewinders, we were told. This information did not add much to my tenderfoot mother's comfort, and occasionally these unwanted visitors did slither across our yard. We children were taught to be on guard against them, as well as against scorpions, centipedes, and tarantulas.

One exceedingly hot day—hot even for the desert—we were trying to maintain some slight degree of comfort by means of fans and cooling drinks. Suddenly we heard the rumble of an approaching train and soon after, the well known cry, "The Mojaves are coming!"

Yes, the Mojaves certainly were coming! In the clear desert distance we could discern the slow moving freight train, far up the track toward Newberry. On top of the cars, swarming like insects, were the gaudy red and yellow decked forms of the Mojave women and the tall, dark ones of their men.

Accustomed as was every dweller in the desert to such sights, we nevertheless watched with great interest while the train drew up at the station and the crowds of strange dark people descended from their lofty perch. True to their Indian nature, they uttered never a word, but deposited their gaudy blanket rolls, their only encumbrance, upon the sand near the tracks and there, under that broiling midday sun, evidently wearied by their long journey, one after another dropped off into heavy sleep.

But to one fat, wrinkled old squaw this hard couch on the hot sand was evidently distasteful. After trying vainly to make herself comfortable with the rest, she gathered up a dirty old sack and, without further ado, crossed the street, deliberately opened our latched front gate, and walked in.

Mother watched her approach from behind the locked screen door with some uneasiness, for she judged, from past experience, that she would ask for, or help herself to, anything she might fancy, from an ice cold drink to our best Sunday bonnets.

But it was soon evident that this woman wanted only a quiet nap. She marched straight up the steps to the shady veranda and, depositing her dirty sack before the front door without so much as "by your leave," threw herself down upon it and went to sleep. There she lay, obstructing the doorway for hours, while no one dared to disturb her slumber.

At last we were led by a mighty grunt to believe that she had awakened, and the belief was soon confirmed when a dishevelled form appeared before the locked screen and a dirty hand shook it until it trembled on its hinges.

"Ugh," she grunted, "heap hot, you get dinner?"

"No," mother answered politely, but fearfully, taking courage from the locked screen. "No dinner today. You go now? Goodbye."

And then, such a look of rage and disgust crossed that squaw's face. Doubling up her grimy fist, she shook it before our faces, and muttered ominously, while her wild black eyes never left ours.

"White squaw, no good. Kill white squaw—burn house!" And giving the door a parting kick, she took up her bed and departed, all the while threatening us with her angry eyes and muttering curses.

As if this were not enough excitement for one day, that night there appeared on the scene, we knew not from whence, a character who I believe has long since disappeared from western life—a grizzled itinerant leading his dancing bear. All the populace, including the visiting Mojaves, gathered in the wide moonlit street to watch the bear perform.

The master holding the chain, which was fastened to the animal's steel muzzle, brought him slowly up on his hind legs. Then to his master's rhythmic chanting, "De, da, de,—de, da, de,—de, da, de, de," the great bear cavorted about in a clumsy sort of dance.

The Mojave braves holding the center of the stage with the bear and his master, burst into shouts of delighted laughter. One huge young

Indian seized another by his long black hair and pulled him about in laughable imitation of the dancing bear, meanwhile chanting "De, da, de,—de, da, de,—de, da, de, de." This was the first indication of Mojave humor that any of us had ever seen, and it was really funny.

Next day, the Mojaves still lingered in Daggett. Mother, still a little fearful, insisted that we children stay close at home. She was trying to amuse us by reading a story, when suddenly the great black faces of two Mojave men were pressed close against the window pane. Hands shading their eyes, they calmly surveyed the interior of our big living room. Out of sheer fright and nervousness, I began to giggle.

"Don't laugh. Don't notice them," warned mother in an undertone. But the hand that held her book trembled.

After a few minutes, which seemed hours, evidently having seen all they cared to see of the white man's civilization, they passed on toward their desert camp. But on the way out they nonchalantly helped themselves to our cherished pets—four adorable, little fat puppies, which we had placed in a box, with their mother, on the cool side of the house.

This was too much! When we children discovered our cataclysmic loss, we set up a loud wailing. Even mother, inclined to temporize with all Indians, was roused to action. She notified the town constable and with a small posse he rode out to the Indian camp and recovered our pets.

We were told by an old desert rat that the Mojaves undoubtedly had intended to cook and eat our puppies. But we never really knew whether it was hunger, or malicious mischief, which, in return for our inhospitality prompted them. After a few days the whole band left town and we never again saw our uninvited guests. But we took warning from these experiences and never again so rudely refused the request of a Mojave Indian.

*From Carita Selvas. "Life on the Desert." *Desert Magazine* 16.6 (June 1953): 20–21.

The Mojave: Afterlife to an Aesthetician

(1901)

Art professor and aesthete John C. Van Dyke showed that the desert could serve a higher purpose than as a Great Grinder meting out fate for blind greed or, contrariwise, as a subject for rosy childhood memories. An object of pure beauty, made more thrilling by lurking real or imagined dangers, it could provide meaning (of sorts) for an otherwise meaningless life.

Drawing on the transcendentalists, but with a twist, the sophisticated art professor from Rutgers College (now University) ascended San Gorgonio peak, overlooked the Mojave, and had a vision at the end of his celebratory work. Civilization is doomed, the earth and humankind along with it, but we can thrill that, long after we're gone, the whole globe will have turned into a shimmering desert, its minarets "fretted with golden fire" as in ultimate loveliness the planet spins off into eternity.

Such was his *frisson,* one much applauded by elitist art devotees in the salons back East. In their panic, the spiritually challenged can fly off, clinging to a desperate, if high-voltage, Götterdämmerung. In the course of this, Van Dyke, wresting a strange hope from a gloomy Darwinism, wrote a pivotal book, the first devoted to praising the desert for its beauty, and one after more than a century still setting the airy standard for desert aficionados who may not fully understand the desperation fueling this work of aestheticism.

C OME TO THE EASTERN SIDE of the peak and look out once more upon the desert while yet there is time. The afternoon sun is driving its rays through the passes like the sharp-cut shafts of search-lights, and the shadows of the mountains are lengthening in distorted silhouette upon the sands below. Yet still the San Bernardino Range, leading off southeast to the Colorado River, is glittering with sunlight at every peak. You are above it and can see over its crests in any direction. The vast sweep of the Mojave lies to the north; the Colorado with its old sea-bed lies to the south. Far away to the east you can see the faint forms of the Arizona mountains melting and mingling with the sky; and in between lie the long pink rifts of the desert valleys and the lilac tracery of the desert ranges.

What a wilderness of fateful buffetings! All the elemental forces seem to have turned against it at different times. It has been swept by seas, shattered by earthquakes and volcanoes, beaten by winds and sands, and scorched by suns. Yet in spite of all it has endured. It remains a factor in Nature's plan. It maintains its types and out of its desolation it brings forth increase that the species may not perish from the face of the earth.

And yet in the fulness of time Nature designs that this waste and all of the earth with it shall perish. Individual, type, and species, all shall pass away; and the globe itself become as desert sand blown hither and yon through space. She cares nothing for the individual man or bird or beast; can it be thought that she cares any more for the individual world? She continues the earth-life by the death of the old and the birth of the new; can it be thought that she deals differently with the planetary and stellar life of the universe? Whence come the new worlds and their satellites unless from the dust of dead worlds compounded with the energy of nebulae? Our outlook is limited indeed, but have we not proof in our own moon that worlds do die? Is it possible that its bleached body will never be disintegrated, will never dissolve and be resolved again into some new life? And how came it to die? What was the element that failed—fire, water, or atmosphere? Perhaps it was water. Perhaps it died through thousands of years with the slow evaporation of moisture and the slow growth of the—desert.

Is then this great expanse of sand and rock the beginning of the end? Is that the way our globe shall perish? Who can say? Nature plans the life, she plans the death; it must be that she plans aright. For death may be the culmination of all character; and life but the process of its development. If so, then not in vain these wastes of sand. The harsh destiny, the life-long struggle which they have imposed upon all the plants and birds and animals have been but as the stepping-stones of character. It is true that Nature taxed her invention to the utmost that each might not wage unequal strife. She gave cunning, artifice, persistence, strength; she wished that each should endure and fulfil to its appointed time. But it is not the armor that develops the wearer thereof. It is the struggle itself—the hard friction of the fight. Not in the spots of earth where plenty breeds indolence do we meet with the perfected type. It is in the land of adversity, and out of much pain and travail that finally emerges the highest manifestation.

Not in vain these wastes of sand. And this time not because they develop character in desert life, but simply because they are beautiful in themselves and good to look upon whether they be life or death. In sublimity—the superlative degree of beauty—what land can equal the desert with its wide plains, its grim mountains, and its expanding canopy of sky! You shall never see elsewhere as here the dome, the pinnacle, the minaret fretted with golden fire at sunrise and sunset; you shall never see elsewhere as here the sunset valleys swimming in a pink and lilac haze, the great mesas and plateaus fading into blue distance, the gorges and canyons banked full of purple shadow. Never again shall you see such light and air and color; never such opaline mirage, such rosy dawn, such fiery twilight. And wherever you go, by land or by sea, you shall not forget that which you saw not but rather felt—the desolation and the silence of the desert.

Look out from the mountain's edge once more. A dusk is gathering on the desert's face, and over the eastern horizon the purple shadow of the world is reaching up to the sky. The light is fading out. Plain and mesa are blurring into unknown distances, and mountain-ranges are looming dimly into unknown heights. Warm drifts of lilac-blue are drawn like mists across the valleys; the yellow sands have shifted into a pallid gray. The glory of the wilderness has gone down with the sun. Mystery—that haunting sense of the unknown—is all that remains.

*From John C. Van Dyke. *The Desert: Further Studies in Natural Appearances.* 1901. Introd. Peter Wild. Baltimore: The Johns Hopkins University Press, 1999. 229–33.

A Strange Story by a Governor's Daughter
(1903)

Here's a "mystery" piece. The daughter of a California governor, for many years Abby Waterman ran the family ranch northwest of Barstow. A progressive force in the community, a founder of the local high school and active in the Red Cross during World War I, she gave little public sign of the talent shown in the following, its smoothness and literary sleights of hand marking it the work of a professional.

Did this unmarried ranch woman have a secret writing career? It's an intriguing thought, but after a good deal of effort I have been unable to find one shred of evidence other than this brightly penned story.

September, 1903

THE BALL BOYS had broken jail at Yuma and taken to the desert. When their escape was known, seven hours later, men were sent in every direction seeking their trail. It was lost at the foot of the wall over which the boys had dropped into the sandy road. At daybreak the deputy sheriff, with three men, rode down to the squat adobe house on the bank of the river, and called to the woman frying bacon at an old stove set outside the kitchen door.

"Halloo, Jess! What do you now about this here?"

"About *what* here!" said the woman.

The deputy felt uncomfortable.

"Don't trifle with the law, Jess. You know what I'm talking about. Tell me where's the boys gone!"

"Oh, it's the boys again! And they're gone? You ought to know where, bettter'n I, Sheriff. You've seen more of 'em lately than I have." There was just a glint of triumph in the brown eyes that flashed to his.

The deputy got down from his horse.

"If you hev helped in this here, Jess, we'll send *you* up, this time—mind what I say! We'll search the house, boys."

The woman stepped to the screen door and held it open for the men to pass.

"You are welcome to look," she said. "Pardon the disorder; I was not prepared for such early visitors."

When the men had satisfied themselves that the fugitives were not in the house, they came out and got on their horses. The woman was taking cornbread from the oven.

"Have you had breakfast?" She was smiling at the deputy.

The man was about to repeat his threat; but—he had not breakfasted. The woman poured some coffee, broke off a piece of the hot bread, and handed them to him before he could answer; then did the same for the other men.

"If you are after the boys, you'll have little chance to eat. Better take it while you can."

"Honest, Jess, don't you know where they are?"

Her laugh rang out. "And if I did, would I tell you?" Then, mockingly, "Honest, Jack, I don't know where they are."

The deputy struck the spurs into his horse.

"Come on, boys, we must meet Franks. We'll be down here again, Jess; don't think you've seen the last of us."

"I'll put on a kettle of beans," she laughed.

As they rode away the deputy said:

"If we catch them fellows, it'll be because we keep a close watch on Jess. It'd `a' ben jes' like her to hide 'em right under our noses, though I didn't much look to find 'em in the house when Franks sent me down."

"Do you think she knows?" asked one of the men.

"Knows? Knows nothin'! Couldn't tell what she knows if you was to talk till sundown! That's Jess!"

They found Franks at the calaboose. He sat slouched forward in his saddle while the deputy reported. Then he straightened his heavy frame, pushed his sombrero off his forehead, wiped the sweat from his face and neck with a red bandana, and prophesied:

"If we lose them fellows, it'll be because she helps 'em off. If we catch 'em, it'll be because we're too smart for 'er. We'll watch her!"

"What did I tell you?" said the deputy to his men.

And a watch was put on Jess. And Jess knew.

A year ago she had returned to her girlhood home. She found her two brothers—professional gamblers—making the money which had kept her in a safe and happy life. They were bad men and fit for any crime. But they loved Jess, these two, though they saw no reason to change their lives for her. And when at last, Jess learned this, she set to work to keep their love at any cost, and to save those two heads from the gallows. When they were brought up for robbing the Needles stage and killing one of the posse sent out for them, Jess worked fiercely to get them cleared. She failed. Twice she had sent aid to them in prison. There was no proof of those, but she knew she was suspected. When the deputy told her that the brothers had escaped, she knew she would be watched as carefully as they would be trailed. And how, with eyes everywhere, could she get the money to them, which alone could get them safely out of the country? It was days before hope came to her. Many of the men on the posse she knew. Some had been schoolmates of hers. She ran them over in her mind. Then she sent for the deputy. He had just come off the trail the day before, and was jaded from four days in the saddle and the fierce desert heat. But when Jess sent for him he came. She met him on the porch.

"Sit here, Jack; you look tired out! Is there any news?"

"You know the' ain't."

"Have you found *nothing*, Jack?"

"We know they ain't out of the country; we know that much. They's about corralled, Jess."

"Franks has so many parties out, they are sure to be taken sooner or later," she reflected. "Don't you think so?"

"Yes, they'll be took. It's only a matter of time now, for they ain't got no guns—we know *that* too, Jess."

"And there is five thousand on them, dead or alive. You've been on the trail steadily, haven't you, Jack?'

The deputy wriggled.

"Oh, it ain't the money. I hev to go when I'm sent."

"But if they give themselves up, no one will get the money, will they?"

"Nope."

"If a whole posse took them, five thousand wouldn't be much among them."

The deputy looked at her.

"With the country guarded this way, they can't get much food. Do you think—Jack—they'd starve before they'd give themselves up—starve in some hole?"

The deputy looked at her again.

"Oh, I don't know, Jess."

"Of course, *then*, no one would get the five thousand?"

"Nope."

"Well, it will end soon. Either they'll be taken or—they'll give themselves up—within a week."

"What are you sayin', Jess?"

"You know what I said!"

The woman stood up. The man stood up, too.

"Do you want it?"

"Jess!"

"Do you want it?"

"Do you know where they be?"

"Do you want it?"

"Yes!"

"Swear to me, no soul shall know it!"

"I swear!"

"Then take the watch on this house tonight, and have two horses, good ones, ready for us."

"For us? How am I to know this ain't no trick?"

"Trick? What do you mean? How could I trick you?"

"Get me into their power."

She laughed out. "What do they want of you, Jack? You are not good to eat. Listen! Two men worn by starvation, without arms—*I* know that, too. Did I say week?—they'll give themselves up in two days—"

"How do you know that, Jess?"

"Ask how I know! I know—that's all! If they are to be taken it must be tonight. I can't help them—I may help you—Jack."

"I'll do it," said the deputy.

[[Two double

spaces here.]]

The first light was creeping into the sky when Jess and the deputy rode into the silent, desert "city of La Paz." Years before, La Paz had been a thriving mining town of five thousand people. But, its mines worked out, the place was deserted. The Indians came down and tore the roofs from the houses to prevent the white men from returning to occupy them. They stood now, crumbling ruins—gray and weird in the early light.

"Is it here, Jess?" whispered the deputy.

"Here!" said the woman. "This was the first place searched! It's—further on."

"Not at the Rancheree? Jess! And I told Franks—"

"What good did it do to tell Franks! Him! And you thought of the Rancheree at first? If *you* had been sheriff, Jack, this would have been over two weeks ago." The deputy reined his horse in closer to hers. He said again, exulting, "The Rancheree! And I told Franks!"

Down the sandy street their horses' feet made little sound. A jackrabbit sprang away from a heap of brush and the deputy's horse shied. He struck it with his spurs and swore aloud. His voice sounded strangely in the silent place. The woman gave a quick glance toward a sunken adobe at her right. A giant cactus loomed up by the gap that had been a door. They rode on a few paces.

"Jack, I'm tired out. Let's rest here just a moment. Let me get down and sit on this wall. Somewhere back of that heap there's an old well. Get me some water and I'll be as fresh as can be in no time. Here, I'll hold your horse."

The deputy climbed the wall and then turned hesitatingly back to Jess. She drooped there, below him, with her head bent forward on her arms.

"She's clean beat out," he said to himself, and went on. He could find only where the well had been. Its water had dried in the summer heat. He remembered where there was another, and searched for it. It was dry, too. He turned back to Jess.

At the end of the long sandy street the desert stretched away to the hills. Fleeing along the level plain the deputy could see two horsemen. They were going away from La Paz. He felt for his pistol. He had hung it on the saddle. He ran back up the street. Jess sat where he had left her, idly throwing bits of dirt at a lizard. The horses were not there.

"Did you find the well?" called Jess.

"Where's them horses?" panted the deputy.

"The horses—'is gone,'" said Jess.

*From Abby L. Waterman. "At La Paz." *The Californians* 4.1 (January–February 1986): 24–25.

Wolves on Desert:"
A High Carnival of Crime"
(1905)

The part played by railroads in settling the Mojave hardly can be exaggerated. Besides giving newcomers easy access and providing goods from the outside world, a major role of railroads, at least initially, was to supply the mines and take out their ore, thus making the Mojave's founding economy possible.

Melodrama was another benefit. Railroads allowed city reporters to glide over the mountains, then titillate their middle-class readers. They shuddered at the horror stories from the Mojave's towns, once again proven to be the hellholes and hotbeds of evil that proper urban folks, ignoring their own crime-filled streets, imagined.

꽃

D AGGETT (Cal.) Jan. 31. A high carnival of crime has started in this town.

Toughs and thugs are dropping in from the big cities on every train; they are waiting for the laborers to come in from the Salt Lake Railroad camps, pockets filled with money, now that the gap is closed.

Their grim watch suggests wolves circling the herds with dripping jaws.

The boldness of their crimes is startling.

Early yesterday morning an attempt was made to kill a man for his money in the middle of town within 100 feet of a depot filled with men. A Times man was in the crowd.

All day, two or three young men had been hanging around town, "sizing up" the newcomers as they arrived from "the front" on the construction trains.

One of the spotters was a handsome young fellow with a certain artistic carelessness of dress. His face was stamped with vice. He watched the men along the main street like a cat.

Every now and then he would go up to one and ask for the price of a meal. If the wallet came out and seemed to be fat with money, you could see his eyes glitter.

Early yesterday morning, he put his acquired information to use.

The laborers had gathered in the stuffy little station house waiting for the 2 o'clock overland on the Santa Fe. They had been drinking, most of them. The air was vile with foul "breath"; many of the men were drunk. One, playing the conductor, was signaling to an imaginary engineer and yelling "All aboard."

Came this good looking young man to the doorway. He called to an old man in laborer's dress.

"Aleck wants to see you," he said.

The old man got up and walked out into the night. The men saw him disappear into the darkness toward the town.

In a minute the night rang with his agonized cries for help. He screamed like some maimed animal.

While the men waited horrified, the old man came staggering back into the circle of light about the depot; he was gushing blood from a wound on his head; the gore streamed over his face and clothes. . . .

Fallen women are drifting in from Los Angeles to have a share in the harvest.

Their boldness is only equaled by the male thugs. They are to be seen in broad daylight standing on the porches of their vile little dives in brilliant wrappers.

Yesterday one of the men from the "front," money to burn, started on the rounds of the town with one of these women, both drinking hard at every joint.

He stated to a Times man that, when he was partly under the influence of liquor, two of the woman's male associates fell upon him; they made a sudden rush for him in one of the bawdy houses. One of them beat him over the head with a beer bottle; the other fought him tooth and nail, at last getting the man's finger beneath his teeth and nearly biting it off.

*From Harry C. Carr. "Wolves on Desert After Greek's Cash." *Los Angeles Times,* February 1, 1905: 2: 1.

🔥

Willie Boy: The Pursuit of an Indian Outlaw Transfixes the Nation

(1909)

Probably, little would have come of it besides a local fuss had not President William Howard Taft been passing through the area.

In September of 1909, a young farm laborer murdered another Indian and ran off into the wilds of the Mojave Desert with the victim's teenage daughter appropriated for a bride. Soon after, the girl was found shot dead. However, ghost-like Willie Boy knew the country, and it took many confusing days before a posse cornered him. During the ensuing shoot-out, Willie Boy, running out of ammunition, committed suicide.

Meanwhile, the news of the chase flew over the telegraph wires, and the nation, perhaps too long drowsing in those Edwardian times, quivered with speculations bordering on hysteria. Perhaps the Indians on the several nearby reservations would show sympathy for Willie Boy and rise up in a last-ditch battle against the white man. Then the renegades would attack the President's train! For all its mangling of facts (for instance, there is no such thing as the San Bernardino Desert), this article in the *New York Times* reflects the widespread jitters.

It all may seem a little silly to us now. Yet for a couple of weeks the Mojave Desert had been in the national limelight. Furthermore, the commotion left several issues of what actually happened unresolved, despite the probings of subsequent books and an entertaining, if factually loosey-goosey, movie, *Tell Them Willie Boy Is Here*, starring Robert Redford.

🔥

S AN FRANCISCO, Oct 16. Willie Boy, the Piute Indian desperado, for whom three armed posses have been searching the San Bernardino Desert, was found dead yesterday on the summit of Bullion Mountain, where he had been making his final stand.

He had killed himself with the last shot in his rifle and had been dead several days.

Willie Boy made his stand on the mountain against the pursuing posse of Sheriff Ralphs on the afternoon of Oct. 7, after being followed for ten days across the most barren section of the western desert.

Among the Piute Indians Willie boy was regarded as a Lothario. On Sept. 26 he murdered Mike Boniface, an aged Indian, and fled with the latter's fifteen-year-old daughter. Four days later the pursuing posse found the girl's body. She had been beaten and finally murdered when she became too exhausted to keep up with her fleeing captor.

In the battle on Bullion Mountain Willie Boy wounded three members of the posse, killed three or their horses, and finally forced them to abandon the attack temporarily.

WASHINGTON, Oct. 16. The information that Willie Boy had killed himself brought a feeling of relief to officials of the Indian Service, who feared that the desperado might stir up considerable trouble among the Government's wards on reservations near Bullion Mountain. The Government has been in thorough sympathy with the action of the State's posses, and had taken precautionary measures through its agents in the field to prevent any possible aid being given to the desperado.

*From "Indian Outlaw Killed Himself." *New York Times,* October 17, 1909: 18.

The Harvey Girls: Boon to the Mojave

(1911)

In this rough, sometimes crude, land, where Indian "scares" were still possible well into the twentieth century, the railroads did more than haul in mining equipment and haul out ore.

The Santa Fe line across the Mojave was part of one of the continent's main east-west routes. Bringing badly needed grace to the barren landscape, railroad concessionaire Fred Harvey built a string of lavish hotel/restaurant complexes across the desert, architectural wonders that still astound.

Also astounding in that women-poor region were the imported Harvey Girls who waited table. For the price of a cup of coffee and a slice of pie, miners and cowboys could gaze at that rare vision on the Mojave, a nicely groomed, sweet-smelling young lady—who, alas, had sworn, as a term of her employment, to guard her modesty.

Remnants of this survive. In the process of restoration, the shining Casa del Desierto, described below, a white, multistoried fantasy of turrets and crenelations, gives visitors to Barstow an uplifting surprise.

A HOT, SANDY RAILROAD JUNCTION located on what was known as the Mohave River Bridge in the Mojave Desert was named Barstow in 1886, in honor of a Santa Fe Railway President William Barstow Strong. Barstow, California, was another of those southwestern communities created and sustained by the Santa Fe. . . .

In 1910, the Santa Fe began a major renewal program in Barstow, launching the desert junction into the twentieth century at a cost to the railroad of two million dollars. Renovations included miles of new rails, new machine shops, oil and water stations, and a new roundhouse. The construction of the Casa del Desierto gave Barstow the most extensive and elegant Harvey House in southern California.

Designed by Santa Barbara architect Francis W. Wilson, Casa del Desierto was a pseudo-Spanish-Moroccan complex of reinforced concrete and brick. In Barstow's otherwise styleless landscape, it was a true jewel in the desert. It was a self-contained village, and was the fifth such luxurious hotel west of Albuquerque.

Casa del Desierto was divided into three main buildings, all connected by covered walkways and spacious verandas with colorful, lush, flowering bushes. The Harvey Girls lived on the first floor of a wing behind the main section of the hotel. The male employees lived in the basement of the same area, while the second floor had more guest rooms and accommodations for railroad employees. The manager lived in a large, four-room apartment in the main part of the hotel.

Casa del Desierto had its own bowling alley, swimming pool, library, and theater for employees, plus a laundry, ice-making and crushing facilities, a butchering station, and ice cream plant. The latter was the pride of the house, with up to thirty gallons of ice cream made daily. Young Barstow natives could earn pocket money by peddling the ice cream to train passengers on the platform. Barstow's ice cream was also shipped out to Needles, Seligman, Winslow, San Bernardino, even to Los Angeles and San Diego.

Young Harvey Girls seeking life and possible adventure in the desert West found just what they hoped for at the Barstow Harvey House. Barstow Harvey Girls became outdoor enthusiasts and were part of a community whose social life revolved around physical, outdoor living. Tennis, swimming, hiking, and dancing were favorite pastimes of Barstow's populace, and Harvey Girls often donned trousers, heavy boots, and a sturdy hat for excursions into the desert.

*From Lesley Poling-Kempes. *The Harvey Girls: Women Who Opened the West.* New York: Paragon House, 1989. 165, 166. Reprinted by permission of the author.

John Burroughs: A Famous Eastern Littérateur Visits a Ghost Town

(1911)

Only in relatively recent times has the swelling population of coastal California driven celebrities such as Roy Rogers and Frank Sinatra to seek moments of privacy and a taste of wildness over the mountains and into the deserts beyond. In light of this, the 1911 visit to the Mojave of such as nature writer John Burroughs, one of the most famous men in America around the turn of the nineteenth century, was an extraordinary event. Celebrant of the East's gentle hills and green meadows, John O' Birds did not come to revel in the scenery—in fact, seeing the earth's bare bones troubled him. He came, rather, to visit Mojave resident Mary Beal, an amateur botanist he'd met by chance while he was wintering near the Pacific Ocean. Burroughs, however, was the sort of fellow who made the best of situations, even in the gloom of a rainy day, especially when he had an attractive young lady botanist on his arm. In light of this, we have a unique portrait of Burroughs: the aging nature writer cutting up and looking like a pirate as he picnics in a famous Mojave ghost town, then blazes away impressively with a rifle.

***

THE NAME OF JOHN BURROUGHS brings thoughts of green pastures and verdure-clad hills, woods and running streams. The sylvan and pastoral divinities, which held his affections, are a far cry from desert wastes. But once, as my guest, he spent a little time in the Mojave, and its very strangeness aroused his interest.

It was because of John Burroughs that I first came to the Van Dyke ranch near Daggett. I had become friends with him while I worked in the Riverside library between 1906 and 1910, and had been invited to spend the summer of 1910 at the Burroughs home on the Hudson. But a severe case of pneumonia left me in such condition that the trip was impossible and I had to plan, instead, to go into the mountains to attempt to regain my health.

When Burroughs heard of this he wrote: "I wish you would consider the desert instead." He told me of John Muir's daughter, Helen, who had gone to the desert after suffering pneumonia and had recovered completely. "Write John Muir," he insisted. I wrote and then, at Muir's request, to his daughter and in a week I was on the way to the ranch and life in a tent house.

In January 1911, John Burroughs and his wife were on their way to California, stopping at the Grand Canyon enroute. They planned to stop at Daggett to visit me, but Mrs. Burroughs' health was uncertain and she decided to stay on a few days at the canyon, rather than risk the unknown quantity of a desert ranch or small frontier hotel. But as for Burroughs, he wrote: "I can sleep on a cot or a haymow, if need be."

Owing to a delayed telegram no one met him at the station and he made his way on foot to the ranch, a mile away. But he insisted that he had enjoyed keenly the walk on the desert in the fresh early morning air.

The first day was given over, as might have been expected, to watching the birds and walks about the ranch. The matchless blue of the mountain bluebird fluttering over the winter-browned alfalfa fields, a large flock of tiny pipits, walking sedately about with bobbing heads and tilting tails, robins laughing all over the place, meadowlarks caroling a phrase of springlike melody, flocks of horned larks suddenly springing from the ground and wheeling about with tinkling bits of song, the quick strong flight of the redshafted flicker—even the activities of an industrious gopher—all came in for interested attention.

But the omnipresent white-crowned Gambel's sparrows won "John O' Bird's" heart. Scores of them made themselves at home at my little tent house beside a cottonwood tree. As we sat on the porch they hopped about our feet and fluttered all around us unafraid, chirping and chattering like a lot of happy children at play. He assured me that a little effort and patience would teach them to eat from my hand, and urged me to try it.

The long slope leading to the mountain range at the south offered inviting possibilities so we made a path through its low scattered growth to a higher outlook. The arid waste stretched out below us in wide expanse, the only spots of cultivation to interrupt the desert pattern being the little town of Daggett huddled among the trees and the Van Dyke ranch from whence we had come.

Across the valley the Calico Mountains, deep red and terra cotta, overlaid with a thin veil of purple, were suffused with glowing light. The ethereal blue of the farther eastern ranges, softened by distance, became delicate pastels of pink and mauve in the late afternoon light. John Burroughs saw the beauty and strength of the vast solitude and felt the charm of sky and mountain coloring, but forgot not the human nature in the midst of it. "What is the life of the little town?" he questioned. "What do the people do and what are they like? What are their interests?"

On our way down the slope we met a little brown owl that faced about and bobbed a quick curtsey as if glad to greet and pay homage to "John O' Birds" and Burroughs was as delighted as if it had been a human friend.

All the day the Calicos had been alluring, with their patchwork of color, maroon splotched with orange, green, lavender and tawny. The next morning the sky was partially overcast, the sun peeping through the clouds only at intervals. But the Calicos still beckoned, violet and deep velvety purple under the threatening clouds.

With my horse, Dolly Varden, and a runabout we set forth. As we drove across the desert toward Calico's barren ruggedness, all seamed and scarred, Burroughs exclaimed, "What a contrast to our mountains! You have never seen our Eastern mountains, have you?"

"Never."

"They have long flowing lines, very restful to the eye and to the spirit. How novel they would seem to you, with the farms, scores of them, lying tilted up against the wooded mountains at a gentle angle, basking in the sun. But these mountains are lean, bony, angular, alert and threatening. After the lapse of ages, when time has worn them down and softened them, they may look as ours look. Our mountains were old, old before yours were born."

After a few miles the road crossed a dry lake, smooth and firm as pavement, a mile in width and twice that long whose borders, when the sun shone, gave a perfect illusion of water, reflecting the growth along the margin and even mountains 20 miles away. From the dry lake the way lay up a slope much washed and strewn with boulders and rocks of varied hue, swept down by torrents of water that cloudbursts now and then loose on the desert.

John Burroughs was very much interested in the rock streams and we stopped several times to inspect individual rocks and pick up small specimens.

The clouds darkened and a light mist began to fall as the slope steepened to the uplift of the mountains. Here we were joined by Mr. Clifford, a friendly horseman with whom we had arranged to share our outing. He thoughtfully added to our protecting covers a heavy tarp and a big slicker, welcome acquisitions as the mist soon turned to rain.

A short distance farther up the mountains, the road ended at the ghost town of Calico. There were a few more buildings there in those days, but the only inhabitants were three "chloriders" working in the old tunnels, the Mulcahey brothers of Daggett. We made the deserted mining camp our headquarters for the day. Our horses were installed in the half ruined drugstore and we took possession of the old dance hall. The only reminder of its former gaiety was the wreck of a piano, the keys missing and the front casing gone, leaving the strings and all inside exposed. Linnets were everywhere, flying in and out as if on business bent, and several of their nests were on the rafters.

The door of an old safe, brought in from a rubbish heap, made a good foundation for a small campfire, upon which we made coffee, heated a can of soup and broiled chops. It was still raining half-heartedly after lunch, and we persuaded Burroughs to put on the slicker which, meant for a much larger man, dragged on the ground. Belted up and bloused over, its impeding length was remedied but it made him look like a cross between a friar and a pirate.

When the men returned from their tour of the camp, the rain had ceased and we all went down into Wall Street canyon, upon the east wall of which the old town of Calico had been built. Here was a geologist's paradise, with huge boulders and rocks and more rocks, flung here and there or heaped in disorderly confusion. The walls were worn and eroded and everywhere in structure and substance gave evidence of volcanic disturbance. In certain stretches, the exposed strata were tilted and curved and on end or folded over, bent and twisted into queer figures. Where erosion had scooped out holes in the cliffs, birds had found nesting places.

In an open stretch we indulged in target practice. Though it had been long since he had handled a gun, Burroughs' eye was as true and his arm as steady as that of a youth. And what a picture he made in his friar-pirate garb in that wild setting. Standing erect, with a long-barreled 32 balanced in his outstretched hand, his white hair and beard and gentle expression were strangely at variance with his queer apparel and occupation.

Farther up the canyon the walls became higher and steeper until at last we were brought to an abrupt stop at the bottom of a hundred-foot fall. The whole canyon there was a medley of color, suggesting an artist's paintbox run riot. I had supposed Burroughs himself to be a fair authority on geology, but he seemed to feel inadequate here.

"How I should like to visit this place with an expert geologist," he said. "How I'd like to go through these mountains with John Muir!"

Driving home in the late afternoon, the clearing sky gave us beautiful lights and shadows on the mountains and enchanting sunset colors—a picture of the desert for him to treasure in his memory.

The next morning our naturalist wanted to see the pipits again, and the mountain bluebirds, in the little time before his train arrived. And there they were in the same field as if waiting for us. Then he took a final look at the rugged Calicos and exclaimed, as he had once the day before, "How these mountains show their teeth! I wish you could see my tree-clad mountains. They are fat and smooth as babies."

The Calico Mountains made a lasting impression on John Burroughs. He planned to come back for a desert sojourn. They would drive out and bring a tent for sleeping. They would stay a week so he could loaf and invite his soul, as he said, "And go back to the Calico Mountains again." But always something prevented the trip.

In March 1921, I saw him when he was ill in the Pasadena hospital, and he spoke of it regretfully. "I wanted to see the Calico Mountains again," he said. "I wanted to see those mountains. But I fear I never will. You'll have to see them for me."

Short weeks later he died on the train, going home to his soft green mountains of the East.

*From Mary Beal. "When John O' Birds Saw Calico." *Calico Print* 7.8 (August 1951): 3.

"Th' Only Christian Thing To Do": Death and Death Valley Scotty

(1912)

Phineas T. Barnum knew how we love to be scammed. On the Mojave, a character called Death Valley Scotty filled the bill magnificently. Despite the distances, people flocked to his ornate castle, built with riches from his secret gold mines, so Scotty boasted (but actually from the purse of a Chicago businessman having his own elaborate, longtime joke). Gaping at the anomaly of fantasyland towers rising out of the sandy sweeps, visitors gathered around the former rodeo performer, eagerly lapping up Scotty's bizarre tales of his desert adventures.

However, perhaps beneath the glittering surface of entertaining deceptions lay truths deep indeed. As the jingly slogans of political campaigns and auctioneers illustrate, we crave the simplicities of childhood. Desperately, like children, we want to believe—to believe that vicarious glory is our own, that we are loved unconditionally, that there is no death.

Part of this simply may be escape from humdrum lives. Yet there also may be a survival value here. Especially in hard times, as prevailed almost constantly on the Mojave, where death was all around the early cowboys and miners, what did one have if not faith to pull one through, the childish magical thinking that jokes can cheat even death? Thus, believing, if only for a moment, we, too, become victorious with the poet and the scam artist.

A TRICKLE OF WATER was all that separated life and death. Nowhere in America was the margin between the two so narrow. In a land where everyone was on the move, where neighbors were neighbors for a few months at most, where friendships were transitory and one stranger as suspect as another, there was amazingly little reverence for life, and less reverence for death. A neighbor or passing acquaintance who met an untimely end was given a burial of sorts, with minimum display of grief and scriptural reference. In fact, the ceremony was more commonly seasoned with banter rather than solemnity, and the grave marker perpetuated the spirit of the occasion:

Died July 31, 1887
We didn't know this gent's name.
A proper burying he got the same.

or

Here lies Symanthie Proctor
Who ketched a cold and wouldn't doctor.
She couldn't stay, she had to go.
Praise God from whom all blessings flow.

The short-lived town of Calico kept a poetaster busy for almost a decade composing suitable epitaphs for its hillside graveyard:

Here lies Slip McVey.
He might be here today
But bum whisky and a bad gun put him away.

1882
Beneath this stone, a lump of clay,
Lies Nora Young
Who on this 21st of May
Began to hold her tongue.

1881
Joe F. Kelley
Saloon-Keeper
This one is on me.

Here rests Sadie Arbuckle.
Her demise was
Noted by many men.
Her reputation can

Be quoted by those
Who knew her when.

1882
Joe Crabbe
When I am dead and in my grave
No more whiskey will I crave,
But on my tombstone shall be wrote
They's many a jolt went down his throat.

The lighthearted attitude toward death persisted right down to the days when the first automobile tourists began to invade the Mojave and Death Valley about 1910 or 1912, as exemplified in one of Death Valley Scotty's favorite yarns.

"Yar, I was out prospectin'," he liked to ruminate, "when I come across an old man an' woman. They'd driv up in their auto and the damn thing had broke down. They hadn't et or had a drop of water fer two days. Must've been all of a hundred and fifty miles from anywhere.

"Well, I had my burros, but I give 'em what water and grub I had and started back to get help. Then I got to thinkin'. Time I got back them two would be dead. And they'd sure have suffered to beat hell. Took me quite a spell to figure out what to do."

In telling his story to shocked and spellbound tourists in after years the leathery prospector drolly expatiated on the seriousness in the predicament of the old couple and the hard choice he had to make in relieving them somehow of the frightful agony they inevitably faced. He explained how he couldn't bear to let them die that way. It was not charitable. Then he customarily paused, as if there were no more to tell.

"But what did you do?" someone invariably cued him after a long moment of suspense.

"Oh," he'd reply in slight irritation, conveying to his rapt listeners the impression that they ought to know the answer, "there wasn't any choice. Went back an' shot them, of course. Th' only Christian thing to do."

*From W. Storrs Lee. *The Great California Deserts*. New York: G. P. Putnam's Sons, 1963. 27–29. Copyright © 1963 W. Storrs Lee.

A Human Comet Blazes across the Mojave:
The Los Angeles to Phoenix Uproar
(1914)

Across the Mojave, cowboys and miners came swarming down out of the hills. For days they sang, danced, and built bonfires. They were waiting for a glimpse of Barney Oldfield, The Human Comet, as he blasted past them at incredible speeds over the dirt roads—sometimes reaching thirty, even forty, miles per hour. On his way to winning the famed Los Angeles to Phoenix road race, all the more renowned because it crossed one of the most tortured and unsettled landscapes in America, Barney Oldfield left behind a host of wrecked competitors dotting the Mojave landscape, while one tough rival racer, in a moving wreck, managed to complete the race after making field repairs and steering across the finish line with two fence rails.

The excitement, however, soon died down. Soon, cowboys and miners were chugging across the cactus flats in their own flivvers, likely unaware that the ease of transportation in which they were participating was ringing down the curtain on one of our last frontiers.

PHOENIX, Nov 11. Splashing through several inches of mud with all the speed left in the first American car to finish at Indianapolis last May, and believing himself defeated, Barney Oldfield finished the seventh annual Los Angeles to Phoenix road race with first honors and won the title of "master driver of the world."

Louis Nikrent on the Paige No 8 led the veteran to the tape by seventeen minutes; but when time was figured, the mud-stained Stutz had won by thirty-five minutes and fifty-five seconds. Oldfield drove the 696-mile course in 23h. 1m 3-5s, Nikrent's time was 23h. 35m. 56 3-5s. Beaudet on Paige No. 1, was third in, covering the distance in 25h. 4m. 38 4-5s. Durant and Chevrolet in the Chevrolet No. 2, won fourth place although they finished behind Bramlette in the Cadillac No. 19. Just thirty-four minutes and nineteen seconds separated the Chevrolet and the veteran Cadillac when the time was figured.

The cars did not go inside the fair grounds for the finish as has always been the custom. The rain had put the course under water and it was decided to hold the cars off the track until the speed brushes come off Thursday. For miles out on the desert, automobiles were parked along the course and the railroad with hundreds of motor-race enthusiasts waiting for the desert racers. What looked to be the entire population of Phoenix was lined up along the muddy road from the finish line out several miles through the reclaimed lands. Teams worked on the road until time for the cars to come in and the teams were stationed at several washes for the purpose of giving the drivers assistance if necessary.

When Nikrent in the Paige came down the muddy road, there were cheers for Barney. The car was so bespattered with Arizona gumbo that it was impossible to see the number or even the shape of the radiator. Even the passengers on the "Howdy Special," which had followed the cars over the course, could hardly recognize Nikrent as he drove up to the finish.

Crowds swarmed around the car and it required a force of Arizona militia to clear the course for the next car.

Second to finish was the Cadillac No. 19 with Bill Bramlette at the wheel. This was by far the most unique finish to an auto race ever witnessed in the West. Driving at about thirty miles an hour, Bramlette and his mechanic bumped down the stretch to the finish, steering with a pair of fence rails lashed to the front axle.

A short distance out of Prescott this morning the Cadillac went over a twelve-foot embankment. The crowd of spectators helped to get the car back on the course, but the steering arm was so bent that Bramlette could not turn to the right. He drove on, however, with great difficulty and when overtaken by the Howdy Special, twenty miles out of Phoenix, was in first position, leading Nikrent, Oldfield and Beaudet in place by several minutes.

The Howdy raced along with the old Cadillac for about five miles, to New River.

As Bramlette went into the wash, he jumped from the bank at high speed and broke the steering arm. There was a team at the stream which pulled the machine out after about fifteen minutes work. The driver and his mechanic then broke off two fence rails and lashing them to the axle, steered fifteen miles to the finish by rubbing the rail against the tire like a youngster guiding a hoop, with the broken steering apparatus dragging in the mud under the car.

Barney's finish was not exactly spectacular. He drove through the mud at a dangerous rate of speed and it was one of the prettiest exhibitions of the entire race, but the crowds stood silently watching the Stutz slop from side to side in the road, until within a few yards of the finish, then someone recognized the car by the cigar which Oldfield held in the hole in his mud mask.

Wild cheers broke loose.

*From Al G. Waddell. "Oldfield Thought He Had Lost Race." *Los Angeles Times,* November 12, 1914: 3:1.

Hollywood Thrives on the Mojave

(1910–1920s)

With the expansion of the railroads, the coming of the automobile, and barnstorming pilots landing on the streets of mining towns, the early years of the twentieth century were exciting times in the desert. In fact, the Mojave, isolated as it was and with a tiny population, would make an excellent laboratory for an historical study of the impact of technology on a frontier society. Surely, one of the factors would be the coming of the film crews from Hollywood. Hopping off trains into desert burgs with their megaphones, jodhpurs, and strange paraphernalia, they must have seemed creatures from another world. But all was bonhomie in this bizarre conjunction of tinsel with the down-homest of Americana. The kids got shiny silver dollars for playing extras, and the local cowboys, enlisted on the spot as outlaws or gussied up as Arabs, later got to hoot and holler at each other on Saturday night as they dashed across the silver screen, often set up in a town's saloon.

INDUSTRY HAD COME TO HOLLYWOOD, and from Hollywood it was soon to spread into the desert. During the next decades more wealth was to be taken from the desert on celluloid than ever came from all the gold, silver and borax mines. To help stay the insatiable public appetite for cinema, bad men galloped down the canyons before whirring cameras and bellowing directors, the Children of Israel traipsed through the wastelands again and again, foreign legions marched over the dunes, lusty sheiks dragged maidens into desert harems, whooping savages ambushed stagecoaches in the arroyos; ersatz blood, bullets and passion thrilled audiences the world around. . . .

In 1925 the public was given the ultimate in the man-versus-desert theme, straight from Death Valley. The story came packaged in the famed film called *Greed*, and to this day it can provoke such an overpowering thirst in an audience that viewers invariably stampede from the theatre to the nearest bar.

Erich von Stroheim directed it—130 reels of mining, money grabbing, misery and murder from Frank Norris's *McTeague.* But the theme ran away with the director and he did not know when to stop. Eventually he cut the film to twenty-six reels, insisting that they be shown in two installments. Metro-Goldwyn-Mayer ruled otherwise, trimmed the film down to ten reels, and in the process eliminated all but the bare essence of a story.

But left in with every grim detail was the final episode in which the implacable avenger catches up with murderer McTeague on the broad salt flats of Death Valley. In all the heat of the desert the two fight it out, and just before the pursuer is killed he succeeds in snapping handcuffs on Mac. There, a hundred miles from water, against a horizon of endless salt and sand, Mac finds himself manacled to a dead man. In the fade-out he submissively lies down beside the corpse to await his own fate.

Greed was an artistic triumph and a magnificent box-office flop—one of the greatest flops in Hollywood history. Moving pictures of the day, agreed the critics, had to serve up either amusement or entertainment. Von Stroheim's masterpiece offered neither. There was too much avarice, too much aridity and too much Death Valley. For a year or two the picture even helped to scare tourists away from Scotty's Castle.

Though the desert failed to provide a palatable setting for *Greed*, with its complex moral preachment, it proved thoroughly adequate as a location for the string of Biblical extravaganzas that began pouring from the studios in the twenties. Finding just the right spot to look like the environs of Jerusalem, Mount Sinai, or the Sea of Galilee took some doing on the part of location scouts, but in general the Mojave was a fair double for the Holy Land.

The first *Ten Commandments* set the standard for picture testaments that followed. Cecil de Mille traipsed the Israelites halfway across Southern California, with Pharaoh and the Egyptians in hot pursuit. But the filming chronology had nothing to do with Biblical chronology. Moses picked up the Decalogue in Red Rock Canyon; the great scenes of the Exodus and the crossing of the Red Sea were shot on the sand dunes at Guadalupe, near Santa Maria; while Muroc Dry Lake—now Edwards Air Force Base—bore witness to some of the more chilling plight of the wandering Children.

At Guadalupe a huge tent city was set up, with a compound for 2,500 people and 3,000 animals. And it was there that a major crisis of the screening developed. De Mille was sure that he could get the best performance out of a cast of orthodox Jews, and he scoured Los Angeles for them. Eager to re-enact the critical events in the annals of their fathers, they assembled at Santa Maria in hundreds, trusting that they would be properly provisioned during their acting debuts.

De Mille had the right intentions, but there was some oversight in the commissary department, and the Israelites from Los Angeles walked between the parted billows of the Red Sea as famished as their forebears. For lunch they had been offered nothing but ham. A few made an unfilmed exodus before the cameras started grinding.

For the biggest scene of all, Muroc Dry Lake was chosen. Down the rugged hills to the north, Pharaoh's horses and chariots were supposed to charge and chase the Children into the Red Sea.

The Muroc sequence was so stupendous that there were not enough horses and horsemen in all Los Angeles to fill the bill. A hurry call was sent to the Presidio in San Francisco. Responding cheerfully to the emergency, the commanding general dispatched an entire cavalry brigade. . . .

On *Ten Commandments* de Mille sunk almost $1,500,000, to the dismay of his employers in New York. It was an unprecedented expenditure for a film of the early twenties, but as an indication of the market value of California desert scenery in terms of celluloid, the picture eventually earned over $4,000,000.

*From W. Storrs Lee. *The Great California Deserts*. New York: G. P. Putnam's, 1963. 229–30, 248–49. Copyright © 1963 W. Storrs Lee.

The Mojave: Soul's Desire
of a Wealthy Feminist
(1922)

What a difference a few decades make!

About 1920, two wealthy feminists from Cleveland, itching for a break from their earnest political campaigns, chose not Palm Beach, Newport, or some other fashionable resort but Death Valley for their vacation. The pioneers who almost died there would have been appalled at such a notion.

A great change had taken place in America. Although re-created by the movies, its wildness was quickly disappearing, and the few fenceless, untrampled places left were trumpet calls to urban romantics wanting adventures in dangerous (but not too dangerous) places.

That cultural aspect, however, does not undercut the romance, which for the two matronly ladies took on a life of its own, as, savoring their adventure and feeling young again, they ignored the common wisdom and plunged into the wilderness. Here, reading words beautifully crafted with a talent that soars beyond cliché, while also giving us unique pictures of life in this "magical country," we see the two women, both also artists, at last trembling with genuine anticipation, filled with "a strange, terrible happiness" on the eve of entering their bright, funereal goal.

ACCORDING TO THAT MAP Death Valley was now not more than sixty miles away. We thoroughly startled the inhabitants of Johannesburg, familiarly known as Joburg, by the announcement that we were going there. We did not yet know how startling an announcement it was; but these real dwellers on the desert, intimately acquainted with her difficulties, met our ignorance in a more helpful spirit than any of our other advisers had, even the agreeable druggist. Hardly any one ever goes to places like Joburg just for the pleasure of going, and they seemed pleased that we had come. They described the Panamint Mountains which shut off the valley from that side with a barrier nearly 12,000 feet high. There are only two passes, the Wingate Pass through which the borax used to be hauled and which is now blocked with fallen rocks, and a pass up by Ballarat. They had not heard of any cars going in for some time. Unhappily, Ballarat had been abandoned for several years and we could not stay there unless we could find the Indians, and no one knew where they were. None of the Joburgians whom we first interviewed had ever been to Death Valley.

It was discouraging, but we persevered until we found a real old-timer. He was known as Shady Myrick. We never discovered his Christian name though he was a famous desert character. Wherever we went afterward everyone knew Shady. Evidently the name was not descriptive for all agreed on his honesty and goodness. He was an old man, rather deaf, with clear, very straightforward-gazing eyes. Most of his life had been spent on the Mojave as a prospector and miner, and much of it in Death Valley itself. The desert held him for her own as she does all old-timers. He was under the "terrible fascination." As soon as we explained that we had come for no other purpose than to visit his beloved land he was eagerly interested and described the wonders of Death Valley, its beautiful high mountains, its shining white floor, its hot brightness, its stillness, and the flowers that sometimes deck it in the spring.

"If you go there," he said, "you will see something that you'll never see anywhere else in the world."

He had gem mines in the Panamints and was in the habit of going off with his mule-team for months at a time. He even said that he would take us to the valley himself were he a younger man. We assured him that we would go with him gladly. We urged him—you had only to look into his eyes to trust him—promising to do all the work if he would furnish the wagon and be the guide, innocently unaware of the absurdity of such a proposal in the burning heat of Death Valley; but he only smiled gently, and said that he was too old.

Silver Lake turned out to be the place for us to go after all. He described how we could drive straight on from Joburg, a hundred and sixteen miles. There was a sort of a road all the way. He drew a map on the sand and said that we could not possibly miss it for a truck had come over six weeks before and we could follow its tracks.

"It ain't blowed much, or rained since," he remarked.

"But suppose we should get lost, what would we do?"

"Why should you get lost? Anyway, you could turn around and come back."

We looked at each other doubtfully. In the far-spreading silence around Joburg the idea of getting lost was more dreadful than it had been at Barstow. There was not even a ranch in the whole hundred and sixteen miles. We hesitated.

"You are well and strong, ain't you?" he asked. "You can take care of yourselves as well as anybody. Why can't you go?"

"You have lived in this country so long, Mr. Myrick," I tried to explain, "you do not understand how strange it is to a newcomer. How would we recognize those mountains you speak of when we do not even know how the desert mountains look? How could we find the spring where you say we might camp when we have never seen one like it?"

"You can do it," he insisted, "that's how you learn."

"And there is the silence, Mr. Myrick," I went on, hating to have him scorn us for cowards, "and the big emptiness."

He understood that and his face grew kind.

"You get used to it," he said gently.

It was refreshing to meet a man who looked into your feminine eyes and said: "You can do it." It made us feel that we had to do it. We spent a whole day on a hilltop near Joburg looking longingly over the sinister, beautiful mountains and trying to get up our courage. Happily we were spared the decision. Two young miners at Atolia sent word that they were going over to Silver Lake in a few days and would be glad to have us follow them. Perhaps it was Shady's doing. We accepted the invitation with gratitude.

We loafed around Joburg during the intervening days. The stern, red mountains were full of mine-holes, but most of the mines were not being worked and the three towns were dead. Everywhere on the Mojave Desert mining activity had fallen off markedly after the beginning of the war. The population of the three towns had dwindled away and the few people who remained did so because they still had faith in the red mountain and hoped that the place might boom again. The big hotel at Joburg, which was attractively built around a court and which could accommodate twenty to thirty guests, was empty save for us. We looked at and admired innumerable specimens of ore. They were everywhere, in the hotel-office, in the general store, in the windows of the houses. Everyone had some shining bit of the earth which he treasured. We bought some of Shady Myrick's cut stones and received presents of gold ore and fine pieces of bloodstone and jasper in the rough.

We enlisted the services of the garage to get our car in the best possible condition for the journey across the uncharted desert. The general opinion held that it was too heavy for such traveling; the next time we should bring a Ford. When the two young men appeared early on the appointed morning with a light Ford truck dismantled of everything except the essential machinery they also looked over our big, red car questioningly. They feared we would get stuck in the sand and jammed on rocks; but generously admitted themselves in the wrong when, later in the day, they stuck and we did not. Of course they had the advantage, for we would probably have remained where we stopped; while the four of us were able to lift and push the little truck out of its troubles. It was the most disreputable-looking car we had ever encountered even among Fords, a moving junkpile loaded with miscellaneous shabby baggage, tools, and half-worn-out extra tires. Our new friends matched it in appearance. They looked as tough as the Wild West story-tellers would have us believe that most miners are. We have found out that most miners are not, though we hate to shatter that dear myth of the movies. If you were to meet on any civilized road the outfit which we followed that day from seven o'clock in the morning until dark you would instantly take to the ditch and give the right of way.

The drive was wild and fearful and wonderful. The bandits led us over and around mountains, down washes and across the beds of dry lakes. Often there was no sign of a road, at least no sign that was apparent to us. On the desert you must travel one of two ways, either along the water-courses or across them. It is strange to find a country dying of thirst cut into a rough chaos by water-channels. Rain on the Mojave is a cloud-burst. The water rushes down from the rocky heights across the long, sloping mesas, digging innumerable trenches, until it reaches a main stream-bed leading to the lowest point in the valley. When you go in the same direction as the water you usually follow up or down the dry stream-beds, or washes, but when you cross the watershed you must crawl as best you can over the parallel trenches which are sometimes small and close together like chuckholes in a bad country road, and sometimes wide and deep. One of the uses of a shovel, which we found out on that day, is to cut down the banks of washes that are too high and steep for a car to cross.

Most of the mountains of the Mojave are separate masses rather than continuous ranges. Between them the mesas curve, sometimes falling into deep valleys. Instead of foothills, long gradual slopes always lead up to the rock battlements, the result of the wearing down of countless ages, the wide foundations that give the ancient mountains an appearance of great repose. They are solid and everlasting. The valleys are like great bowls curving up gently to sudden, perpendicular sides. The mesas always look smooth, beautiful sweeps that completely satisfy the eye. It rests itself upon them.

When the valleys are deep they usually contain a dry lake, baked mud of a white, yellow, or brownish-purple color. Crossing dry lakes is a curious experience. They never look very wide, but are often several miles across. You need a whole new adjustment of ideas of distance on the desert for the air is so clear that distant objects look stark and near. What you judge to be half a mile usually turns out to be five, and four miles is certainly eighteen. We were always deceived about distances until we trained ourselves a little by picking out some point ahead, guessing how far it was, and measuring it with the cyclometer. Dry lakes are not only deceitful about their size, but also about their nature. Along the edges is a strange glistening effect as though water were standing under the shore. Often the rocks and bushes are reflected in it upside down, and if the lake is large enough the illusion of water is perfect. You drive across with a queer effect of standing still, for there is not so much as a stone to mark your progress. It is like being in a boat on an actual lake. The sunlight is very dazzling on the white and yellow expanses and the heat-shimmer makes the ground seem to heave. Sometimes you have the illusion of going steeply up-hill.

Nothing grows in the lake-beds, but the mesas are covered with the usual desert-growths, sagebrush, greasewood and many varieties of cacti. A view from one of the ridges is a look into a magical country. Only enchantment could produce the pale, lovely colors that lie along the mountains and the endless variety of blues and pinks and sage-greens which flow over the wide, sagebrush-covered mesas. The dry lake far down in the bottom of the valley shines. The illusion of water at its further edges is a glistening brightness. It is hard to tell where the baked mud ends and the sand begins. It is hard to tell what are the real colors and shapes of things. If you can linger a while they change. The valley never loses its immense repose, but it changes its colors as though they were garments, and it changes the relations of things to each other. That violet crag looks very big and important while you are toiling up the mesa, but just as you are crossing the ridge and look back for the last time you see that the wine-red hill beside it is really much larger.

For a short distance we followed the old trail over which the borax used to be hauled from Death Valley. The familiar name, "Twenty-Mule-Team Borax," was touched with romance. Out of the bottom of that baffling, inaccessible valley, through a pass by the high Panamint Mountains where it is sixty miles between the water-holes, and over this weird country unlike any country we had dreamed existed in the world, this prosaic commodity was hauled by strings of laboring mules. They tugged through the sand day after day and their drivers made camp-fires under the stars. We can never see that name now on a package of kitchen-borax, humbly standing on the shelf, without going again in imagination over those two old, lonely ruts.

We lunched at a spring under a cottonwood tree—Two Springs is its name, the only water on the route. Someone once tried to graze cattle there, and the water came through a wooden trough into a cement basin. During lunch the bandits entertained us with tales of the desert. It has its own ethics. You are justified in killing a man who robs your camp or steals your burros. Out there at Two Springs we realized that it was right. If you lose your food or your pack-animal you may well lose your life. Many a prospector has never returned. The elder of the bandits remarked thoughtfully that he was glad he had never had to kill a man. He knew a fellow who had and who was hounded to death by the memory. He was justified by desert-ethics, but he had no peace in his sleep.

Toward sunset we went down an endless slope among mountains, some of which were red, some yellow, some a sulphurous green, and some black. A black mountain is a sinister object. There is a kind of fear which does not concern itself with real things that might happen, but is a primitive fear of nature herself. Even the bandits admitted feeling it sometimes. It is a fear of something impending in the bare spaces, as though the mountains threatened. A little creeping chill that had nothing to do with the cool of evening kept us close behind the Ford. At the bottom of the rough slope lay a somber basin full of shadow, beyond which rose an abrupt, high ridge of sand. In spite of us the Ford gained there and we saw it far ahead crawling up the ridge like a black bug. It seemed to stop and jerk and stop and jerk again. Then it disappeared over the top. For a few fearful moments we were alone with Mojave. How could rocks and sand and silence make us afraid and yet be so wonderful? For they were wonderful. The ridge was orange against a luminous-orange sky, the sand in the shadowy basin reached right and left, mysteriously shining, to mountains with rosy tops. The darkness around us was indigo, the two crooked ruts of the Ford were full of blue.

Apprehensively, jerking and stopping, stopping and jerking, as the Ford had done, the engine clanking as though it would smash itself to pieces, the radiator boiling frantically, we bucked our way to the summit of the ridge. It looked down on an immense dry lake in a valley so big that the mountains beyond were dim in the twilight. At the far side of the lake stood a group of eight or ten portable houses, bright orange beside the purple darkness of the baked-mud lake. It was the town which we had made that incredible journey to reach. Below us we could see the little truck struggling through the sand. Presently it reached the hard edge of the lake and merged with its dark smoothness. We followed down the ridge in its ruts and drove for three miles straight across the hard lake-bed toward the town, where now a few lights gleamed. The orange faded from the houses and the whole valley became a rich plum-color. It was dark when we came out onto the sand again and drove into the lonely hamlet.

A kindly German couple received us. They were as amazed to see two women arrive in a big car as we were at arriving. Once two men had come in a Cadillac just to see the desert, but they could remember no other visitors with such an unusual object. Mrs. Brauer doubted if we would find much to look at in Silver Lake. We assured her that we found much already and hoped to find much more.

"And where did you think you vas going?" her husband asked, chuckling vastly in the background.

"To Death Valley."

"Mein Gott!"

They conducted us to a one-room shack beside the tin can dump and bade us be at home. Strangely enough we felt at home. The door of the shack faced the open desert, the threshold only three inches above the sand. It stretched away white and still, radiating pale light. The craving which had made us seek a wild and lonely place responded to it. The night was a deep-blue, warm and luminous. A hard young moon, sharp as a curved knife blade, hung over the hills. We went out into the vague brightness among the ghostly bushes, and at last onto the darkness of the lake-bed. Beyond it the sand gleamed on the ridge we had come over. On either side the mountains we had feared were strong, beautiful silhouettes. In the northwest stood the mass of the Avawatz, a pure and noble skyline glowing with pale rose. The Avawatz had been the most fearful mountain of all in the sultry afternoon, a red conglomeration of volcanic hills. We walked on and on, full of a strange, terrible happiness. The trackless, unbroken expanse of the lake seemed boundless, the mountains were never any nearer. We kept looking back for the reassuring gleam of the lamp we had set in the window; presently it was lost. Nothing indicated the whereabouts of the town, we left no footprint-trail on the hard mud, every link with mankind was gone. Before starting we had located the little houses in relation to a certain peak and we felt like navigators in an uncharted sea.

"We must learn to steer by the stars," Charlotte said. "We must always remember that."

We stood still listening to the silence. It was immense and all enveloping. No murmur of leaves, nor drip of water, nor buzz of insects broke it. It brooded around us like a live thing.

"Do you hear the universe moving on?" Charlotte whispered.

"It is your own heart beating," I told her, but I did not believe it.

We had found Mojave.

*From Edna Brush Perkins. *The White Heart of Mojave: An Adventure with the Outdoors of the Desert.* 1922. Ed. Peter Wild. Baltimore: The Johns Hopkins University Press, 2001. 34–50.

Snipers and Riots: Violence along the Railroad
(1922)

The appreciation of beauty may require a certain isolation, a detachment from intrusive realities. While trembling at nature's glories off in Death Valley, Mrs. Perkins had the good fortune of being far removed from some nasty events elsewhere on the desert. For instance, if the railroads eased the Mojave's first settlement, they also were a divisive force. They attained such great power across the state that for years California politicians were forced to take pro- or anti-railroad stances. Reflecting the turmoil was Frank Norris's famed *The Octopus*, a 1901 novel about the railroads' stranglehold on wheat farmers in California.

Along the line in the Mojave, railroads all but ran some towns, and their "bulls," or policemen, hardly a kindly lot, were known for the free use of their clubs. Now and then, violence broke out, with rioting and sniper fire from those who felt themselves unjustly oppressed.

S AN BERNARDINO, July 24. A period of calm in the strike created by the appeal for troops here lasted just eight days, and serious rioting broke out again tonight.

Santa Fe passenger train No. 21 was fired on and Deputy United States Marshal O. S. Greenwood and police with difficulty prevented the storming of a car containing twenty-nine workers brought to the shops here.

Believing that a new crisis is at hand, Deputy Marshal Greenwood tonight appealed for reinforcement. He asked that twenty-five additional marshals be sent here.

Two signal torpedoes were placed on the track near Highland Junction. When the train slowed down shots were fired at the coach containing the workers. Two bullets went though the windows. The strikers had telegraphic information of the particular car in which the workers were arriving.

When the train reached the station, strikers numbering about 300 attempted to reach the car. The entire police force of the city and the deputy United States marshals struggled with the crowd. Two marshals were knocked down. One arrest was made by the government agents.

Greenwood demanded the removal of one police officer who, he charged, released a striker placed temporarily in his custody. The marshals were first to draw their guns, so closely were they pressed.

It was apparent tonight that the lull since the Mayor and Sheriff appealed to the Governor for troops was merely the result of the strikers trying to impress inspectors sent here by the State and the Regular Army.

*From "Santa Fe Train Fired Upon." *Los Angeles Times*, July 25, 1922: 1: 1, 2.

Booze Makes Beasts, Not Gods
(1925 or 1926)

Although violence often is overplayed in Western history, nonetheless the wisdom of some old desert rats holds true: that, without the civilizing influence of women, on the desert isolation can turn a man either into "a god or a wild beast." Booze didn't help. As per the following grim account.

DURING PROHIBITION IN 1925 or 1926, Nick Gegg, an immense German fellow, lived in a cabin at Arrastra Spring while prospecting and making moon-shine. Gegg shared his cabin with Claude Yake, who was raised in Pahrump Valley. The two got in a serious argument. Yake grabbed a shot-gun and blew off Gegg's right hand. With his left, Gegg reached under his pillow and pulled out a pistol but was unable to release the safety. Then Yake knocked the pistol out of his hand and picked it up. Yake told authorities that Gegg came at him and as he fled backing down the hill, he shot and killed Gegg. But a witness who came along after the shooting thought that from where the cartridges were it looked like Yake pursued Gegg and shot him. Reportedly George "Daddy" Rose, who soon arrived on the scene collected the cartridges and moved them to substantiate Yake's story.

*From Larry M. Vrendenburgh. "Fort Irwin and Vicinity: History of Mining Development." *San Bernardino County Museum Association Quarterly* Special Publication 94.1 (1994): 89. Reprinted by permission of the San Bernardino County Museum Association.

The Happy Beginnings of Aviation
(1926)

When Barney Oldfield, The Human Comet, blasted across the
Mojave in his Stutz, he was but a precursor of yet more amazing
marvels. Technology came quickly to the desert, a silver, glittering
herald of rapid growth throwing the new society badly out of kilter
with the Mojave's limited resources. Nonetheless, many residents
rejoiced at the newfangled incursions. As one old-timer chuckled
approvingly to me, remembering his first sight of an airplane flying
over his mountain cabin, "Why, it looked just like the pictures I'd
seen in the magazines!"

I N THE BEGINNING there were four of them, and since it was the mid-
Twenties they naturally were called the Four Horsemen, an adoption
of the sobriquet of the era's most famous backfield.

They weren't football players; they were flyers, among the nation's
first in regularly scheduled commercial aviation. They flew between Los
Angeles and Salt Lake City. Up one day and back the next.

One of them crashed in a blinding snowstorm in January of 1930, and
his body was found the following July; one retired early from commercial flying to a ranch in Montana; one now is retired and living in
Oregon; one died peacefully in his sleep in 1964.

The record books say their story began the morning of April 17,
1926, in Los Angeles and Salt Lake City where one of the nation's first
regularly scheduled commercial airline flights originated. In Los Angeles
the pilot was Maury Graham; in Salt Lake City, C. N. (Jimmy) James, a
former Signal Corps flyer. They had been selected to make the inaugural
flights by tossing a coin with the other two original pilots of Western Air
Express (now named Western Airlines), Fred Kelly and Al DeGarmo.

Operations Vice President C. C. Moseley, a World War I combat flyer
and army test pilot, had been picked to organize the flying end of the

airline. He selected the Four Horsemen from a National Guard squadron of which he was commandant. First hired was Kelly, a quiet, whimsical, lanky six-footer—an ex-army pilot who brought grace and coordination to flying. Kelly was soon joined by DeGarmo, a ruddy-faced, husky, former army flyer, and Graham, a handsome World War I aviator who, with James, completed the flight crew.

The morning was bright and clear when James left the corrugated steel hangar of a Salt Lake City airport and started toward a small biplane parked at the end of the landing strip. Among the fair-sized crowd on hand to see him off were politicians with lasting messages to deliver, a pretty girl to christen the plane, airline officials with what they hoped was the look of eagles in their eyes, and mechanics to spin the prop and remove the chocks from the wheels.

Whereas all but the mechanics were dressed in their Sunday best, James's tall, broad-shouldered frame was attired in faded khaki riding breeches, high-laced boots, a V-necked, heavy pullover sweater and a .45 revolver strapped to his waist.

The plane, frail and clumsy by today's standards, looked trim and ready to James that morning. He circled it slowly, thrumming a strut here, checking a gauge there, moving the propeller slowly to determine the cylinders were not frozen. As he passed the wheels of the stationary landing gear, he kicked the heavy cord tires in much the manner of a man about to buy a used car.

Built by the Douglas Aircraft Company, the plane was powered by a 415-horsepower Liberty engine, its so-called tunnel radiator remounted in front of the engine, rather than underneath, on rubber shocks to eliminate vibration and prevent possible damage from landing on rough fields. The craft was capable of carrying a 1,000-pound payload at a speed of 115 miles per hour. Its ceiling was 15,000 feet and its range was 600 miles.

"The mail was in, and I was all ready to go except for starting the engine," recalled James, in an interview prior to his death ten years ago, "when I felt a peculiar thudding on the front of the plane." Leaning over the side, James watched the governor's daughter attempting to christen the plane by smashing a bottle of Salt Lake water into the propeller.

James suggested she hit the bottle on the wheel's hub cap instead. The plane christened and the speeches made, James fired up the engine and took off.

There were several thousand persons on hand to welcome Jimmy when he set down on the 4,000-foot runway of Montebello and taxied to a hangar converted from an old movie studio. "I was very tired," James remembered. "My face was blackened by soot from the exhaust pipes." As the welcoming committee was picking up the first-flight souvenirs, word was received that Maury Graham had arrived in Salt Lake City on schedule.

On the second day of operation James took off at 7:30 A.M. in a slight drizzle, dodging clouds and squalls to Cajon Pass by flying very low along the highways with which he was familiar. When he found it would be impossible to get through the pass CFR (contact flight rules), he pulled up to 9,000 feet by jumping between broken, overlapping cloud layers.

Instrument flying was virtually unknown in those days, so James had to feel his way up through the soup. After climbing, leveling off, doubling back and climbing again for several minutes, he decided he could not get on top to proceed, and returned to land on a small pasture at the foot of Cajon Pass.

James walked to the highway and hitched a ride several miles to a phone, to advise operations at Vail Field that he was down because of weather and would either return to home base or sit it out till the weather lifted.

He decided to go on. After four attempts he wriggled through Cajon Pass. When he left Las Vegas, he ran into weather trouble again and, forced down to about twenty feet, he followed the railroad tracks below. Since there was no radio beam for aircraft in those days, the pilots had decided to follow the Union Pacific Railroad tracks between Salt Lake City and Los Angeles. They agreed to fly to the right of the rails, where possible, so they would not hit oncoming aircraft in bad weather.

"Going up Rainbow Canyon, which is where the Union Pacific cut through the Mormon Range, I thought I was flying about as low as I could and slowed my forward speed by rapidly fishtailing and zigzagging. It was while hugging the ground that I was suddenly aware of a rapid swish beneath me. I knew then there was still navigable air between me and the ground, for that was Maury Graham passing underneath me on his return flight from Salt Lake. He, too, was hugging the rails and feeling his way through the canyon."

From this second day's experience in foul weather, the pilots knew that they would have to do something about improving their weather reports.

Engineers on the Union Pacific cooperated by sending ahead reports. Their advice was not too helpful, however, since they studied weather from railroading requirements, which were considerably different from those of flying. Farmers assisted too by phoning in weather data from telephone boxes along the railroad tracks.

Forced landings were not uncommon in those days not only because of bad weather, but motors sometimes conked out without warning. The pilots knew the air route between Los Angeles and Salt Lake City as well as the backs of their hands, for they laid it out themselves before operations began.

Six months before their historic first-day flights, James, Kelly, Graham, DeGarmo and a reserve pilot, Eldred Remelin, started out from Los Angeles in two trucks to familiarize themselves with the terrain over which they would fly. With them they took several hundred yards of three-foot-wide canvas stripping and hundreds of foot-long steel stakes. This equipment was used to mark emergency landing fields with a huge canvas T to indicate the best direction for landing. They laid out 105 canvas Ts, some of which were still visible until a few years ago.

The truck caravan drove to Salt Lake City on one airway, returning on another, and inspected all alternate routes along the way. They stopped often to ask residents about seasonal weather conditions, precipitation, winds and other data.

Special pains were taken to study the type of earth before establishing an emergency field, for ground that looks all right from the air often will not carry the weight of an airplane. This was particularly true of the alkaline and sandy soils over which most of the route went.

A close relationship sprang up between the pilots and farmers who more than once afforded refuge to the downed flyers. Rather than by name, the families were known to the pilots by the location of their property or the number of children who would come out to wave at the planes. One such family that occupied a special place in the hearts of the early pilots were the Bonners, who tended a government intermediate landing field near their home on the edge of a lonely desert in southern Utah. When her husband was killed in an accident in the early Thirties, Mrs. Bonner provided for her eight children by continuing his role as caretaker of the field. She turned on the landing lights at night and turned them off every morning. After hearing of her husband's death, the airline pilots took up a Christmas fund for the Bonners, although they had only seen the family from 2,000 feet.

The week before Christmas in 1935 a pilot dropped Mrs. Bonner a camera and a note asking her to take pictures of the family and send them to Western's home office. She did this, and from the pictures the pilots determined the sizes of the eight Bonner kids.

A couple of days later Kelly glanced down as he passed over the Bonner residence. He saw "Merry Xmas, Western Air Express Pilots" painted on the roof of the house. On the return flight Kelly snapped a picture of the housetop greetings with all eight children in the front yard.

On Christmas day, Kelly, dressed as Santa Claus, dropped gifts for the eight children and an envelope containing money for Mrs. Bonner, all donated by Western personnel.

Though early birdmen had more than their share of thrills, they occasionally became bored flying long hauls over seemingly endless desert wastes. To break the monotony they would dive down and buzz herds of wild horses and antelope. A favorite trick was to overtake a train traveling about sixty miles an hour in open country. If there was a head wind, the pilot would dip low and, traveling alongside, slowly overhaul the locomotive. When the plane and locomotive were even, the pilot would move in close until his wing tip almost touched the engineer's elbow. The first inkling the startled engineer had that there was an airplane anywhere near was when he would look out of his cab to see a begoggled pilot grinning devilishly at him. Then, with a wave, the aviator would soar out of sight.

"This caper was mild compared to its nighttime counterpart," James recalled. "We would approach a train head on with all wing light out. Keeping well out of the engine's headlight range, we'd wait until that closely calculated moment when we'd suddenly loom up dead ahead coming right at him. Then, we'd turn on all our lights and pull up over the locomotive. . . ."

The night of January 10, 1930, Maury Graham was forced down in a snowstorm between Las Vegas and Salt Lake City. When the weather cleared, Graham's friends hedgehopped the rugged area for days looking for him, but to no avail.

The following June, when the snow melted, the wrecked plane was found, but no trace of the pilot. "On July 16," according to the *Las Vegas Age* (which for many years each July ran this same account), "Major Richard McDonald, who had pressed an unremitting search for the lost pilot, identified a body discovered in a canyon leading toward the highway about five miles from the wrecked plane as that of Graham. The body was flown to Los Angeles by a Western plane and following funeral services there, the ashes were taken by Fred Kelly, Maury's closest friend, and somewhere on the flight of the mail plane between Los Angeles and Salt Lake City, the ashes were given back to the mountainous area in which he had perished. . . ."

In the beginning, Western had six M-2 Douglas biplanes. These were augmented by three more, shortly after start of operations. By 1934, nearly all these valiant craft had been washed out in wrecks or sold.

Only one plane remains. Rechristened the *Escalante II*, after James's original ship, plane number nine is now crated and stored in a warehouse; I saw it about five years ago, trussed to the rafters of the WAL hangar at Los Angeles International airport. When, in 1936, Western celebrated its tenth anniversary, they borrowed the lone surviving craft so that James could fly it back over the original route. A rendezvous was arranged a few miles south of Salt Lake City, where James, in the M-2, and Kelly, in a Boeing 247, came over the airport together before landing.

After that, the airline lost track of number nine until about 1945 when it was rediscovered standing outside a San Diego flying service hangar. WAL bought it for $350 FOB Burbank, and shortly thereafter number nine made its last fight.

It took six days, 100 gallons of gas, a burned-out piston and four forced landings to get the little plane home safe. And today its trail, like the other trails of the flying Four Horsemen, has been all but erased by jet streams of supersonic aircraft, piloted by engineers with their eyes not on the railroad tracks below, but on outer space.

*From Rockey Spicer. "Four Horsemen of Flight." *Westways* 66.1 (January 1974): 40–43, 44, 45. Reprinted by permission of the Automobile Club of Southern California.

✺

The Bottomless Womb

(1929)

There is more than one way to take a trip.

In the process, to see a piece about the Mojave Desert begin with a reference to modern Swiss painter Paul Klee is something of a jolt. Desert-lover Edwin Corle was a scriptwriter for radio in Los Angeles, and it shows in his chromatic writings about the Mojave, with pieces often driven more by romantic enthusiasm to turn out dramatic prose than concerns for accuracy. Nonetheless, here he brings the two impulses beautifully together in creating a truly frightening piece.

✺

I N 1929 PAUL KLEE, a Swiss painter, completed at Düsseldorf in Germany a painting which is neither red nor pink in its totality of color, but varies in degrees of mauve. It shows a little man swimming upstream in what might be a vaginal canal, and as he is progressing it appears that his body is losing its general adult form and he is returning more and more into the shape of an egg. His little eyes are set determinedly close together, he is concentrating upon his goal, and his arms and legs are rapidly becoming vestigial—a few more strokes, and he will be entirely ovoid. He will have arrived at his destination, which can be none other than the womb, and which, directionally, would be located in the eyes of the observer. Klee called the painting by a name which may be freely translated as "refuge" or "retreat" in English. The work has singleness, purity, and no doubt greatness. For his freedom and high degree of originality and his complete cleavage from conventional painting, Paul Klee was branded by the Nazi government an anarchist in art, whose depraved mind should no longer be allowed the privilege of living in Germany. Klee returned to democratic Switzerland and continued his great work until his death in 1940.

Also in 1929, when Klee was at work on his little man returning to a state of gestation, a prospector named Jack Mitchell roamed into the Providence Mountains in the Mojave Desert, sixty miles west of the town of Needles, looking, of course, for gold. The year 1929 would seem, at first glance, to be the only thing that Messrs. Mitchell and Klee had in common. But that is not quite so.

One painted a concept, and the other experienced it. Klee executed the abstraction; Mitchell entered the womb of space-time.

Jack Mitchell was not a conventional prospector. He had been a real estate operator in Los Angeles, and in his transactions he had acquired some mining interests in Arizona. This led to his being bitten by the gold bug, and he proceeded to spend something more than a hundred thousand dollars in the development of his Arizona gold mines. He found some gold but not enough and finally came out in 1929 with nothing. And 1929 was a bad year to start all over again. He could not go back into real estate; so, reduced to the status of a hard-rock prospector living on bacon and beans, he went on looking for gold.

He has yet to find the gold, but his search has been far from barren. High up on the alluvial fans of the Providence Range is the old Bonanza King mine. Mitchell decided to give this area another look in the hope of discovering some low-grade ore. His chief discovery proved to be a lot of bats. When they returned to their home with the first dawn, Mitchell noticed from where he was camped that not one bat but hundreds of them all entered the same cleft of rock. A little climbing through mountain chaparral, and a few blows on the rock disclosed a small aperture.

If all the bats had gone inside, the area within must be a fairly respectable cave. So Mitchell forced the entrance, clambered over rubble, and found himself in a small cavern formed by erosion. But there were no bats. In the rear of the cave was a further opening, not much larger than a stovepipe. Apparently the bats had a cave within a cave, and Mitchell investigated further. It was half a day's work to force this second entrance, and Mitchell picked away until he had broken through into a long, dark passage which led on into the depths of the Providence Mountains. On the ceiling, asleep for the day, clung the bats, disturbed somewhat by this intrusion. Half a dozen of them swept past his head in soundless arcs and dips.

Exploring as best he could with no equipment, Mitchell found passageways and grottoes and large halls and amphitheaters, all more or less bounded by innumerable stalactites and stalagmites. He could not go very far into this series of caverns until he had some cave-exploring implements; so he returned to the daylight of the desert mountain range. . . .

Among the caverns thus far opened there are three or four separate entrances, and some of the caves do not communicate. One of them began like any ordinary series of halls, grottoes, and passageways and then turned straight down into a deep shaft many feet across, which precluded further exploration until somebody could be lowered by a rope. There was no way to estimate the depth of the shaft; flashlight beams failed to show anything, and dropped flares went down and finally out. A tossed rock or pebble obviously ricocheted against the sides in its downward course, but there seemed to be no final plunk of its hitting bottom. So Jack Mitchell decided to go down and see.

With his co-workers he got 1200 feet of rope, and they constructed a bosun's chair and a windlass, allowed for stress and strain and Mitchell's weight (he is close to two hundred pounds), and were careful to guard against the ropes' rubbing against the face of rocks near the top of the shaft. Lashed securely in this swinging seat and armed with flashlights and a little food and water, Mitchell was ready for a journey straight down into darkness. The plan was that when he hit bottom he should extricate himself from his roped security and explore further, and perhaps the others could be let down gradually and a new base established at the bottom of this crude elevator. Then they could work on from there. So far the plan has failed, and miraculously Jack Mitchell is still alive to tell the tale. With everything ready and seemingly every precaution taken, the descent began. Mitchell went down in darkness in order to conserve the light which he would need as his drop in space progressed. He waved to the men at the top, and jokingly they began to pay out the rope. That was the last they saw or heard of Mitchell for two days.

When they were finally able to get him back he was unconscious, badly cut by the chafing rope, which had worked into his hips, without any supplies of any kind, and ready for a hospital.

When you are deep in the chilled darkness of a cave, weirdly illuminated by artificial light which serves only to accentuate the eeriness of your base, since the light is unnatural and increases the rock and stalagmite grotesqueries, and you are surrounded in all dimensions beyond that light by impenetrable blackness, time becomes a relative matter. What seems like eternity may be merely minutes, and what seems like minutes may be hours or even days. Nobody at the top thought very much about it during the first half-hour. Slowly the rope was paid out—once they thought they could see flashes of light as Mitchell was searching the walls of the shaft to learn the nature of the rock or to see if there were level passageways leading off. Once somebody at the top yelled "Hallo!" But the chasm simply swallowed the hail and sent back no echo.

Now 1200 feet is a long drop. In order to get a visual image, recall that the Washington Monument is 555 feet high. But those at the top continued to pay out rope while waiting for a hail from below to tell them that Mitchell had reached bottom. The hail never came. On went the rope until 800 feet were out. There was nothing for those on top to do but to keep on letting Mitchell down into space. Now it was impossible, by leaning over the edge, to see any light down in the shaft at all. Nine hundred feet—ten—eleven—the men exchanged troubled looks; could it be that there was still more to this shaft? Then they came to the end. Every bit of the 1200 feet was out—and where was Mitchell?—no sound, no light, no signal.

They waited.

The waiting was nerve-racking. When it had been an hour they looked at their watches. Odd—the watches said it had only been eleven minutes since the rope had been completely paid out. They waited some more. Had Mitchell hit bottom just at 1200 feet, perhaps, and wandered off, exploring down there below? No—the weight indicated that he was still in the bosun's chair. Then what was he doing? Should they pull him back up? Or was he not yet ready to make the ascent? Why the hell hadn't they planned a more definite system of signals and communication? And they had thought that every emergency had been allowed for—and now, they didn't know for sure what they should do next. Dissension arose. One was for bringing him back; another was for waiting fifteen minutes more. The fifteen minutes went by. At last the men began to be afraid. This deathlike stillness was unendurable. Mitchell was definitely still in the bosun's chair—there was no doubt of that. Perhaps he had never reached bottom. The only thing to do was to bring him up; then, if they had blundered, at least everybody was safe and a second attempt would be possible.

They yelled down to Mitchell that the ascent was about to begin. Just in case he was not ready they waited an extra five minutes. Then he would have secured himself safely again, granted he had ever had any reason for attempting to free himself from the strait jacket of the roped chair. No answer came back from the chill blackness. They began to reverse the windlass. It wouldn't reverse. They put more pressure on it. It didn't budge. In spite of the chill in the clammy atmosphere they broke into a sweat. No amount of exertion could make the windlass bring the rope up out of that black hole. They labored furiously over it for ten minutes—ten minutes? That was odd, for their watches said it was already an hour since they had called down that they were about to begin the ascent.

For another half-hour they worked, but the windlass was jammed, and there was no way to put any concerted effort on the rope strong enough to maintain itself while the 1200 feet were brought up. Mitchell must have felt a series of jerks and pauses and sickening drops as the men tried to use muscular power to no avail. They called down to him but got no answer; they dared not throw flares down for fear of striking him. Outside, the sun was setting and the desert was cooling, but to the men in the cave, night and day were one. They tried again and again to devise some way of bringing Mitchell back from the depths. Nothing worked, and too violent attempts increased the hazard that something might happen to weaken the rope. And if *that* should break . . .

It was impossible to take the windlass apart and repair it without removing the final few feet of rope, and if that were attempted Mitchell's weight 1200 feet below might pull them all over before they could secure it in any certain way. Moreover, the windlass had been constructed and braced well out over the black opening so that the rope might be safe from the danger of scraping sharp rocks on the sides of the chasm; it was in a position that made it doubly dangerous to work on. In other words, they were faced with repairing a piece of machinery which they hardly dared touch.

The next day dawned, and the weary crew weren't aware of it. There was desperate talk of one of them going for help, but where to go and what to ask for was another problem. The nearest town of any size was Needles on the Colorado River, more than sixty miles away. It was a climb of fifteen minutes to the surface, a run of fifteen more over a narrow mountain trail to the nearest automobile, and then an hour's drive to Needles. Explanation in Needles. Ideas. Men. Help. Then an hour and a half more back to the cave. That meant four hours at least before any help of any nature could be hoped for.

Then one of the men looked at the rope and turned paler than before. It was turning slightly, almost three-quarters of a circle, and then turning back. That meant that their efforts, plus Mitchell's weight, had started a twisting motion. If it were three-quarters of a circle at the top, allowing for the play in the weave of the rope, Mitchell must be making three or four revolutions clockwise and then three or four counterclockwise, 1200 feet down below. Besides the sickening sensation of those rhythmic revolutions, it meant an additional strain on the tensile strength of the rope, and unless it were stopped it would eventually so weaken that one life line that it would surely give way.

An improvised and dangerous platform had been constructed about the windlass, and one of the men was out on that, risking his own neck should he make one slip.

Another exclaimed, "The fire department!"

The others thought he had gone crazy, but he repeated the idea. Fire departments have been known to rescue children from cisterns and cats from trees, but could one bring a man out of a 1200-foot abyss? The man who thought of the firemen was about to dash off for Needles to implore their help when the man on the windlass said, "It looks to me as if it ought to work—let's just try it once more."

He scrambled down, and the weary crew tried again. They began to turn slowly, steadily, and the big roller revolved, pulling up the rope slowly, while the men strained and waited for the rope to slip. Somehow it didn't. It had caught, and the roller continued to turn and bring the rope up at a tedious pace, which, to those who labored, seemed to be a foot a minute. Actually it was much more than that; nevertheless it was a good five-hour job to bring the 1200 feet to the surface of the cave. With it they brought the unconscious form of Jack Mitchell. They swung him to safety and cut him out of the bosun's chair and managed to revive him. And then, like the exhausted crew of a racing shell, the men themselves collapsed.

Within twenty-four hours Mitchell had recovered sufficiently to be able to tell his version of the story. He had gone down into darkness, not using his flashlight until he was about a hundred feet below. At this point the cylindrical walls were further apart, and he could tell that he was in a much larger opening than farther above—something like the interior of a huge inverted funnel. Galleries and ridges and corridors led off in various directions, and different geological strata were visible. Once he thought he heard rushing water. But sound was difficult to distinguish in this cavern. The water sound may have been only a hail from above, entirely distorted to his ears. About halfway down, the walls retreated so far that he was simply descending in darkness, and his light was not sufficiently strong to pick up any further rock formations in any direction. After an interminable time he was aware that the descent had stopped. There seemed to be a faint glow far above from the lights around the windlass, but he could not be sure. At last he understood that he was at rope's length, 1200 feet deep into the belly of the Old Woman of the Mountain. He cast his flashlight in every direction—right, left, forward, backward, up and down. The strong beam revealed absolutely nothing but Stygian blackness, no matter how he played it. He was suspended in an immense chamber of black emptiness. No man had ever been here before, and what lay about him or how far the huge chamber extended he had no idea. He ignited a flare and dropped it. It fell burning, a reddish comet falling away from him and disappearing below. He could not say that he heard it strike any bottom. It burned, it dropped quickly away, and then was gone.

For hours he hung in this dead, silent, black womb of space-time. He became weary; his legs became numb; he had to fight a terrific impulse to go to sleep; his mind became torpid. There was no purpose in anything. He was not afraid. There was nothing but nothing and there was nothing to be afraid of. All of that material world of light and sun and shade and color and day and night seemed an unreal dream. All that thing he had thought he lived in was an unreal world on some other planet. No, not some *other* planet—just any planet—for he was in the cold, black emptiness of interstellar space. He was not afraid of falling, for no longer did he have a sense of up or down or north or south. He was alone in the universe. All other men were dead—no, they hadn't been born yet. Which was it? It didn't matter whether man had appeared yet or whether he had to wait another million years to be born—for it was all instantaneous. Time was a hoax. Now he understood it. Time was a silly jest that men believed in, or had believed in if they had lived, or would believe in if they hadn't lived yet. But here, in the womb of universal nothingness and allness, space and time were both simultaneous—this was the quintessential pin point of all directions at once through space and through time. It was all possible points in the cosmos; it was all possible points in conscious time; it was the cosmic center from which some demiurgic force could jestingly create a world and call himself Jehovah or Brahma or Baal.

No longer had he been here in the plexus of consciousness for an hour or two or a day; hours and days were a chimera of limited experience. He had been here for an instant; he had been here forever—it was the same thing. He was not living, he was dead, and in this unlimited death was a meaning which limited life never knew.

After a long time he awoke. There was a breath of cool air. He was moving now through the desert of interstellar space, passing at a distance star clusters, galaxies, island universes of nebulae, some of which contained planets with life on them, and vaguely he had a sensation of pain. Ropes were cutting through his clothing into the flesh of his hips, and he was conscious of a stirring round and around, and then a reversal, around and around. The womb was shaking him loose. He was going to be expelled into life. He was going to be imprisoned into human consciousness; he was going to be born. . . .

This is the story you may easily miss if you happen to visit Mitchell's Caverns. Just how great these caves may be or how far they extend into and under the Providence Mountains and the Mojave Desert is still conjecture. Jack Mitchell is still going on with the slow work of further exploration. Some day in the future they may be mapped and made accessible, but that day is a long way off. But you may be sure that Mitchell will be there for the rest of his life. He declares he has learned more from the caves than he can tell. A descent into darkness holds no terrors for him. And as for the still unplumbed bottomless pit, for that womb of the Old Woman of the Mountain he has great reverence. There are a few words to be said about it above in the limited light of day. Mitchell smiles slowly and says with simple firmness, with determination unalterable: "I shall go back."

*From Edwin Corle. *Desert Country*. New York: Duell, Sloan and Pearce, 1941. 55–57, 59–65.

❧
The Worst Town on the Desert
(1930s)

In contrast to people in more refined, longer-settled areas, Mojave residents produced relatively little writing. This is understandable. In that rough-and-tumble land of tobacco-chewing cowboys and gnarly miners, folks had practical things, such as making a living, on their minds, not creating a lasting literary legacy.

For this we're all the more fortunate to have the writings of rancher Dix Van Dyke. The son of a novelist and the local "judge," or justice of the peace, as was his father, Dix offers a whimsical portrait of Daggett, a once-wild boom town ghosting before his eyes yet lost in its dream of frontier days. Daggett, by the way, is still there, slouching a bit and looking very much the way Dix describes it here.

❧

EW PEOPLE WOULD CALL IT A TOWN. It is not incorporated, it is not a center of bustling activity. Its unpaved streets—mostly one-track roads for occasional cars—wind through stunted vegetation that struggles for existence in the desert. Most of its unpainted houses are veterans of more than half a century of grim battle with the elements. There is nothing in its battered, nondescript appearance to inspire a chamber of commerce or boosters' club to send out invitations to prospective home-seekers.

But I'll wager my last dollar bill that no community in California can show the spirit that survives in Daggett. It may have the ear-marks of a ghost town, but no one who lived here back in the adventurous days has ever been satisfied to call another place "home." Even those who moved away and established themselves in settings of green lawns and vine-clad houses return once in a while to visit with oldtimers who refused to leave the wilderness.

Back in 1882, when the Southern Pacific built a line eastward from Mojave to meet the Atlantic and Pacific Railroad that was creeping westward from the Colorado River, Daggett was born. Railway officials decided that a good place for a station would be alongside the Mojave River, six miles south of Calico, a mining camp which was beginning to pour a stream of silver into the San Francisco mint. Their choice proved to be even better than they had expected when borax was discovered in the Calico Range.

Daggett was a man's town—a rendezvous for miners and an outfitting point for roamers of the desert who came from distant places, or perhaps to have a spree. Most of those who sinned did so openly, and their frailty was regarded with tolerance. But if one became intoxicated and went out looking for trouble . . . he always found it!

One of our great peacemakers was Robert Finley Wilson, a Civil War veteran possessed of a gloomy, saturnine nature, who was elected constable. He commanded great respect from all who knew him because his belligerence made him "a bad man to have trouble with." One day a stranger in his cups started a disturbance, and Bob ordered him to shut up. The answer was a fist aimed at Bob's general direction. In a flash, Bob felled him with a club, and continued to maul the prostrate man until he was completely subdued.

John Ralphs, the sheriff, was a perfect frontier type—a huge, brawny individual with a shaggy thatch of hair and a big moustache. His very appearance and deep, resonant voice was enough to intimidate most wrong-doers, and his reputation for fearlessness was known in every corner of the desert. The deputy sheriff, however, was a small, frail chap; the sort you might expect to see behind a ribbon counter. One day, I remarked to Old Bob that Ralphs had shown rather poor judgment in selecting such a puny assistant.

"Never you mind that feller's looks," Bob retorted. "They don't make 'em no better. He's got the nerve, and that's what it takes!"

Well, the name of that deputy was W. S. McNabb. He studied law, and many years later was appointed United States District Attorney for Southern California.

None of our peace officers happened to be at Alec's saloon one night when hostilities began. Before the tumult subsided there was gun-play, and a Mexican sprawled on the floor. Doc Pitman, the coroner, was a jolly soul who enjoyed visiting a desert saloon and making merry with the boys. In due time, he arrived for the inquest. But to his disgust he could not find one witness to the shooting, although the saloon had been crowded.

The jury returned a quick verdict of death at the hands of persons unknown, which ended the matter. From this incident Alec's place became known as the Bucket of Blood, and acquired an unsavory repute. Its fame spread to the ears of a traveling salesman who decided to have a look at this bit of the "wild west." Entering boldly, he walked up to the bar, laid down a half dollar, and ordered a drink. Over his shoulder came the hand of a husky ruffian and grabbed the coin. Turning to beat a fast retreat, the victim was stopped by another man who laid down the law.

"Oh no ye don't my friend! Ye ain't gettin' out o' here until ye set up the drinks fer the house!"

A thoroughly frightened salesman reached into his pocket and brought out a five dollar gold-piece. While the crowd collected for its refreshment, he bolted out of the door and raced across the tracks to the station, where he stayed until the next train carried him out of town for good.

Daggett's only lynching avenged a murder climaxing a feud between a borax wagon teamster and his swamper [helper]. After a return trip from the mines, the swamper made a bee-line for a saloon, and filled up with whiskey. Several hours later, he told his story to another teamster and asked his advice. Mostly in a spirit of fun, the other asked, "Why don't you kill him?"

The next morning, a man passing by the shack where the two men slept, heard a feeble groan. Going inside, he found the teamster lying unconscious on his bed. Just outside the door lay a wagon spoke covered with gore and hair from the victim's head. Within two hours, he died.

The swamper was promptly rounded up and jailed. So too was the teamster, whose bad advice had been overheard by another man. But even the most persistent questioning failed to get a confession from the swamper, who maintained that he had no memory of what had happened during the previous night. Quickly the rumor spread through town that the suspect was about to be released for lack of evidence, and that report was like a spark in dry grass. A mob collected, held a short council, and then went to the jail. Taking both men out, they hurried them to a telegraph pole. Two ropes were thrown over the single cross-arm, two nooses were knotted, and in almost no time the two culprits were "dancing on air." After a minute, the teamster was lowered to the ground and advised to leave the confines of Daggett within an hour. It wasn't necessary to give him a second hint.

There was something in the code of those oldtimers that demanded prompt and unwavering justice. At the same time they were a generous lot, and never failed to help a man who was down and out. But there were very few among them who had any religious leanings, and I suppose this was the reason why no church was ever built in Daggett. One revivalist stopped to look the place over and became grief-stricken because of its godlessness. So he made arrangements to hold meetings in the schoolhouse. They were well attended, and the congregation proved to be very generous when the plate came around. All of this proved to be highly encouraging to the worthy gentleman of the cloth. After a week had passed, he came to the point and asked all who were saved to stand up.

None stood.

Then after a fervid exhortation, he appealed to all those who *desired* to be saved to stand up.

Not a soul moved from his seat.

The good parson was so horrified that he shook the dust of Daggett from his feet and vowed that this was the worst town he had ever seen. But this, after all, was a libel. Most of the inhabitants were industrious, honorable men who kept their word and paid their debts. Many of them had come from older mining camps in California and Nevada. They were not a pious people.

Daggett is still on the map, but it isn't the town it used to be in the old days. Silver mining took a nose-dive, and Calico became a ghost city. The borax company moved its center of operations to Death Valley when large deposits of Colemanite were found in the Funeral Range. One after another, houses were vacated by families who went away to find new occupations. Business fell off, and the stores dwindled to one establishment. Saloons dried up for lack of patronage.

And so you will see a stage that is not crowded with actors these days. But some of the scenery and trappings remain to prove that Daggett was a typical outpost of the frontier.

*From Dix Van Dyke, as told to Philip Johnston. "Old Times in Daggett." *Westways* 35.2 Part One (February 1943): 16–17. Reprinted by permission of the Automobile Club of Southern California.

The Dry Mojave Slakes the Cities: Prohibition

(1930s)

Traditionally, the motto "root, hog, or die" has been the watchword on the desert. There, both resources and money were scarce, and people did whatever it took to make a living. As Clifford Walker points out, Prohibition came along at just the right time to pick up the slack for the local people during a slump in farming and the mining industry. Stills proliferated across the desert. Somewhat ironically, the dry Mojave took on the role of wetting the whistle of greener places.

As here, people tend to treat that era lightly, conveniently forgetting that bootlegging had a darker side, with Tommy guns and organized crime arriving on the desert, undermining the local law, causing human misery, and validating the corruption we'll see later on in Ramona Stewart's exposé of small-town rottenness.

For years, Professor Walker traveled the outback, interviewing the aging moonshiners. Here is his analysis of the times and a homey reminiscence from one old-timer.

PROFITS IN DESERT AGRICULTURE, railroading and mining kept thousands of families with good incomes from the 1900s to the end of the first World War. But as the wartime demand for agricultural products to feed starving people in Europe declined, prices fell, and many farmers had trouble making mortgage payments in the 1920s, especially on marginal farmland. After the war, demand for copper, lead and tungsten fell, prices fell, mines closed, and smaller desert railroads suffered. Therefore, with some "rails" (railroad workers), homesteaders, farmers and miners struggling to make a living in the postwar recession and the "farmers' depression" of the 1920s, desert residents did not realize they were in what would later be called "The Roaring Twenties."

Upon this background came prohibition and a demand for another product—alcohol. The desert had water, springs and ranch wells all over the place. Flowing underground much of its course across the Mojave

Desert, the Mojave River held a great aquifer of what seemed like an endless supply of fine water just below the surface of the dry riverbed. Ranchers and miners who turned to moonshining knew the desert had the advantage of distance and isolation from the dry squads' sorties coming out of San Bernardino, Riverside and Independence, county seats of three inland counties. Water, isolation and labor created the three ingredients for favorable moonshine operations.

As with every area of California local moonshiners set up small operations, big enough to supply local demand; other booze makers supplied family needs and needs of their neighbors making a little profit to pay expenses.

Large liquor wholesalers in Los Angeles paid for stills to be built or encouraged ranchers to make moonshine and bought it from them. The syndicate, for lack of a better word, often had a conspirator lease a ranch, then set up a liquor operation. For fourteen years liquor flowed from the Mojave Desert into the Los Angeles basin, an endless supply of liquid wealth. Such a supply existed that if a few stills were not knocked over, the price of moonshine would drop and it did drop in 1929 and the early 1930s.

"If the desert gets any wetter, Noah will have to build an ark"—these words were uttered in frustration and with a little jest about the deserts of Riverside and San Bernardino counties.

Local constables, charged with enforcement in their townships, had the unenviable duty to stop violators who were usually their friends or neighbors, often people they grew up with. Moonshiners were decent folks, struggling to make a living and if they made some moon on their homesteads or at an abandoned mine or desert spring, the constable generally looked the other way. Walt Wilhelm, pioneer gas station owner east of Yermo who started his station when the road to Las Vegas was sand and gravel, had respect for the desert bootlegger: "All decent men." Wilhelm assisted Constable Tom Williams and later, in the 1930s, became constable himself.

Penny Morrow, constable of Oro Grande, born in Barstow in 1885, said the same thing: "I didn't go out looking for them or I would have had to arrest all my friends and neighbors."

If someone made bad booze, Constable Melvin "Red" Butler of Victorville searched out the culprit to put him out of business. He frowned on unscrupulous moonshiners who used five-gallon metal cans for their stills or old car radiators for the coils—creating poison. He did not molest makers of quality liquor. Other constables basically felt the same way: J. W. Everett of Ludlow, Jim Lucas of Daggett, and Ed Harris of Barstow.

Constables solved community problems such as drunkenness, drunk driving and disturbing the peace, especially if the culprits were from big cities. If someone issued a complaint of selling intoxicating liquors, constables investigated and made arrests if appropriate and if expedient. Since the WCTU, Anti-Saloon League and vociferous church groups weren't the force in the desert they were other places, there were few complaints about miners coming into town Saturday night to play pool, drink a little moonshine and kick some tailings off their boots. If they kicked too much, the constable acted. . . .

The Owl, Silver Dollar and Monkey House
By George Pipkin, Trona

The Owl is not a bird. The Silver Dollar was not money and the Monkey House was not a zoo; in Red Mountain they were houses of pleasure for many and houses of tragedy for some. They proffered the nearest social services for the many single men employed in Searles Valley and a few married ones too, as well as the miners who worked the Rand Mining District.

The casinos flourished illegally during the days of prohibition when the country was supposed to be dry. In its heyday the town had many names. Take your pick: Hampton, Osdick, Inn City, Sin City, Gin Town and finally Red Mountain, coming from a landmark, the big red mountain against which it nestles.

The Monkey House has been gone for many years. It was destroyed late one night after everyone had gone home by a dynamite blast set off by a disgruntled miner who claimed he'd been gypped in the place by a blackjack dealer, given knockout drops by the bartender and rolled by one of the girls.

The Silver Dollar which was owned and operated for many years by Jimmie Holcomb burned. When rebuilt, the place was changed to The Palace.

Only the old Owl remains intact as it was originally built and enlarged back in the early 20s by C. H. "Slim" Riffle. My friend, Slim, made a fortune out of the Owl; part of which was used to finance a Dodge-Plymouth dealership which was located in a big building across the highway from the Owl. The business was not insured and when it burned, Slim lost $175,000. Why wasn't it insured? Because of the scarcity of water. What little there was sold for 3/4 cent a gallon and there was hardly enough to drink, let alone waste on fires. . . .

A unique saloon was the Dugout. It was located in a cellar between Red Mountain and Johannesburg astride the county line. Half was in San Bernardino County and half in Kern County. Whenever the owner received a tip that a raid was coming from one county, he would move the liquor stock across the room into the other county. This worked real well until someone got their wires crossed and both counties raided simultaneously.

In the Argus fire station, there's a valuable antique, an old Stutz fire truck, vintage about the year 1926. The Stutz was Trona's first fire truck and W. E. Tripp the first fire chief. The truck was purchased from the city of Colton and while being driven to Trona by the late Charles "Pee Wee" Cameron, it created quite a commotion in Red Mountain. It was during prohibition and after dark Pee Wee drove through the town with red lights flashing and the siren going full blast. Thinking that an unexpected raid by the law was about to take place, the girls and gamblers scattered into the darkness while the bartenders, trying to get rid of the evidence, dumped a lot of booze down the drain. We know for sure that for a long time Pee Wee wasn't welcomed in Red Mountain.

*From Clifford James Walker. *One Eye Closed, the Other Red: The California Bootlegging Years*. Barstow, California: Back Door Publishing, 1999. 70–73, 102, 103–04. Reprinted by permission of the author.

The Mojave as Cultural Icon
(1937)

Despite the seamier side of small towns and the easily forgotten reality of William L. Manly clawing himself across the tortures of the Mojave, the general public was developing a cotton-candy picture of the desert as a wonderland, a place of self-fulfillment, even retirement. Responsible for this, for all the romantic words, was the abrupt arrival of technology, allowing flocks of newcomers not only to project their happy notions on a formerly despised landscape, but also to live out their fantasies in comfort. This requires some background.

Far into modern times, much of the Mojave remained "primitive." Other than a few major thoroughfares across the desert, many roads remained sand traps, and electricity didn't come to outlying areas until the 1940s and 1950s.

Since early settlement, the small and isolated population had depended on the railroad, mining, and ranching for hardscrabble livelihoods. Then around the time of World War II the influx of affluent people began. Often retirees, former tourists, and military families, they viewed the desert as a place of pleasure, not of grinding work—a pleasure made possible by powerful new automobiles—most of all by air-conditioning—and other recent amenities of civilization.

Both reflecting and effecting the shift was *Desert Magazine*. It was founded in 1937, primarily by land developer Randall Henderson, and significantly enough about the time that electric cooling became available and paved roads were spreading across the Mojave. In his magazine entrepreneur Henderson downplayed the fearsome aspects of the desert proclaimed by early travelers and substituted a rosy dream. For nearly half a century thereafter, readers could dip into *Desert Magazine* and, through articles on travel, gem collecting, and ghost towns, enter a fascinating world.

No doubt, Henderson was sincere in his happy view of the desert as an uplifting, if not spiritual, place for people sensitive to nature, yet he was a visionary in other respects as well. Out of the raw landscape he helped carve the new town of Palm Desert, just south of the Mojave and now a booming, upscale resort of fancy boutiques surrounded by acrylic-green golf courses. Still standing, nobly forbearing in the midst of the tinseled show, is the former magazine's charming Santa Fe-style headquarters, now a steakhouse, at 74225 State Highway 111. One dream has superseded another. We may doubt that, if one comes to the desert with friendliness, as the writers assert, the desert—heartless thing that it is—is capable of giving back friendship in return. The unacknowledged nub behind this appealing and popular fiction, one prevailing to this day, is that comfort born of technology has triumphed over Manly's reality. A little test. Anyone doubting the above might try driving across the Mojave in summer with the air-conditioning turned off.

॥

ONE IS A GRIM DESOLATE WASTELAND. It is the home of venomous reptiles and stinging insects, of vicious thorn-covered plants and trees, and of unbearable heat. This is the desert seen by the stranger speeding along the highway, impatient to be out of "this damnable country." It is the desert visualized by those children of luxury to whom any environment is unbearable which does not provide all of the comforts and services of a pampering civilization. It is a concept fostered by fiction writers who dramatize the tragedies of the desert for the profit it will bring them.

But the stranger and the uninitiated see only the mask. The other Desert—the real Desert—is not for the eyes of the superficial observer, or the fearful soul or cynic. It is a land, the character of which is hidden except to those who come with friendliness and understanding. To these the Desert offers rare gifts: health-giving sunshine—a sky that is studded with diamonds—a breeze that bears no poison—a landscape of pastel colors such as no artist can duplicate—thorn-covered plants which during countless ages have clung tenaciously to life through heat and drought and wind and the depredations of thirsty animals, and yet each season send forth blossoms of exquisite coloring as a symbol of courage that has triumphed over terrifying obstacles.

To those who come to the Desert with friendliness, it gives friendship; to those who come with courage, it gives new strength of character. Those seeking relaxation find release from the world of man-made troubles. For those seeking beauty, the Desert offers nature's rarest artistry. This is the Desert that men and women learn to love.

141

Nearly every creed and industry and locality has its journal—except the Desert. Here, within the boundaries of Arizona, California, Nevada, New Mexico and Utah resides a great family of human beings—the highest type of American citizenship—with a common heritage of environment and interest and opportunity, yet residing for the most part in regions that are remote from the so-called cultural centers.

This is the last great frontier of the United States. It will be the purpose of the *Desert Magazine* to entertain and serve the people whom desire or circumstance have brought to this Desert frontier. But also, the magazine will carry as accurately as possible in word and picture, the spirit of the real Desert to those countless men and women who have been intrigued by the charm of the desert, but whose homes are elsewhere.

This is to be a friendly, personal magazine, written for the people of the Desert and their friends—and insofar as possible, by Desert people. Preference will be given to those writers and artists—yes, and poets—whose inspiration comes from close association with the scented greasewood, the shifting sand dunes, the coloring of Desert landscapes, from precipitous canyons and gorgeous sunsets.

The Desert has its own traditions—art—literature—industry and commerce. It will be the purpose of the *Desert Magazine* to crystallize and preserve these phases of Desert life as a culture distinctive of arid but virile America. We would give character and personality to the pursuits of Desert peoples—create a keener consciousness of the heritage which is theirs—bring them a little closer together in a bond of pride in their Desert homes, and perhaps break down in some measure the prejudice against the Desert which is born of misunderstanding and fear.

It is an idealistic goal, to be sure, but without vision the Desert would still be a forbidding wasteland—uninhabited and shunned. The staff of the *Desert Magazine* has undertaken its task with the same unbounded confidence which has brought a million people to a land which once was regarded as unfit for human habitation.

We want to give to the folks who live on the Desert—and to those who are interested in the Desert—something that will make their lives a little happier and a little finer—something worthwhile. In the accomplishment of this purpose we ask for the cooperation and help of all friends of the Desert everywhere.

*From Randall Henderson and J. Wilson McKenney. "There Are Two Deserts." *Desert Magazine* 1.1 (November 1937): 5.

Route 66: "A Nice Green Place"
(1939)

"It don't take no nerve to do somepin when there ain't nothin' else you can do." The loftiness of *Desert Magazine* was not on the minds of the Joad family when, about the time Randall Henderson was writing his poetic words, these migrants crossed the Mojave during the Depression.

In the 1930s, thousands of poverty-stricken farmers, refugees from the Dust Bowl, streamed across the Mojave on U.S. 66 in hopes of finding work in California's fabled agricultural region waiting on the other side. Often they made the crossing at night, more to increase the chance that with the cooler temperatures their battered trucks would survive the ordeal than for personal comfort.

Radiators boiling over, however, wasn't their only worry. Periodically the California authorities turned back the unwanted Okies and Arkies, a possibility the distraught Mrs. Joad got around in a unique way.

PA CALLED, "Good-by, Mister and Mis' Wilson." There was no answer from the tent. Tom started the engine and the truck lumbered away. And as they crawled up the rough road toward Needles and the highway, Ma looked back. Wilson stood in front of his tent, staring after them, and his hat was in his hand. The sun fell full on his face. Ma waved her hand at him, but he did not respond.

Tom kept the truck in second gear over the rough road, to protect the springs. At Needles he drove into a service station, checked the worn tires for air, checked the spares tied to the back. He had the gas tank filled, and he bought two five-gallon cans of gasoline and a two-gallon can of oil. He filled the radiator, begged a map, and studied it.

The service-station boy, in his white uniform, seemed uneasy until the bill was paid. He said, "You people sure have got nerve."

Tom looked up from the map. "What you mean?"

"Well, crossin' in a jalopy like this."

"You been acrost?"

"Sure, plenty, but not in no wreck like this."

Tom said, "If we broke down maybe somebody'd give us a han'."

"Well, maybe. But folks are kind of scared to stop at night. I'd hate to be doing it. Takes more nerve than I've got."

Tom grinned. "It don't take no nerve to do somepin when there ain't nothin' else you can do. Well, thanks. We'll drag on." And he got in the truck and moved away.

The boy in white went into the iron building where his helper labored over a book of bills. "Jesus, what a hard-looking outfit!"

"Them Okies? They're all hard-lookin'."

"Jesus, I'd hate to start out in a jalopy like that."

"Well, you and me got sense. Them goddamn Okies got no sense and no feeling. They ain't human. A human being wouldn't live like they do. A human being couldn't stand it to be so dirty and miserable. They ain't a hell of a lot better than gorillas."

"Just the same I'm glad I ain't crossing the desert in no Hudson Super-Six. She sounds like a threshing machine."

The other boy looked down at his book of bills. And a big drop of sweat rolled down his finger and fell on the pink bills. "You know, they don't have much trouble. They're so goddamn dumb they don't know it's dangerous. And, Christ Almighty, they don't know any better than what they got. Why worry?"

"I'm not worrying. Just thought if it was me, I wouldn't like it."

"That's 'cause you know better. They don't know any better." And he wiped the sweat from the pink bill with his sleeve.

The truck took the road and moved up the long hill, through the broken, rotten rock. The engine boiled very soon and Tom slowed down and took it easy. Up the long slope, winding and twisting through dead country, burned white and gray, and no hint of life in it. Once Tom stopped for a few moments to let the engine cool, and then he traveled on. They topped the pass while the sun was still up, and looked down on the desert—black cinder mountains in the distance, and the yellow sun reflected on the gray desert. The little starved bushes, sage and grease-wood, threw bold shadows on the sand and bits of rock. The glaring sun was straight ahead. Tom held his hand before his eyes to see at all. They passed the crest and coasted down to cool the engine. They coasted down the long sweep to the floor of the desert, and the fan turned over to cool the water in the radiator. In the driver's seat, Tom and Al and Pa, and Winfield on Pa's knee, looked into the bright descending sun, and their eyes were stony, and their brown faces were damp with perspiration. The burnt land and the black, cindery hills broke the even distance and made it terrible in the reddening light of the setting sun.

Al said, "Jesus, what a place. How'd you like to walk acrost her?"

"People done it," said Tom. "Lot a people don it; an' if they could, we could."

"Lots must a died," said Al.

"Well, we ain't come out exac'ly clean."

Al was silent for a while, and the reddening desert swept past. "Think we'll ever see them Wilsons again?" Al asked.

Tom flicked his eyes down to the oil gauge. "I got a hunch nobody ain't gonna see Mis' Wilson for long. Jus' a hunch I got."

Winfield said "Pa, I wanta get out."

Tom looked over at him. "Might's well let ever'body out 'fore we settle down to drivin' tonight." He slowed the car and brought it to a stop. Winfield scrambled out and urinated at the side of the road. Tom leaned out. "Anybody else?"

"We're holdin' our water up here," Uncle John called.

Pa said, "Winfiel', you crawl up on top. You put my legs to sleep a-settin' on 'em." The little boy buttoned his overalls and obediently crawled up the back board and on his hands and knees crawled over Granma's mattress and forward to Ruthie.

The truck moved on into the evening, and the edge of the sun struck the rough horizon and turned the desert red.

Ruthie said, "Wouldn' leave you set up there, huh?"

"I didn' want to. It wasn't so nice as here. Couldn' lie down."

"Well, don' you bother me, a-squawkin' an' a-talkin'," Ruthie said, "'cause I'm goin' to sleep, an' when I wake up, we gonna be there!

'Cause Tom said so! Gonna seem funny to see pretty country."

The sun went down and left a great halo in the sky. And it grew very dark under the tarpaulin, a long cave with light at each end—a flat triangle of light.

Connie and Rose of Sharon leaned back against the cab, and the hot wind tumbling through the tent struck the backs of their heads, and the tarpaulin whipped and drummed above them. They spoke together in low tones, pitched to the drumming canvas, so that no one could hear them. When Connie spoke he turned his head and spoke into her ear, and she did the same to him. She said, "Seems like we wasn't never gonna do nothin' but move. I'm so tar'd."

He turned his head to her ear. "Maybe in the mornin'. How'd you like to be alone now?" In the dusk his hand moved out and stroked her hip.

She said, "Don't. You'll make me crazy as a loon. Don't do that." And she turned her head to hear his response.

"Maybe—when ever'body's asleep."

"Maybe," she said. "But wait till they get to sleep. You'll make me crazy, an' maybe they won't get to sleep."

"I can't hardly stop," he said.

"I know. Me neither. Le's talk about when we get there; an' you move away 'fore I get crazy."

He shifted away a little. "Well, I'll get to studyin' nights right off," he said. She sighed deeply. "Gonna get one a them books that tells about it an' cut the coupon, right off."

"How long, you think?" she asked

"How long what?"

"How long 'fore you'll be makin' big money an' we got ice?"

"Can't tell," he said importantly. "Can't really rightly tell. Fella oughta be studied up pretty good 'fore Christmus."

"Soon's you get studied up we could get ice an' stuff, I guess."

He chuckled. "It's this here heat," he said. "What you gonna need ice roun' Christmus for?"

She giggled. "Tha's right. But I'd like ice any time. Now don't. You'll get me crazy!"

The dusk passed into dark and the desert stars came out in the soft sky, stars stabbing and sharp, with few points and rays to them, and the sky was velvet. And the heat changed. While the sun was up, it was a beating, flailing heat, but now the heat came from below, from the earth itself, and the heat was thick and muffling. The lights of the truck came on, and they illuminated a little blur of highway ahead, and a strip of desert on either side of the road. And sometimes eyes gleamed in the lights far ahead, but no animal showed in the lights. It was pitch dark under the canvas now. Uncle John and the preacher were curled in the middle of the truck, resting on their elbows, and staring out the back triangle. They could see the two bumps that were Ma and Granma against the outside. They could see Ma move occasionally, and her dark arm moving against the outside.

Uncle John talked to the preacher. "Casy," he said, "you're a fella oughta know what to do."

"What to do about what?"

"I dunno," said Uncle John.

Casy said, "Well, that's gonna make it easy for me!"

"Well, you been a preacher."

"Look, John, ever'body takes a crack at me 'cause I been a preacher. A preacher ain't nothin' but a man."

"Yeah, but—he's—a *kind* of a man, else he wouldn' be a preacher. I wanna ast you—well, you think a fella could bring bad luck to folks?"

"I dunno," said Casy. "I dunno."

"Well—see—I was married—fine, good girl. An' one night she got a pain in her stomach. An' she says, 'You better get a doctor.' An' I says, 'Hell, you jus' et too much.'" Uncle John put his hand on Casy's knee and he peered through the darkness at him. "She give me a *look*. An' she groaned all night, an' she died in the next afternoon." The preacher mumbled something. "You see," John went on, "I kil't her. An' sence then I tried to make it up—mos'ly to kids. An' I tried to be good, an' I can't. I get drunk, an' I go wild."

"Ever'body goes wild," said Casy. "I do too."

"Yeah, but you ain't got a sin on your soul like me."

Casy said gently, "Sure I got sins. Ever'body got sins. A sin is somepin you ain't sure about. Them people that's sure about ever'thing an' ain't got no sin—well, with that kind a son-of-a-bitch, if I was God I'd kick their ass right outa heaven! I couldn' stand 'em!"

Uncle John said, "I got a feelin' I'm bringin' bad luck to my own folks. I got a feelin' I oughta go away an' let 'em be. I ain't comf'table bein' like this."

Casy said quickly, "I know this—a man got to do what he got to do. I can't tell you. I can't tell you. I don't think they's luck or bad luck. On'y one thing in this worl' I'm sure of, an' that's I'm sure nobody got a right to mess with a fella's life. He got to do it all hisself. Help him, maybe, but not tell him what to do."

Uncle John said disappointedly, "Then you don' know?"

"I don' know."

"You think it was a sin to let my wife die like that?"

"Well," said Casy, "for anybody else it was a mistake, but if you think it was a sin—then it's a sin. A fella builds his own sins right up from the groun'."

"I got to give that a goin'-over," said Uncle John, and he rolled on his back and lay with his knees pulled up.

The truck moved on over the hot earth, and the hours passed. Ruthie and Winfield went to sleep. Connie loosened a blanket from the load and covered himself and Rose of Sharon with it, and in the heat they struggled together, and held their breaths. And after a time Connie threw off the blanket and the hot tunneling wind felt cool on their wet bodies.

On the back of the truck Ma lay on the mattress beside Granma, and she could not see with her eyes, but she could feel the struggling body and the struggling heart; and the sobbing breath was in her ear. And Ma said over and over, "All right. It's gonna be all right." And she said hoarsely, "You know the family got to get acrost. You know that."

Uncle John called, "You all right?"

It was a moment before she answered. "All right. Guess I dropped off to sleep." And after a time Granma was still, and Ma lay rigid beside her.

The night hours passed, and the dark was in against the truck. Sometimes cars passed them, going west and away; and sometimes great trucks came up out of the west and rumbled eastward. And the stars flowed down in a slow cascade over the western horizon. It was near midnight when they neared Daggett, where the inspection station is. The road was floodlighted there, and a sign illuminated, "KEEP RIGHT AND STOP." The officers loafed in the office, but they came out and stood under the long covered shed when Tom pulled in. One officer put down the license number and raised the hood.

Tom asked, "What's this here?"

"Agricultural inspection. We got to look over your stuff. Got any vegetables or seeds?"

"No," said Tom.

"Well, we got to look over your stuff. You got to unload."

Now Ma climbed heavily down from the truck. Her face was swollen and her eyes were hard. "Look, mister. We got a sick ol' lady. We got to get her to a doctor. We can't wait." She seemed to fight with hysteria. "You can't make us wait."

"Yeah? Well, we got to look you over."

"I swear we ain't got any thing!" Ma cried. "I swear it. An' Granma's awful sick."

"You don't look so good yourself," the officer said.

Ma pulled herself up the back of the truck, hoisted herself with huge strength. "Look," she said.

The officer shot a flashlight beam up on the old shrunken face. "By God, she is," he said. "You swear you got no seeds or fruits or vegetables, no corn, no oranges?"

"No, no. I swear it!"

"Then go ahead. You can get a doctor in Barstow. That's only eight miles. Go on ahead."

Tom climbed in and drove on.

The officer turned to his companion. "I couldn't hold 'em."

"Maybe it was a bluff," said the other.

"Oh, Jesus, no! You should of seen that ol' woman's face. That wasn't no bluff."

Tom increased his speed to Barstow, and in the little town he stopped, got out, and walked around the truck. Ma leaned out. "It's awright," she said. "I didn't wanta stop there, fear we wouldn' get acrost."

"Yeah! But how's Granma?"

"She's awright—awright. Drive on We got to get acrost." Tom shook his head and walked back.

"Al," he said, "I'm gonna fill her up, an' then you drive some." He pulled to an all-night gas station and filled the tank and the radiator, and filled the crank case. Then Al slipped under the wheel and Tom took the outside, with Pa in the middle. They drove away into the darkness and the little hills near Barstow were behind them.

Tom said, "I don' know what's got into Ma. She's flighty as a dog with a flea in his ear. Wouldn't a took long to look over the stuff. An' she says Granma's sick; an' now she says Granma's awright. I can't figger her out. She ain't right. S'pose she wore her brains out on the trip."

Pa said, "Ma's almost like she was when she was a girl. She was a wild one then. She wasn' scairt of nothin'. I thought havin' all the kids an' workin' took it out a her, but I guess it ain't. Christ! When she got that jack handle back there, I tell you I wouln' wanna be the fella took it away from her."

"I dunno what's got into her," Tom said. "Maybe she's jus' tar'd out."

Al said, "I won't be doin' no weepin' an' a-moanin' to get through. I got this goddamn car on my soul."

Tom said, "Well, you done a damn good job a pickin'. We ain't had hardly no trouble with her at all."

All night they bored through the hot darkness, and jackrabbits scuttled into the lights and dashed away in long jolting leaps. And the dawn came up behind them when the lights of Mojave were ahead. And the dawn showed high mountains to the west. They filled with water and oil at Mojave and crawled into the mountains, and the dawn was about them.

Tom said, "Jesus, the desert's past! Pa, Al, for Christ sakes! The desert's past!"

"I'm too goddamn tired to care," said Al.

"Want me to drive?"

"No, wait awhile."

They drove through Tehachapi in the morning glow, and the sun came up behind them, and then—suddenly they saw the great valley below them. Al jammed on the brake and stopped in the middle of the road, and, "Jesus Christ! Look!" he said. The vineyards, the orchards, the great flat valley, green and beautiful, the trees set in rows, and the farm houses.

And Pa said, "God Almighty!" The distant cities, the little towns in the orchard land, and the morning sun, golden on the valley. A car honked behind them. Al pulled to the side of the road and parked.

"I want ta look at her." The grain fields golden in the morning, and the willow lines, the eucalyptus trees in rows.

Pa sighed, "I never knowed they was anything like her." The peach trees and the walnut groves, and the dark green patches of oranges. And red roofs among the trees, and barns—rich barns. Al got out and stretched his legs.

He called, "Ma—come look. We're there!"

Ruthie and Winfield scrambled down from the car, and then they stood, silent and awestruck, embarrassed before the great valley. The distance was thinned with haze, and the land grew softer and softer in the distance. A windmill flashed in the sun, and its turning blades were like a little heliograph, far away. Ruthie and Winfield looked at it, and Ruthie whispered, "It's California."

Winfield moved his lips silently over the syllables. "There's fruit," he said aloud.

Casy and Uncle John, Connie and Rose of Sharon climbed down. And they stood silently. Rose of Sharon had started to brush her hair back, when she caught sight of the valley and her hand dropped slowly to her side.

Tom said, "Where's Ma? I want Ma to see it. Look, Ma! Come here, Ma." Ma was climbing slowly, stiffly, down the back board. Tom looked at her. "My God, Ma, you sick?" Her face was stiff and putty-like, and her eyes seemed to have sunk deep into her head, and the rims were red with weariness. Her feet touched the ground and she braced herself by holding the truck-side.

Her voice was a croak. "Ya say we're acrost?"

Tom pointed to the great valley. "Look!"

She turned her head, and her mouth opened a little. Her fingers went to her throat and gathered a little pinch of skin and twisted gently. "Thank God!" she said. "The fambly's here." Her knees buckled and she sat down on the running board.

"You sick, Ma?"

"No, jus' tar'd."

"Didn' you get no sleep?"

"No."

"Was Granma bad?"

Ma looked down at her hands, lying together like tired lovers in her lap. "I wisht I could wait an' not tell you. I wisht it could be all—nice."

Pa said, "Then Granma's bad."

Ma raised her eyes and looked over the valley. "Granma's dead."

They looked at her, all of them, and Pa asked, "When?"

"Before they stopped us las' night."

"So that's why you didn't want 'em to look."

"I was afraid we wouldn' get acrost," she said. "I tol' Granma we couldn' he'p her. The fambly had ta get acrost. I tol' her, tol' her when she was a-dyin'. We couldn't stop in the desert. There was the young ones—an' Rosasharn's baby. I tol' her." She put up her hands and covered her face for a moment. "She can get buried in a nice green place," Ma said softly. "Trees aroun' an' a nice place. She got to lay her head down in California."

*From John Steinbeck. *The Grapes of Wrath*. 1939. New York: Viking, 1989. 300–11. Reprinted by permission of Viking Penguin, a division of Penguin Group (U.S.A.) Inc.

The Mojave Blooms: Crying Out

(1941)

Yes, people do cry out with that laughter that may be a close relative of pain when the desert blooms. Mostly, however, they are visitors; and, although many a spring the seekers go home disappointed
because the desert remains its barren self, the phenomenon has
enjoyed such publicity as to be assumed a regular magical event—as
if each season the prophet appeared on schedule to show his
extravagant powers.

To me, the psychology of this has always seemed a little strange.
Yes, when once every few years the right conditions of moisture
and temperature coincide, tiny seeds that have lain dormant for
years explode into what they were intended to become. Then the
desert assumes an extraordinary variety of colors, especially by
comparison to its usual drab patience. But I have always been puzzled by the human reaction, for the sudden florescence, too, is a
perfectly natural part of desert life. It should be seen as if a wondrous animal had strangely appeared before us, then disappeared—
an event treasured in the heart, true, but best not robbed of its
innate dignity by an irrelevant human cry.

NOT EVERY SPRING does the stone roll back like this, but only
when the rain and the snows and the sun combine fortuitously
to decree it. I had not seen the miracle before, road-runners though we
had been for years, crisscrossing the southwestern wastes in all directions, across the Antelope Valley and down into Death Valley, beside the
Salton Sea and over the Yuma dunes, across Nevada sagebrush, Arizona
mesas, alkaline playas of the Amargosa Desert, spaces of the Gila Desert
where solid things have the unreality of mirage. I knew occasional flow-
ery spots, brief blossomings licked by blast of wind and blaze of sun; I
knew the secretive blooming of the desert shrubs, in flowers without
petals, or lonely corollas falling beside some seepage of water in the high

clefts of the hills, where even the bees, you'd think, would not thread their way to find them. Dusty, wiry, naked but for thorns, resinous, bitter, sparse, the desert brush and cacti are admirable for enduring where they do at all; they are, like the scorpions and centipedes and rattlesnakes of their environment, much to be respected. In a sort of dead and silvery and almost invisible way, they are even beautiful, as the ghosts of Tamerlane's Tartars might look, if one had an hallucination of their passing in a blur of heat and whirling dust.

But here to my feet, that April morning, swept a radiant populace of flowers, sprung overnight, it seemed to me, from what had looked barren soil. As anyone will cry out involuntarily at an unexpected sharp pain, so there was no stopping the laughter that rose in the throat at the sight. . . .

In all, those April days yielded to my vasculum some seventy-five species. Large as this number sounds, it is not a greater variety than would be found at a corresponding stage of seasonal development anywhere else; what brought delight was the sheer abundance of the bloom, the feeling that we were besieged by an army of little flowers. The bees were drunk with them; they came in thousands from only the Mojave knew where. I saw the hummingbirds flash by in such a state of excitement that they looked as if they had been shot sideways out of a cannon with a twisted bore. They seemed unable to settle their scattered brains on anything; they went so fast I couldn't follow them with my glasses to identify which of California's many kinds of hummer they were. We used to wonder, at the ranch, how far this flood of rare flowering washed across the desert floor. You couldn't tell; you only knew it went on to the rim of the horizon. And you knew it was brief. It must be loved while you had it, like the song of the thrush in the southern states. Something that each morning you dread to find gone at last, whelmed by the advance of summer heat.

Camp Clipper: "Dear God, Bless This Food"
(1943–1944)

Jack Mitchell, the man we saw suspended in a cave, was a colorful Mojave character who ran a resort (of sorts) on the slopes of the Providence Mountains. When World War II came, Jack and wife Ida witnessed the invasion of thousands of Army troops, in training for battle in North Africa.

In this heartwarming anecdote, the couple also witnessed something else, something they didn't comprehend. The military had come to stay, for the great spaces of the Mojave were most amenable for bombing ranges and rocket testing and other needs of modern warfare. Today, vast sweeps of the Mojave are occupied by the Army, Navy, Air Force, and units of less overt identification. Some nights the Mojave skies are ablaze with artillery fire. General Patton's tank tracks, still visible, were but a portent. Both locals and outsiders may gripe about the continuing intrusion that places huge chunks of the Mojave off-limits to the public, but the hard truth of the matter is that the Mojave's economy, always shaky, would go flat without the continuing infusion of federal dollars.

Living in simpler times, the Mitchells foresaw none of this. The following reproduces the original without editing.

W ATCHING NIGHT ARTILLERY practice from our front porch was like having a grandstand seat for a huge Fourth of July fireworks display, only our exhibit was on a much larger scale. Tracer ammunition shot across the sky leaving patterns in bright color, to fade slowly as they were replaced by fresh patterns of cross-fire plaid or radiant sunbursts of sparks.

Troops at practice were divided into a Red Army and a Blue Army. Sometimes thousands of men from one of the many nearby training camps scattered about the Mojave Desert would come to battle it out with the troops of Camp Clipper, just as intercollegiate teams meet for a New Years football game.

Under the canopy of bright fire, the ground troops had to crawl on their bellies to avoid being hit by the live ammunition. When these boys were sent overseas they would be well seasoned to the swish and ping of real bullets.

We know of one lad who never made it overseas, for his fate was sealed by the combined forces of desert and battle life. Crawling through a trench under fire one night, he suddenly found his face within inches of a rattle snake, coiled and ready to strike. Because of the nearness of the other soldiers behind him, he was unable to retreat, and the trench was too narrow for him to move to either side. He panicked and jumped up exposing his body to the machine gun fire. Of course he was killed instantly. His life was sacrificed just as heroically as if he had been charging an enemy line.

"The 33rd Infantry Division has been alerted for a move overseas." This was the solemn announcement of General Millikin to all his troops assembled in the outdoor theatre one Sunday afternoon in May.

We received word that same night when Captains Madden and Turnbull returned home. For several days there was much excitement and great activity packing and crating supplies for the move to who knew where. Immunization shots were the chief subject of conversation among the few men who visited us in the succeeding weeks.

Early in June the troops broke camp and left, and Camp Clipper was deserted except for a small detail left behind to guard and maintain it for its next occupants. Ida and I felt deserted too, for we had come to love the bustle and excitement of army activities. We would miss the companionship of our guests.

In a matter of a few days, the camp was humming with activity again, for the 93rd, a division of colored troops from Fort Huachuca, Arizona, replaced the 33rd division. Soon we were entertaining these boys from Brooklyn and Chicago and the south. Desert life was so strange to them that we always figured they deserved special credit for the way they took their training.

One group of these men was detailed to repair our road right up to our property. We were very grateful, for this was a help to us as well as to the men who marched over it. We got permission from their captain to show these men our appreciation by inviting them to a chicken dinner.

The boys arrived by jeep all grinning happily in anticipation of the fried chicken. When Ida had the table piled high with golden fluffy biscuits and crisp southern fried chicken, bowls of thick cream gravy and jars of homemade jams, she called our company to the dining room. With big eyes and good appetites they sat down at once. One lanky lad with arms like buggy whips reached out hastily for the platter of chicken.

"Wait just a minute, boy," ordered the sergeant in charge, as he placed a restraining black hand on the lad's long arm. "The Mitchells have invited us up here to their house for a nice dinner, and we ain't gonna eat a bite of it until we've thanked the Lord for such nice folks who is so good to us."

All heads were bowed, and the sergeant's deep voice broke the silence. "Dear God, bless this food, of which we is about to partake, and give us the rememberin' always of the gratitude we feels for the goodness of the Mitchells."

By January of 1944 the 93rd had received their orders to move overseas, and once more only the guards were left at Camp Clipper. It was next occupied in May by about 350 Italian prisoners of war, who were sent in to post the artillery duds which were lying everywhere making the area unsafe for us desert rats, especially for the prospectors who were anxious to get back to their diggings.

The non-commissioned officers in charge of the Italians had a good thing while it lasted. Their prisoners didn't know one kind of stripe from another, so they saluted every man in khaki for fear of neglecting an officer. The Italians seemed to appreciate the courtesy of the American soldiers in command of them. During an assignment on the desert, the sergeant gave the order, "At ease." One prisoner who spoke a little English told of his surprise that they should ever be put at ease in the presence of a superior officer.

By October the prisoners of war and their soldier guards were removed, and Camp Clipper was completely dismantled. What equipment and materials and supplies couldn't be used elsewhere were burned or buried, and the only sign that this had once been a bustling community was the roadways between the rows of barracks. But time will reclaim these too, and soon this part of the desert will look like it has for thousands of years. The desert winds will re-seed the ground and someday it will blossom again with sage and creosote brush.

*From Jack Mitchell. *Jack Mitchell: Caveman.* Torrance, California: privately printed, 1964. 125–27. Reprinted by permission of the author.

Slime in a Small Town

(1946)

Up until quite recently, desert towns were tough places. This brief excerpt peels back the pleasant exterior of a Mojave community to show the deputy sheriff, judge, and other prominent citizens deeply involved in the gambling and prostitution lying at its secret heart.

Quite by accident I discovered that, although fiction, this is no made-up scandal but a *roman à clef*. This happened when one of my Mojave friends found an old used copy of *Desert Town* with a yellow paper slipped in the pages. To one side, this listed the main characters, then matched them with the names of the townspeople portrayed. Once we were on the trail, a little checking showed that the Chuckawalla of the story is Barstow, California, that the characters ring true to life, and that this sort of sleaze was common in the small Mojave towns of the day. The writer, so I've been told, was a young lady from San Francisco, still in her early twenties, who got the inside scoop for the book by working as a secretary in the local Highway Patrol office.

Under the title of *Bitter Harvest,* the novel was serialized in *Collier's* of November 24, December 1, and December 8, 1945. It made Barstow's people even less happy when in 1947 Paramount turned the book into a movie, *Desert Fury,* starring Burt Lancaster. But by then Ramona Stewart was long gone.

F RITZI HAD REPRESENTED HER FORTUNES as being much greater than they were. Before they had spoken to one another half an hour, the Judge knew that she had in mind opening a saloon in Chuckawalla. And being a man with an eye for making honest money, he was easily convinced that a small investment might repay well, especially when his money would mix with the gold of a large Eastern syndicate. He invested.

And when, three weeks after the opening, he discovered that there was no Eastern syndicate (Fritzi had never said there *was*; she had only hinted), but that the Purple Sage was broke and about to close, taking with it his investment, he was almost frantic.

At this point, Fritzi installed the roulette wheel. As the Judge, because of his position, never entered the Purple Sage, he knew nothing about it for five weeks. Then word of it filtered through town until it reached his ears.

Furiously, he stormed down to Fritzi's rooming house and demanded an explanation.

Fritzi smiled up at him and the look in her eyes made him uneasy. That dark expressive glance reminded him that no matter how he might deny knowledge of the gambling wheel, Chuckawalla would never believe him. He was a partner in the Purple Sage, though no one knew it yet—and Fritzi had it in writing. After a long bitter silence during which they gained stern knowledge of one another, Fritzi brought out the saloon's books and sweetened this knowledge with the last month's profits. It was the real beginning of their partnership. By the end of another month, the Judge had loosened up enough to suggest a faro table to accommodate the overflow from the wheel.

For the next year and a half, life flowed smoothly. The Purple Sage's reputation spread through the whole desert area, and cattlemen and railroad people traveled as much as a hundred miles to empty their pockets into Fritzi's till. The Judge bought a valuable tract of land which he had coveted for ten years, while Fritzi moved from the rooming house to a little rented place on the Judge's street. She began driving a new automobile.

There was another blow yet to fall. The old Sheriff's deputy, who had been in such poor health for some time that he could scarcely bother with a town cleanup, died. The next week, Pat Johnson was sent up from the county seat to take his place.

It was a bad moment when Judge Lindquist looked up from his armchair and saw Pat's tall, raw-boned frame filling his doorway.

Pat took off his ten-gallon hat and held out his hand. "Hi yah, Judge! Let's clean up the town," he bellowed heartily.

After a short struggle with panic, the Judge regained his composure and invited Pat to sit down.

"Clean up the town?" he asked mildly.

Pat lit a cigar and threw the burnt match into the fireplace. "There's always a certain amount of cleanin' up for a new deputy. You know that, Judge."

Berle nodded quickly. "Oh! I see what you mean. I thought for a second you meant something definite."

"You know anything definite?"

Too late, the Judge pulled back from the trap. Pat had the knowledge he had been seeking.

"Hear there's some gamblin' in these parts," he said easily.

"Harrumph. . . . You're certain?"

"Sounds that way. Bad."

"Er—yes. Of course, if it's true."

"Lot of money in gamblin'."

The Judge looked up hopefully. "Yes, Mr. Johnson?"

"Always is in these things that's against the law."

Berle's hopes sunk. "Yes, yes. Shocking."

"Sure is." Pat stood up and jammed his hat back on his head. "Well, I better be takin' off. Got a lot of work cut out for me. Better get at it."

There was agony in Berle's glance. "It'll take you several days to get settled?"

"Nope. Always travel light. I can start the job right away."

"A glass of wine before you go?"

Pat shook his head. "Never touch it," he said. "Well, Judge, see you in court!"

Before Berle could recover himself enough to rise, Pat had let himself out the front door and was gone.

Ten minutes later, while the Judge was still talking to Fritzi on the phone, Pat walked into the Purple Sage. Fritzi hung up the phone when her bartender came to the back room to announce his arrival. She inspected herself calmly in her wall mirror while the wheel was being hidden, and then, when everything was in order, she walked slowly out to the bar.

"Have a drink?"

Pat was already sitting at the bar. "What does it cost me?"

Fritzi smiled. "On the house."

"Then I'll have a drink."

She settled herself on the stool beside him and took out a cigarette. He made no move to light it, and she seemed not to notice.

"What'll it be?" the bartender asked.

"Whiskey. Just bring the bottle," Pat said.

With the bottle between them, Fritzi and the new deputy drank in silence for nearly an hour. At five o'clock, when several railway men came in, Fritzi suggested they go to the back room, and Pat nodded in appreciation of this discretion.

At six o'clock they started on their second quart. Neither one of them showed the effects of the first quart and they were beginning to respect each other. Pat saw that Fritzi made no attempt to make him drunk or to hedge on her share of the drinking. And Fritzi knew that she was on trial.

At nine o'clock, Pat leaned back in his chair and yawned. "Hear you got a roulette wheel," he said.

"Got a faro table too," Fritzi said.

He nodded. "How's business?"

"We aren't broke yet."

He stood up. "You're a smart woman."

She said nothing and finally he took a half-smoked cigar from his shirt pocket. "Now, I don't want to start nothin' here in town, 'less I have to. Just so long's there ain't a lot of fights and nobody gets hurt, I believe in co-operatin'. Within reason, you know."

"I think we'll get along all right," Fritzi said.

"Maybe. No reason why we can't."

He stuck his hat on his head and walked out without ceremony.

Fritzi ordered the wheel set up again and the back room was opened for business.

The next day, Pat received two hundred dollars in twenty-dollar bills through the mail. There was no note enclosed.

*From Ramona Stewart. *Desert Town*. New York: William Morrow, 1946. 26–30. Reprinted by permission of HarperCollins Publishers.

Urges: Jackrabbit Homesteads and Cloudbursts

(1940s)

Following their romantic urges to "get away from it all," starting in the late 1930s and accelerating after World War II Americans flocked into the Mojave. They were claiming their patches of the desert by building cabins on five-acre plots made available by the government on generous terms.

Many of these "Jackrabbit" homesteads as they were called became playthings, the weekend getaways for city people eager to build with their hands and get close to nature. However, despite the buoyant spirits, close to nature often proved too much, for the newcomers found that Paradise had its flies. Big ones. The fierce heat, bad roads, lack of water, scorpions, tarantulas, rattlesnakes, lightning storms, and other perfectly natural circumstances eventually drove many of the enthusiasts back to the comforts and safety of the city, leaving the host of leaning shacks one can still see dotting the Mojave in some places.

However, a few people stayed, reveling in the challenges of "pioneering" that set their adrenaline rushing with new thrills. As here, in a chapter titled "The Cloudburst," the authentic account of that great irony on the bone-dry Mojave: too much water all at once.

It might be added as a point of interest that this book, written by an amateur, sometimes gushing with clichés, published by a vanity press, nonetheless is one of the primary documents for the southern Mojave—a book now of local fame, offered at high price in used bookstores, and invaluable to historians for its wealth of details. This is simply because it is one of the very few full-length early firsthand accounts of its kind for the area and, indeed, one of the rare examples of its kind for the Mojave as a whole. So, given the circumstances, even this modestly talented kitchen-table writer of the desert achieved an important niche, scribbling away in a little cabin still standing on the outskirts of Yucca Valley.

I T WAS MID-SUMMER; but since we were going to furnish wood for Doleta, John and I planned to begin early to build our winter supply by getting a few loads at a time when we were in a picnic mood. On a pleasant day, when clouds were scattered here and there, we knew that the higher altitude where we found our wood would be cool and restful. One very promising morning we headed the old truck toward the southern rim. Doleta, who by that time usually went with us, had other chores that day, a circumstance which for her proved fortunate. Going several miles farther up the mountain than usual, we found on a westerly slope an unexplored area. The wood was so plentiful that it took us no time to get our load, so we scouted around for a while, hoping to find the discarded horns of mountain sheep for our collection. Already we had polished and mounted several pairs of cow horns and one set of deer antlers.

Lunch was over, and we were putting some interesting rocks in the truck when John, observing the cloud formation, remarked that he didn't like its looks and thought it best to start back home immediately. We coasted down the grade about two miles and had entered an old river bed when the storm, in all its wildness, struck us. The cab of the truck had a top, but there was no glass in the windshield or the sides. The rain came down in sheets, and the wind lashed it madly against us! Still coasting, we stood up to protect our faces. To be heard above the fury of the storm, we had to shout to each other! The question uppermost in our minds was whether we should keep going, running into we knew not what, or try to make it on foot to higher ground.

Foamy water swirled about us. The old truck bounced over debris washed down from the mountain sides; at times it leaped over obstacles. By then we knew there was nothing we could do but go on! The maddening wind would have taken our breath so completely that climbing through gushing water and over sliding rocks was out of the question. Already our cold, soggy clothes were clinging to our bodies!

The stream bed was getting deeper. The roar of the thunder grew more deafening! Streaks of jagged lightning leaped from one cliff to another! I looked at John's face, and it was grim. By that I knew that he thought our case was a desperate one, almost hopeless! With all the voice that I could muster, I shouted in his ear, "PRAY!" A slight grin relaxed his tension. It might have given him courage to think that I believed that we still had a chance, or he might have been reminded of a recent razzing he had given me about my childlike faith in talking over my problems with the Spirit Father.

We were going downhill but still had several miles to cover before we could leave the river bed. Although the storm did not diminish, the old truck never gave up its steady momentum. John could brace himself at the wheel, but a sudden swerving of the truck would throw me over; at times I almost fell from the cab! At a sickening flash of lightning or a sharp crack of thunder, John would look reassuringly at me, knowing I was always terrified during an electric storm!

At last we were nearing the 29 Palms Highway. To take our regular trail from there was not feasible; but by going somewhat to the west, we ran out of the path of the rushing current. Hoarse from shouting, and drenched and beaten by the wind-lashed water, we amazed Doleta as we stopped by her place to tell her about our experience. It was difficult for her to realize the extent of the storm, as there had been only a light shower on our hillside. For more than an hour we three sat on our front porch, listening to the roar and watching the powerful flow of water as it came down from the mountains from which we had just escaped.

A few days later, when we went back to the same place to get another load, we discovered that had we remained on the spot where we were gathering wood that fateful afternoon, we would have been safe, as the ground in the higher mountains showed no indication of even a light shower.

*From June LeMert Paxton. *My Life on the Mojave*. New York: Vantage Press, 1957. 63–65. Copyright © 1957 June LeMert Paxton.

Dying Hard: The Myth of Abundance
(1952)

Old ideas die hard. When the Europeans landed on our shores, they struck out across the continent on a rampage of exploitation. Forests, minerals, water—all seemed endlessly abundant.

Along such lines, one of *Desert Magazine's* most popular features presented articles and maps leading readers to places where jasper, opals, and Indian petroglyphs might be found. Almost inevitably people flocked to such sites and took what they wanted. A few left the areas in shambles, destroying these for all who would come after.

It should be said in all fairness that in later years editor Randall Henderson underwent a "conversion" and became an ardent preservationist of the desert, fighting against just such a limited outlook he promotes here. Meanwhile, however, his response to complaints about the magazine's contribution to the vandalism leaves one dumbfounded. "There will always remain great expanses of unknown land"—that is precisely the willful blindness that almost destroyed a continent.

D URING THE LAST MONTH two letters have come to my desk expressing criticism of that great fraternity of hobbyists known as rockhounds. One of these letters is from Edwin J. Wright of Whittier, California. Mr. Wright's criticism also is directed at the editorial program of *Desert Magazine*. Perhaps it will help clarify the situation if I will publish his letter and my answer. Mr. Wright wrote:

"Two years ago I got mad at you *Desert Magazine* people—and in a way, I am still mad. Perhaps I am wrong. But, although I am still upset, I offer constructive criticism. Please take in good faith what I have to say.

"I have roamed the desert a lot—for pastime. I love getting out in God's country. What I have found has not amounted to much materially, but the pleasure I have derived is beyond calculating. And I owe it to no one but myself. I don't want anyone to tell me where to go or what to see. I find it myself, and reap the full satisfaction.

"Now, why did I get mad at *Desert Magazine*?

"Because you are always harping on those rockhounds who higrade sites and leave fields looking like bombs had landed there. Often they finish up the job by battering up the road markers, scattering boxes, cans and debris about.

"Sometimes you criticize their doings, but you continue to encourage them, giving them all the help you possibly can by publishing maps with field trip stories.

"Why not write the stories and forget the maps? Let general directions suffice, and make the rockhounds hunt their own specimens. The true rock lover will derive more sport from seeking out his own location and gathering his rocks from unspoiled country.

"I am a mechanical and civil engineer. I have been in California long enough to have earned the title of native son. There was a time when I could go to the desert and be assured of finding natural beauty, and escaping this gang that runs all over you. Now, I am not so sure."

In answer to this letter, I wrote Mr. Wright as follows:

"I do not expect to convert you to my way of thinking, but I would like to give you a glimpse at least of a somewhat broader view than is expressed in your letter.

"From the day of its inception it has been the mission of *Desert Magazine* to break down old prejudices and fears which your forefathers and mine felt toward this arid land. We publish maps to bring people out into the desert country for wholesome recreation, and to help them find their way around.

"Mineral field trips merely are one phase of that general program. We publish maps showing the way to scenic canyons, historical landmarks, ghost mining camps and reclamation projects. Perhaps there are a few people who follow these maps and take purple glass from the ghost towns, cut their initials in the trees in the Palm Canyons, and leave their rubbish beside the historical landmarks—but only a few do that. It is my view that the good purpose we serve in bringing people out into the sunshine and clean air of the desert far more than offsets the evil that is done by the few. Generally, the kind of people who vandalize the landscape and toss beer cans into the roadside gutters are not the kind of people who read this type of magazine. You well know that we crusade constantly against that kind of thing.

"As for the rockhounds, are they any different from the prospectors who have been roaming over this desert land for the last 100 years, seeking precious minerals—and mining them whenever and wherever they are found?

"True, when one of them finds a good field, they all rush in to share the good specimens—but haven't miners been doing that ever since gold first was discovered in California?

"The difference is that most of the rockhounds have to earn a living at an occupation which keeps them on the job five or more days a week. They do not have time and equipment to go out seeking new fields. If they are to get any reward for their desert field trips they must depend on the tips given by their Mineral Societies, by their fellow rockhounds—or by *Desert Magazine*.

"There is no one to grub-stake the rock collectors, and so they do their week's work and then in the few hours that are left they rush out to pick up what they can in the mineral fields—and many of them spend their remaining leisure time cutting and polishing these stones into beautiful gems.

"Tramping the desert is good for people—whether they are seeking camera pictures, botanical specimens, or just plain rocks. The broad view held by our *Desert Magazine* staff is well expressed by these four lines which came to my desk this week in a poem by Claude C. Walton of Evanston, Wyoming:

Here a soul can grow in stature, reaching
    to the very stars,
And a heart forget the prison of convention's
    rigid bars.
These are things that make me love it,
    God-forsaken though it be—
Oh barren land, in your domain a man
    is free—is free!

"This is a big, big desert. The rockhounds have found access only to a few tiny corners of it. There will always remain great expanses of unknown land where prospectors like yourself may go to find your own minerals—and beauty."

*From Randall Henderson. "Just between You and Me." *Desert Magazine* 15.2 (February 1952): 42.

Charles Manson:
Doing the Devil's Business on the Mojave
(1969)

"Please, let me go," begged the pregnant actress, stretched by the neck with a rope slung over a ceiling beam in her mansion; "All I want to do is have my baby." Her pleas did no good. In the following screaming melee, she was stabbed sixteen times, then the word "Pig" written on her front door in her own blood.

The nation reeled back in horror at that bloody evening in the summer of 1969. However, if the public learned that, during an orgy of gore in the Hollywood Hills of the Los Angeles area, five people in the same house were variously shot, stabbed, and their bodies mutilated, the country would reel back once again, this time in utter disbelief, when the next night a similar slaughter occurred not far away.

Today, the Sharon Tate–LaBianca murders, dark with the name of Charles Manson, are seared in the cultural memory as senseless lunatic acts carried out under the direction of a sociopath; Manson's piercing black eyes continue to stare out at us from the crypt of his soul. Less often remembered is that, after the two nights of horror, Manson and his murdering band, following an old tradition of criminals, fled the law into the canyons of Death Valley. There the Satanist led his "Family," drug-soaked, deadbeat youths crazed for murder and group sex, in continuing orgies.

Natural conditions in the Mojave, sometimes described as hellish for its barrenness and heat, pale beside the demonic qualities some humans have brought to the desert. In the following, Bob Murphy, the ranger who was in charge of Death Valley at the time and helped track down the murderers, reveals their twisted lives.

S ANDRA COLLINS was carrying a baby about one year old, who had been named Zezozose Zadfrack Glutz. He had scabs over his nose and under the left eye, having been injured in some manner several days earlier. Rachel Morse was also carrying a baby who appeared to be about two to three months old and was called Sunstone Hawk. He had a badly sunburned face. From the actions of Pugh and Morse, the officers assumed they were their children, respectively, but later they were to find that Susan Atkins was the mother of Zezozose, and Sandy Pugh, the mother of Sunstone.

Hailey and Pursell decided it was time to go back down Goler Wash and bring Soupspoon, Clem and Randy back to the Barker ranch. On their return they isolated their handcuffed prisoners from the women.

Steuber and George, accompanied by Deputy District Attorney Gibbons, were guarding the women. Susan Atkins approached the officers and, pointing to Clem, asked the officers to "unhook him." When George asked the reason he was told, "I want to take him behind the buildings and make love to him one more time." She explained, "He's about the best piece I've ever had, and I may never see him again."

All but two of the females were armed with sheath or belt-type knives. The officers noted that they were collectively similar in expression, reaction, and communication, and seemed at peace with themselves. Their reaction toward their situation was casual to the point of nonexistence. They took off or exchanged clothing in as off-hand a manner as other persons change hats, disrobing and urinating in the presence of the officers like animals. All prisoners gave aliases and it was not until long after their booking at the jail in Independence that their true identities were learned . . . .

They overheard voices and estimated that there were at least six persons in the house. When the additional officers arrived, a plan of approach to the Barker house was made by radio. Leach made a wide swing across the wash, screened from the house by brush, to a location about two hundred feet to the south. Powell was just off the east side of the building and Curran off to the northwest. Schneider moved up the wash toward the front door. Pursell came off the ridge to the north to a location behind a small outbuilding adjacent to the house and facing the back door.

Suddenly the back door opened and a woman walked into the yard. She had a towel wrapped around her head. She stopped and coughed several times, spat into the dirt, and walked back into the house. It was Diane Bluestein.

Pursell thought, "If she looks up, we're done for."

The back door closed behind her. It was 6:30 p.m. and growing dark rapidly. Ward was close to Pursell's position, and Leach and Schneider were covering the front door. Pursell moved quickly to the back door, flung it open, and for protection moved against the outside wall to the left of the doorway. He ordered all the occupants to hold their positions and place their hands on their heads. There was no response. The order was loudly repeated. A rather slow compliance followed his second order.

Pursell saw a man to his left facing the opposite direction, three women to his left in the kitchen and three other men either sitting or standing around the large kitchen table in the center of the room. Pursell had the men back out to the doorway one at a time with hands on their heads. Each was then passed to the officers who had assembled on the porch outside the back door. After four men were removed from the house, three women were ordered to go out of the house, one at a time, which they did. The men and women followed these orders without comment.

When the kitchen was cleared, Pursell entered the house and picked up a homemade candle burning in a China mug, the only illumination in the now dark building. With it, he conducted a search of the other rooms. He had been in the house before, and was familiar with the floor plan.

He went to the bathroom, which had the usual fixtures but was largely nonfunctional.

He was forced to move the improvised candle around a bit; it made a poor light. He lowered it to the wash basin and a small cupboard below. He observed long hair, like a wig, hanging over the top of the cupboard door, which was partially open. Almost at once, fingers extended through the hair and began to move. Pursell said, "Don't make any false moves." A figure emerged from the cupboard.

As his subject emerged from his cramped quarters, he said with some jocularity that he was glad to be out of the cupboard because it was cramped in there.

The man was clad entirely in buckskin; he looked very different from the others apprehended by the officers. Pursell suspected that this man was the leader of the group, a guy named Charlie. When Pursell asked his name, he replied, "Charles Manson . . . ."

In Pursell's arrest report he noted that Manson insisted that he was Jesus Christ . . . .

At Barker Ranch the officers started walking their subjects down to the two 4x4 Park Service pickups. Most of them were loaded in the back of one pickup while the others followed to provide light. Manson noticed the ranger uniforms and asked, "How come you guys are hassling me? You should be out telling people about the flowers and animals . . . ."

At the ranch they found a guitar, Cathy Gillies' purse, a sizeable food supply and other items that indicated the Family intended to stay at the ranch all winter. Their inventory included fourteen cartons of candy bars, eight large rolls of cheese, four gallons of peanut butter, three gallons of honey, five half-gallon jars of jam, two half gallons of jelly, five huge boxes of crackers, three boxes of graham crackers, two cases of canned milk, forty gallons of wheat germ, corn meal and flour, and four large cans of smoking tobacco. There were other items in small quantities but not much variety. They also found many items of clothing, mostly women's.

The bathroom where Pursell had apprehended Manson from under the wash basin was inspected. It was filthy. The toilet was full of urine and water only dripped into the rusted holding tank.

"You could probably flush this thing only once every twenty-four hours," Leach observed.

There was not much furniture in the front room or in the bedroom. A king-size mattress so dirty even a dog would shun it was in the middle of the front room floor. Someone had defecated in the corner of the living room. An interesting pincushion was found by Murphy. The stitches were cut and inside was a buckskin bag containing an amber or cream-colored powder. The rangers speculated it was a cheap form of heroin, Mexican brown, prized by the family for a special event.

*From Bob Murphy. *Desert Shadows: A True Story of the Charles Manson Family in Death Valley.* 1986. No place: Robert Murphy, 1993. 83, 90–91, 94,100. Reprinted by permission of the author.

The Story of the Wooden Children
(1974)

Is it something in the water?

Wherever fans of the Mojave gather, they begin swapping stories, trying to outdo one another in tales about the weirdos, oddballs, eccentrics, and just plain lunatics hiding out in the sandy nooks and crannies of this desert. Among my favorites is the one about the hermit who one day heard a divine voice. It told him to walk to Death Valley, construct a cross, drag it back, and erect it on a hill behind his trailer.

Obediently, the ragged man did as the Voice instructed, schlepping for days across the sands and lugging the cross he'd made of old mining timbers back toward home. However, worn-out and thirsty, he paused partway in a little town, propped the cross against a fast-food place, and went in to beg a drink of water.

When he came out, someone had stolen his sacred burden, and he ran about wild-eyed, stopping cars and asking if anyone had seen his cross.

After the laughter dies down from a number of such accounts, the conversation inevitably turns to the cause. Does the desert simply attract misfits who elsewhere might be institutionalized, or is there something about the desert itself that over time unhinges even normal people?

The answer has never been found. However, one thing is sure. The tale-telling may be lighthearted, but the stories often contain a serious core touching on the yearnings and pathos found in the lives of all of us. As in this story of the wooden children, told here by one of the desert's foremost journalists.

Today, a life-sized child, sporting a red dress, lives in Barstow's Mojave River Valley Museum. Probing further complexities is *Possum Trot: The Life and Work of Calvin Black, 1903–1972*, a documentary in video produced by Allie Light and Irving Saraf in 1986.

ALLIE LIGHT and her 14-year-old daughter, Julia, were driving through the Mojave desert in 1974 when they noticed what appeared to be a yard full of scarecrows. It was one of those roadside attractions with a neglected look about it, the kind of place tourists often pass by.

Light stopped the car anyway. Walking around the property, about eight miles east of Barstow on Highway 15, she and Julia saw dozens of solemn-faced homemade dolls, some mounted on carrousels. In the wind, the wooden platforms groaned and the dolls jerked like puppets.

The Lights were about to head on down the road when they saw an old woman sitting on the porch of a nearby shack.

"She was quite a sight, dried and burned looking and wearing a dress she had lived in for a long time," Light wrote in her journal entry of June 20, 1974. "Her hair was matted and full of bobby pins. She was hard of hearing, but needed to talk in the worst way."

Ruby Black explained that her husband, Calvin, had spent nearly 20 years carving the dolls, rigging them with wires and speakers so they could sing. The power of the wind made them dance. Since Calvin had passed away two years before, Ruby had stayed up nights with the coffee pot on and her shotgun nearby, guarding the imaginary community they called Possum Trot.

When Ruby Black died in 1980, there was no one left to protect the wind-powered puppet theater, and no interest among the local community in saving it.

"They [the Blacks] were mostly disliked, people thought the place should be torn down," Light said from her San Francisco home in a recent telephone interview.

Los Angeles folk art dealer Larry Whiteley purchased all 86 of Calvin Black's dolls, as well as the signs and other paraphernalia that made up Possum Trot.

Today, 14 years after Calvin Black's death, his creations are in demand among folk art collectors on both coasts. Individual dolls have sold for as much as $30,000, said Whiteley, who displays the last 15 dolls remaining for sale in his gallery on La Brea Avenue.

The dolls Calvin Black never wanted to see separated—he asked Ruby to burn them upon his death—now travel to museums and galleries all over the country. . . .

Born in 1903 in Tennessee, Calvin Black taught himself to carve dolls out of corncobs as a boy. When he reached puberty, other boys began to tease him about his hobby and he burned all 200 corncob dolls he had made.

At age 17, Calvin won a $100 prize at the county fair singing opera in a woman's voice—another talent he would later apply to his work at Possum Trot.

He joined the circus, working as a bodyguard for a snake woman. But his favorite things in the circus were the Kewpie dolls; he hated to see people win them and take them home.

Calvin married Ruby in 1933. She was 18 years old and had never been away from home before from "Monday to Sunday," she once said.

The two traveled West. Calvin took various jobs in Northern California, including panning for gold. But the poor circulation in his legs due to diabetes was aggravated by standing in icy water all day. In hopes that a warmer climate would improve his health, the couple purchased a tract of land sight unseen from a magazine ad, and moved to the Mojave desert in 1953.

Restricted to bed until his legs began to feel better, Calvin passed the time by carving dolls.

In an interview with Saraf and Light in 1976, Ruby Black said: "We didn't never have any children. I lost the first one and I never could carry any more. It's the only real disappointment I had purt near 38_ years [of marriage], cause I really love children."

Allie Light asked, "Were the dolls like children?"

"He called 'em our children," Ruby replied.

The Blacks lived on about $40 a month made by selling soda pop—as well as turquoise, quartzite and other rocks—to tourists. They had no electricity (Calvin ran his tape recorder on a gasoline-powered generator) and no telephone. They couldn't afford doll-making supplies. So Calvin would wait until a motorist plowed into a utility pole on the highway, then he'd go out and retrieve the lumber. He used redwood from the downed poles to craft his dolls' faces. The noses, arms and legs were carved from softer sugar pine.

Ruby was billed as gown maker to the dolls (she collected discarded clothes from the Barstow dump and cut them down to size); but the show was all Calvin's.

"Ruby was very jealous of the dolls," Allie Light said. "She complained because Calvin would be off with the dolls and she'd be left alone. There was a real, deep resentment about Calvin's other life."

Tim Brehm, now a photography instructor at John Burroughs High School in Burbank, got to know the Blacks while photographing them on a number of occasions from 1968 to the mid-'70s. He once described a Calvin Black show in an interview with Light and Saraf. Brehm sat alone in a small room with broken television sets on one side of him and sand sifting through the ceiling. There were about 20 dolls on stage.

"You'd sit on this very uncomfortable bench, and then he [Calvin] would get up in front and he would give a deadpan monologue to kind of get things rolling. Then he'd walk back of this little booth on the left-hand side and you'd see him starting to fumble away with some tapes.

"He had rigged up a unique system of various tape recorders and different tape cassettes that were wired to the different dolls. You would see a conversation taking place with Calvin and a doll, and maybe the doll would start to talk and introduce a song."

At the end of the show, guests were asked to place coins in the kitty boxes next to their favorite performers. Calvin used the money to purchase necklaces, perfume and even store-bought dolls for his girls. "The Beautiful Dolls of the Desert Wasteland," as he advertised them.

"It became obvious to me, after I watched several of these shows, that this entire show was a representation of Calvin's life," Brehm said. "Actually each doll was a representation of someone he'd known in his life. It was a very personal thing to him."

Allie Light believes that the dolls expressed a feminine side of Black's personality. What makes Calvin Black a source of fascination and inspiration to collectors and others, she said, is that he chose to spend most of his time not in the real world, but in a world he had created.

"Most people forget how to live in the imagination," Light said.

In the late '70s, Larry Whiteley learned that Calvin Black's widow was living in the desert alone. Art dealer Whiteley said he offered through a contact to sell a doll or two so that Ruby could move out of her shack and into a trailer. But the offer was refused; Ruby would not sell a doll for any price.

Ruby Black was discovered dead by a minister making a home visit in 1980. The dolls were removed by a neighbor who was conservator of the property and stored temporarily in a nearby warehouse. Larry Whiteley drove out to the desert and made a bid on what was left of Possum Trot.

For the first year he owned the work, there were no buyers, Whiteley said, and he began to wonder if people had been right when they told him the dolls were junk. (One museum even advised that they be burned, Whiteley said.)

What attracted Whiteley was the directness of Calvin Black's work. "It was painted on instinct rather than academic training," he said. "Real folk art is made by people who don't make it to sell. They were just expressing themselves.

"Each doll is totally individual," he added. "All the faces look alike when you first look at them. Then, after a while, none of them look alike."

Allie Light and Irving Saraf purchased a doll from Whiteley. Her name is Miss Sherion Rose. There's also a photograph of Calvin and all his dolls in the couple's living room.

"It's sort of crept into our lives," Allie Light said of their connection to the Blacks. She and her husband sometimes find themselves quoting Calvin and Ruby in their exchanges, she said.

Light said that what made Calvin Black great was his compulsion, and his obstinate respect for his own taste. It didn't matter if some tourists thought Possum Trot was creepy. (Light's daughter, now a TV anchorwoman in El Paso, couldn't wait to get out of there the first time she visited.) But it didn't matter what anyone thought—Calvin loved his dolls.

*From Ann Japenga. "The Reincarnation of Possum Trot Theater." *Los Angeles Times* (December 7, 1986): 6: 1, 30, 31. Reprinted by permission of the *Los Angeles Times.*

An English Critic's Desert Aesthetics
(1982)

The thundersome treatise about desert beauty turned out by erumpent art critic John C. Van Dyke caused a problem going largely unacknowledged by the many desert enthusiasts following in Van Dyke's footsteps. We may agree that the desert overwhelms with its beauty, but what, indeed, makes the desert beautiful? Intellectually rigorous while remaining emotionally committed, English art critic Peter Reyner Banham at once constructs an aesthetic theory while avoiding the easy sentimentalism that has become the accepted stock-in-trade of many writers on the desert.

B EHIND US, something—a cloud, a mountain—occluded the setting sun, and the landscape ahead seemed suddenly darker, and that was fine because just after the next or next-but-one turn of the Interstate, the lights of Las Vegas would come into view, and they need a dark background. But I had not reckoned with the optical effects of that deceiving desert air, still heated by the ground below and full of the haze of the afternoon. The towers of lights and the changing skysigns were there all right, but wavering dizzily and fractured into flickering filaments and ripples of pink and electric blue and gold, floating above a reflecting pool of mirage in the purple air. If you sought an image of the dissolution of a corrupted civilization you could hardly have done better; yet the effect was more gentle and poetic than that, more like a dream city dissolving in its own ecstasy.

It didn't dissolve, of course. It became more solid and profane as we approached and the sun came out again to confuse the issue further. But for maybe half a minute it had been an incredible image of an architecture of light drowning in light more beautiful than its own. The great terminal oasis had become the ultimate optical illusion. . . .

Few of us in our daily round will ever see adjectives separated from nouns in this way; we see red tomatoes and green apples and yellow bananas. But we don't see the colors apart from the fruits; and it took a long time for even the most sophisticated men of antiquity to be able to make much verbal discrimination between color—the poverty of color words in Greek, even as late as Plato, is now almost proverbial and makes us wonder how many colors they could even visually discriminate.

So the disembodied colors that haunt (we have no other word for it) the desert eerily short-circuit a process of reasoned discrimination that has cost Western Man long centuries of verbal exercise of the faculty of reason. But in making her particular celebration of this short circuit, Helen Frankenthaler is also drawing on respectable traditions in Modern Art since about the time of the post-Impressionists. Color and form have long been two separable topics of painterly discourse—often within the terms of a single painting—from the dislocations of early Cubism to the final efflorescence of color-field painting in the 1950s.

That is why I am still unwilling to give up the idea that there may be some congruence between the look of the deserts and some abstract art; but I cannot advance this idea in the comforting and reassuring guise of an iconography that I learned in youth or as a student of art history. The whole matter is too appropriately tenuous for that, and in many ways my responses are too strong to be so neatly explained. However, it was somewhat reassuring that this particular train of thought should have been opened up by a work of art, for *Indian Redscape* is a fine and commanding painting that would probably have stuck in my visual memory anyhow. And it is bound to gratify one's vanity if one finds that the preoccupations of the day are answered by major works, rather than no account trivia.

For the desert is not trivial. Even if one only skitters across its surface in leisure clothes and casual shoes, even if every night's destination is a surprise-free franchised motel, there is still something large and mysterious about the experience of being in it. The first old-timer with whom I ever swapped value judgments about the Mojave phrased it thus:

Ah love thuh Desert. Used to live on thuh Coast, work for thuh State of California, got muhself transferred up here. Wouldn't move 'way agin. Ain't no two ways 'bout it: yuh either loves the desert or yuh hates it. . . . Ah love it!

Every move, every gesture, every facial expression, every turn of phrase suggested role playing—even the accent sounded acquired. Yet I know (from what I learned about him later) that he was not codding me, nor codding himself. If you love anything as fundamentally inhospitable to the lazy and self-indulgent human race as a desert, then you may well have credibility problems, even within yourself. It may be a necessary support and comfort to adopt a guise that has been codified and sanctified by art (if only the movies) and speak through a *persona* that seems more appropriate than one's own.

Behind the play-acting, however, I think there was truth. There are no two ways about the desert; there are no middle opinions; and I have never met anyone who was just a "mild" desert lover. And it could be that the old-timer's B-movie prose was a way of controlling responses that surprised him as much as mine had already surprised me, for this was already my second visit to the Mojave and I knew that I was over my ears, committed and out of my depth.

And something of my long-term uneasiness and fascination with the desert derives, I suspect, from my never having found a suitable disguise or function with which to designate my relationship to this landscape I love. I feel sure that if I could be a professional old-timer, a Ranger for the BLM, or the line man who services the telephone that rejoices in the call number Landfair 1, I could be able to use words like *beautiful* without wondering what I mean by them, and how I came by the responses that drive me to use words like that.

Clearly, the desert has done to me what it has done to many of us desert freaks—it has made me ask questions about myself that I would never otherwise have asked. And since I have no convincing answers to those questions (*Indian Redscape* is only a clue, not an answer), I have not done what one has been supposed to do in deserts ever since the time of Moses—I have not "found myself." If anything I have lost myself, in the sense that I now feel that I understand myself less than I did before.

What I have truly found, however, is something that I value, in some ways, more than myself. Beauty may indeed lie in the eye of the beholder, but that eye must have an object of vision, a scene on which it can fasten, and I have found that scene, and appropriate objects of scrutiny within it, and that light and that color. And all this I knew (I believe) from the very moment that my eye was taken by the vision of that ethereal luminous mist on that first morning on the Mojave. The desert hath me in thrall, and I am happy to say that I am still astonished to discover that this is so.

*From Peter Reyner Banham. *Scenes in America Deserta*. Salt Lake City: Gibbs M. Smith, 1982. 208, 226–28.

The Last Word on Las Vegas

(1982)

The state of Nevada has no income tax. It doesn't need one. Paying its bills, thousands of tourists come tumbling in. Surrounded by the sugar highs of an artificial Egypt, phony pirate fights on an artificial ocean, and, yes, even an artificial (and air-conditioned) desert, they gamble their money away, then in a state of shock leave with their shrunken wallets. The locals rejoice for the fatuous hordes bearing their tax burden.

Paralleling this is a storm of inspirations making up another benefit, but perhaps a more onerous one. So much has been written about Sin City, both by heated moralists rending their garments at the Godless ticky-tacky and by heady celebrants of our modern Sodom and Gomorrah, that the anthologist is left paralyzed. It would seem impossible to draw one selection representing all from the welter of battling prose. For that, one rejoices, having found the final word on Las Vegas.

. . . it will never make noble ruins. . . .

From Peter Reyner Banham. *Scenes in America Deserta*. Salt Lake City: Gibbs M. Smith, 1982. 43.

Murder on the Mojave

(1992)

Although the exact number is not known, thousands of mine shafts dot the Mojave. Also unknown is the number of bodies at their bottoms.

The fact is that, despite the fine words over the years about the desert's natural beauty, the Mojave has been a violent place—perhaps more violent today than ever before. One sheriff's deputy told me that more bodies are found annually in the desert portions of San Bernardino County than in any other county in the United States. This is entirely believable. People in highly populated Los Angeles with embarrassing corpses on their hands, as in the grim but fairly common incident recorded below, find it convenient to drive east over the mountains and use the desert as a funereal dumping ground. Add other darkling factors. The desert not only is a hotbed for the manufacture of methamphetamine and trafficking in other illegal drugs; some of its residents, unable to cope with "normal" society, have fled to desert shacks where, with whirling minds, they await their real or imagined pursuers. And then there are the hard-headed militia types with crates of Uzis in their barns, getting prepared. They hold to all kinds of political beliefs, to left and right, as well as off the charts; but they have one thing in common: When the revolution breaks out, they are ready to declare the Republic of the Mojave. Given such things, one is not surprised at crudely lettered signs such as one I saw nailed to a front gate: "If You Want To Find Out About The Afterlife, Trespass On This Property."

The everyday traveler enjoying the desert on the standard tourist routes is unlikely to encounter any of this. However, it is unwise to knock on the door of a lone cabin or investigate unusual activities in progress, unless one doesn't mind being greeted with a gun in his or her face.

RANCHO CUCAMONGA. The aunt and grandmother of a 5-year-old girl whose body was found five weeks ago in the Mojave

Desert were rearrested in Los Angeles on Friday. The aunt was charged with murder and the grandmother with being an accessory to murder.

The aunt, Renee Lloyd, 32, and grandmother, Bertha Toombs, 49, were initially arrested in September when the body of Marquishia Candler was found east of Victorville. But both were released two days later after police said they did not have enough evidence to hold them. . .

Lloyd and Toombs told Culver City police Sept. 22 that Marquishia had disappeared during a shopping trip at the Fox Hills Mall. In the days that followed, Toombs appeared on television to ask help in finding the missing girl.

When police summoned Lloyd and Toombs to the Culver City station for further questioning Sept. 28, the women admitted that the first story was a fabrication. They said that Marquishia had drowned accidentally in a bathtub at Toombs' home in Ontario.

The women told police they panicked after the girl died and Lloyd dumped Marquishia's body beside a lonely stretch of road in the Lucerne Valley. Lloyd directed police to where the body was found and both women were placed under arrest. At that time, Lloyd was booked on suspicion of murder and Toombs was booked on suspicion of being an accessory to the crime.

*From Eric Malnic and Christopher Heredia. "2 Relatives Arrested in Girl's Death." *Los Angeles Times,* November 7, 1992. B: 1, 8. Reprinted by permission of the *Los Angeles Times.*

Area 51:
The Military Base that Doesn't Exist
(1994)

For the military, the Mojave is a beautiful place. Relatively accessible to technology centers on the West Coast, the desert's great, uninhabited expanses nevertheless offer the isolation and nearly endless runways on dry lakebeds for conducting experiments. Sometimes, these are funded by untraceable "black budgets" best kept from the eyes of the public.

To flip things over, the situation makes a rich breeding ground for the imagination. On raw peaks overlooking the infamous Area 51 (significantly only a hundred miles north of Las Vegas, another dreamland) one encounters gaggles of voyeurs. Sometimes in horned Viking helmets and sporting whimsical names such as Captain Eric and Psychospy, the enthusiasts wait for hours straining to glimpse the rumored flying saucers secreted below, evidenced by weird lights that occasionally leap out of the darkness to put on dazzling, if ephemeral, nighttime displays.

It's tempting to dismiss such avid observers with a wink. Yet are they any stranger than the strange (and likely far more ominous) things going on down there or any more extraordinary than what's indicated by the extraordinary measures the government takes to hide its own activities?

O N ANOTHER NIGHT, with our headlights off and taillights disconnected so they won't flash when the brakes are applied, Jim Goodall and I pilot our Toyota Land Cruiser along the dirt roads and bumpy trails just north of the base. For a few miles, we drive within the sight lines of a security post; then we pass behind some low ridges. We head for a slope where Campbell had earlier positioned a large military camouflage net. Shrouded in the netting, our parked truck resembles another mound of greenish scrub in the partial moonlight. On foot, we lug our gear up the hill.

Campbell hikes to our campsite the next morning, and things on the summit remain peaceful until noon. Then we hear the distant whumping of a Blackhawk. Adrenaline flows. This aerial visit lasts four hours.

We watch the Blackhawk circle below us, then finally swoop down to sandblast a barren hillock about two miles distant. Peering through his binoculars, Goodall is suddenly seized with a laughing fit. "They're assaulting my old lawn chair! I left it there months ago." Security men emerge from vehicles and take possession of the area near the chair, as the helicopter widens its search pattern, sandblasting every clump of vegetation in the area.

The search expands, covering several square miles. Eventually, Campbell's car, tucked into a ditch under a gray cover, is spotted. Sheriffs note its license number.

We remain rolled up like armadillos under small, gnarled evergreens, where we weather dozens of helicopter passes undetected. Finally, the security forces give up and leave.

Definitely no secret airplanes tonight, we realize, so we decide to seek some real food and hot showers. We retreat to the Little A Le Inn (pronounced "alien"), the sole watering hole in the hamlet of Rachel. The bar's walls are covered with UFO memorabilia and a large Goodall photo of the secret base. "We heard someone penetrated the base perimeter," says Pat Travis, as she takes our orders.

Proprietors Pat and Joe Travis serve food and drink to a mix of cowboys, UFO buffs, and base workers. The latter are generally congenial but strictly observe their secrecy vows: "I'd tell you, but then I'd have to kill you," they like to say if questioned about Groom Lake. . . .

Two nights later, several of us venture out again. After an uneventful evening watching from Freedom Ridge, we fall asleep. At 2:00 a.m., visitors with bright flashlights arrive: a sheriff and a security guard in camouflage. When the sheriff demands to search through our bags for cameras, my companions stubbornly assert their civil liberties. The sheriff backs down when we ask to see a warrant. Because the Groom lake base is officially unmentionable, a judge can't issue a warrant alleging infractions in the vicinity; it's an odd Catch-22 the government has concocted for itself.

*From Stuart F. Brown. "Searching for the Secrets of Groom Lake." *Popular Science* 244.3 (March 1994): 84. Copyright © 1994 *Popular Science Magazine*. Reprinted by permission of Time4Media, Inc.

Locals as Dolts

(1996)

Ranching has had a long history in the Mojave. Early Anglo settlers brought along their cattle and turned them loose on a land considered good for little else but grazing.

Yet not actually "good" for grazing. In fact, with its sparse vegetation and desperately little water, the Mojave makes a poor place for growing hamburgers. Worse, still, too many cattle have ravaged the land, putting the delicate, rain-poor ecosystem into a tailspin. The public's recent realization of this has turned the once-romanticized rancher into a vile character. As a result, the government has put the squeeze on grazing across leased federal lands. Today, for example, the historic OX Ranch is no more.

Urbanites tend to gloat over this, thinking that the villainous ranchers finally have received their due. I'm not so sure. Not so sure that the situation is as simple as the "enlightened" outsiders imagine. The root problem with the Mojave is not too many cattle but too many of a far more destructive creature—people. The cattle may be gone, but the growth of retirement communities, huge military installations, and tourist motels continues apace—obliterating precious habitat and sucking down the water table at an exponential rate far beyond the ability of any rancher.

I FINALLY HOOKED UP WITH Overson by phone at six thirty in the morning. He told me that he was coming toward Goffs that day and I could ride along with him if I wanted to. When he picked me up at the schoolhouse, I noticed that he had his rifle on the seat beside him—not on a rack in the cab's rear window—and that, as he got out of the truck and walked bowlegged on his boots around the tailgate, he was still wearing his spurs.

He was small but sinewy, simultaneously sharp and blunt. "First of all," he said as I got into his truck, "I don't care about what you're doing at all. It don't mean nothing to me to be in a book." He spit some snuff juice into a bowl and, having thus established his independence, explained that he was out checking water lines and tank float valves. "I own sixteen of the main water rights in this area. Springs, windmills, over a hundred miles of pipeline—the land where the water is. That's the key to the desert; water is the whole thing." Indeed, if it weren't for such artificial developments, much of the Mojave would be naturally off-limits to livestock.

We pulled out from the schoolhouse and onto Goffs Road. As we drove south through the desert, Overson scanned the landscape for cows. "Cattle get fat on yucca blooms," he said, referring to the creamy-white blossoms I'd seen in Lanfair Valley. "Eating those, they might go two weeks without water. Then, when they get thirsty, they start a-walking down this way. I gotta watch 'em, or they'll go all the way to the Colorado River."

He told me he'd come to the East Mojave from St. John's, Arizona, fifty years earlier, when he was three years old. "I went to work for the OX Ranch when I was eleven," he said. "My father was a rancher till he went to work for the railroad. He was right across the road at that stockyard there. He got killed by a train when I was about fifteen. When I got married, all I had was a bedroll, a saddle, and a pickup payment. After a while, I managed to get a one-third interest in the Kessler Springs Ranch—a hundred cows, one bull, and two saddle horses. I kept on buying cattle, and later I bought my partners out. Bought the Sand Dunes Ranch at Kelso and sold it; bought the Valley Wells Ranch, sold it. Then I bought the OX Ranch. Now I got seven thousand acres of deeded land and close to nine hundred thousand of grazing land, not counting two ranches I take care of. It's not all BLM [Bureau of Land Management] land—I don't know how many sections of railroad land I lease—and it's not as big as it sounds. With this country here, cattle don't use a lot of it but once every three or four years."

The weather was overcast with occasional raindrops—not as chilly as it had been earlier in the week, but consistent with the recent pattern of repeated spring rains. "This is what you want," said Overson. "Warm rains out of Los Angeles, San Diego, and Mexico. March will make you or break you as far as feed conditions on the desert. It's unpredictable—

with the wind blowing, it can freeze or dry the ground out. The secret is having moisture in the ground before it dries out. What you *don't* want is storms from the north; that just brings cold and snow and humps up your cattle. In most countries you have only one season, but here you have two: spring and summer. The spring of the year is your payday. We ship the cattle in June, and when we start work, we need seventeen or eighteen head of broke saddle horses and five or six of us riding 'em.

"The OX is the most productive ranch in this country," Overson went on. "It can carry as much as twenty-five hundred mother cows all year long. That black grama grass up at Carothers is as good a grass as there is anywhere; steers come off there in June weighing seven hundred pounds. A lot of ranches that people think are so great still have to feed hay in winter, and that stuff is getting expensive. But the OX Ranch has feed year-round."

We turned east toward the Colorado River, where the country was characterized more by creosote bush than by Joshua trees. "This is a coarser grass in here," Overson observed. "You see that peanut cactus? When the ground gets so dry that cattle eat that, you gotta either sell 'em or move 'em. The needles foul their stomachs up. A lot of this country is only used three or four months out of the year. It's low, and in warm weather it's dry. The cattle would rather have green, so you move 'em up into the cooler country. I move cattle around all over. People from other places don't understand that. How the hell can you have all your cattle in one place in the desert country?"

When Overson expressed disdain—as he did with the last sentence—he dipped his head forward and wagged it from side to side as if imitating the posture of a prattling fool. "If a lot of the people who are against grazing came out here and lived a couple of years, they wouldn't be against it," he claimed. "*People* is what ruins the country—not cattle."

*From David Darlington. *The Mojave: A Portrait of the Definitive American Desert*. New York: Henry Holt, 1996). 110–12. Copyright © 1996 David Darlington. Reprinted by permission of Henry Holt and Company, LLC.

The Locals Revolt

(1996)

As we've touched on, many urbanites escape their cities by driving out into the Mojave on weekends and holidays. Such tourists, often considering themselves staunch environmentalists, yet living and working in some of the most ecologically disturbed areas on the planet, view the Mojave as a place for their pleasure, one that should be a pristine landscape offering a romantic focus for their dreamings. Getting in the way of this are the everyday people who actually make a living on the desert, few in number and lacking political clout. They feel defenseless against a government which, responding to pressure from the politicians representing urban power centers, seems determined to chase off some of the Mojave families that have lived out on the desert for generations.

Ironically, in a sharp example of unintended consequences, in some cases at least, government policy is backfiring, not making the Mojave a more peaceful place but encouraging destruction through crime and hooliganism, just as the following Mojave resident warned.

. . . THE GOVERNMENT has been around out here for a long time and nobody can match the government when it comes to major impacts. Take Operation Desert Strike of 1964, for example, when 250,000 troops with all manner of equipment swarmed across the East Mojave tearing apart the desert like no vandal ever dreamed of. Or take the recent die-off of 45 or more big horn sheep in the Old Dad Mountains which seems attributable to government bungling and lack of effective coordination between government agencies. There's no way you or I could ever eliminate 45 big horn sheep if we dedicated our lives to it—but government is big enough to do the job. Look at all the historic structures BLM has destroyed in the East Mojave over the last twenty years—Weavers Well in the Old Woman Mountains, the buildings at Kingston Springs, the buildings of the headquarters of the Yates Ranch at Valley Wells. . . .

But, we must accept that when President Clinton signed the California Desert Protection Act into law on Halloween Day 1994, *he condemned our way of life on the desert to oblivion*. He started these quiet, restful, and historic lands down the road to the great norms of society and behavior that are being experienced on the streets of Washington, D.C., Little Rock, San Francisco, and other "cultural centers." The area will become crowded with pushing, lawless, impatient, rude people demanding to be cared for at every turn by a welfare government. There is no visible way for us to change it or even influence this result to any significant degree. In a lot of ways I will not try to change it because the forces of evil that produced the California Desert Protection Act are virtually overpowering. Our exchange with this well-meaning group of NPS [National Park Service] and BLM professionals was to share views and concerns based on our experience in the hope it might somehow help. More importantly, we shared insights about history that I think will be useful to them and to us.

In many ways, unfortunately, government comes across as uncaring as ever. It is clear from meetings like this and inputs from other directions that NPS doesn't care about the people that live out here. They never did and they never will. They resist taking the necessary steps to ameliorate the fears and concerns that land owning, tax paying citizens have. The intense negative reception they have received was expected—it must say in the National Park Service manual somewhere that when a new park is established and locals are deprived of their lifeways, they'll be mad. The manual must say, "Just let them (the tax payers) thrash around, like a puppy being introduced to a leash, and eventually, they will get tired, calm down, go away, or acquiesce and accept the benevolent presence and oversight of Big Brother."

*From Dennis Casebier. "National Park Service Officials Visit Goffs Schoolhouse." *Mojave Road Report* 157 (November 1996): 8, 9. Reprinted by permission of the author.

Talking with the Spirits:
The California Desert Protection Act
(1997)

If, despite his bad grammar and hokey ways, one thing can be said for rancher Overson it's that at least he lived on the land, struggling with its hardships and making an honest living.

In contrast, there's something fey about writers breezing into the desert from distant cities, then letting loose with pent-up New Age imaginings.

That the desert is a wonderful place—one of many intrigues, a humbling place, awesome in its spaces, its multiple, ever-changing blends of beauty and harsh conditions bringing us back to much of our essential selves, and thus for all these reasons and more deserving to be treasured—we won't dispute. But does the desert, then, "hold all life's passions" and "awaken all one's senses"? And do desert nights magically propel one "into infinity"? I think not. Unless the enthusiasts will themselves into believing such things. This has the false ring of urban romance imposed on the desert.

That is, now we're encountering not appreciation of nature, but self-serving narcissism. This hardly is "loving" the desert but turning it into what it is not, "loving" it only because the emotional spillage serves desert enthusiasts' needs. Otherwise, they'd leave the horned lizard at peace.

Yet the reality may well be, in one of life's continuing ironies found on the Mojave, that it takes just such a warm, pink, and fuzzy-wuzzy fog of shallow but appealing emotionalism on the part of politically powerful urban populations to sustain the movement for preserving the desert.

❧

SOMEWHERE OUT THERE is a land grand enough to hold all life's passions and contradictions, to expand one's soul with vast possibilities, to awaken all one's senses.

To find it, search north from the Mexican border up through the

California desert via backroads and wilderness areas, through the lost and forgotten and least-explored outback. Find those places least written about. Ask locals. Be adventurous. Expand into infinity in a desert night. Take on the night vision of an elf owl, the radar of a leaf-nosed bat, the ears of a kit fox, the vibration sensors of a Gambel's quail. Turn off the radio. Turn off the stereo. Get out of the vehicle and walk. Gaze at the desert with the eyes of an eagle, then with the eyes of a snake. Sit for long periods of time in silence, listening. After a while, the desert will speak to you.

Time in the great deserts of the West is very different from city time. Because the earth's crust is sliced open, and so many objects from past history lie preserved in the dry, clean air, desert time is like layers of clear plate glass. You can drop down through them, intersecting lives separated by centuries. In the desert, antiquity is interlayered with the present—as when ancient rock art lies within military testing grounds. Sitting near a wall painted with a giant shaman figure created two thousand years ago, you may think you hear a foot thud on the hardpacked desert floor and turn swiftly to see no one. You may imagine the shaman dressing as, then actually becoming, a god in order to call the rain. You may hear the ladder creak as he emerges from a sacred cave, having performed a healing ritual.

Or you may hear the hoof beats of a seventeenth-century padre gingerly riding from one hardship to the next, seeking native people to convert, inserting Old World Spanish saints into the native pantheon.

Or you may overhear a voice from a century ago, an old white prospector having a talk with his mule, demanding from the desert too much, too soon, and too easy.

Simultaneously, you may hear contemporary Chemehuevi people chanting clan songs that will continue their tradition down through the ages, or hear a researcher mumbling at his Global Positioning Satellite navigator as he tracks desert tortoise.

In the desert, you will meet animals possessed with people-wisdom. You will glimpse Coyote, the Trickster, darting in and out, through the edge of cities, sewing an urban civilization uneasily onto the desert. The daredevil jackrabbit will dash two inches in front of your car bumper, making bets with his cronies about how close he can come to death. He will always win. The horned lizard, all pimpled and lumpy, will lie passively in your hand, too stuffed with sun and insects to object.

In your imagination, you will find yourself conducting interviews with the men who hunted with *atl-atl* twenty-six thousand years ago over near Barstow. You will find yourself chattering across time, across language, and across cultural gaps with the Ancient Ones as if they stood in your kitchen. Which, at your campfire, they will. They will teach you the rich variety of uses for the plants and animals. You will find your sensory perception far lacking compared to their own. Yet the longer you remain in wild places and outside your vehicle, the more your hearing, smelling, touching, electromagnetic radar, and vibration sensors will return to you.

Nowhere else on earth is geologic time so exposed as in a desert. There, you will travel swiftly through geological eras as you pass through highly eroded mountains, bizarre volcanic necks and cones, endless salt playas, and towering sand dunes in sensuous curves of pink and tan. You will pass through brick red and black dorsal fins jutting eight hundred feet up out of the earth as if stegosaurs cavorted just under the ground, past long black snakes of glassy lava one hundred feet high, through badlands as colorful as an artist's palette, through narrow, contorted canyons, through limestone caverns, and through the world's largest Joshua tree forest. Each profusely flowering cactus, each hidden desert waterfall and plunge pool, will open senses you barely knew you had.

The fragile California desert stretches 100 miles from east to west and 240 miles from north to south. For ten long years, hundreds of American citizens worked to protect its remarkable wild lands, which include three of the great deserts of the world—the Mojave, the lower tip of the Great Basin, and the northern wedge of the Sonoran. On October 31, 1994, President Clinton signed the California Desert Protection Act into law, protecting another 3.57 million acres of land as wilderness. The sixty-nine new wilderness areas are as different from one another as topography can be—from high alpine snow fields discharging roaring streams to dry, barren salt playas—and they will take a lifetime to explore.

The Desert Protection Act created two new national parks, Death Valley and Joshua Tree. At over 3.3 million acres, Death Valley is now the largest park in the lower forty-eight states. Joshua Tree was increased to 793,000 acres by including natural ecosystems which had previously extended beyond the former monument boundaries. The act also established the dramatic landscape between Interstates 15 and 40 as the Mojave National Preserve, the newest addition to the National Park Service. In addition, wilderness habitat adjacent to Anza-Borrego and Red Rock Canyon State Parks has been greatly expanded.

*From Susan Zwinger. *Still Wild, Always Wild: A Journey into the Desert Wilderness of California*. San Francisco: Sierra Club Books, 1997. 9–11. Reprinted by permission of the author.

The Desert Tortoise: "Walking Raviolis"
(1999)

It's amazing what humankind will squabble over.

This antediluvian and fierce-looking (but entirely harmless) creature emerges from its burrow in late spring, lumbers about for a bit, then retreats, spending some ninety percent of its life underground, avoiding the winter cold and the summer heat.

It's the desert tortoise, and it has become a cause célèbre on the Mojave. One faction of activists self-righteously rends its garments, maintaining that the plummeting population of the reptile confirms the general slumgummery of the human species. The reformers support an elaborate system of fences, refuges, and teams of pickup trucks cruising the desert highways to save tortoises lumbering across the pavement. Another faction chortles that such frenzy is yet another example of a government gone beserko with a fabricated cause used as an excuse for ever more elaborate federal intervention.

One thing seems certain. The number of tortoises is falling. About a foot long, the critters are stepped on by horses, shot by vandals, and suffering rapid loss of habitat from metastasizing condominium complexes. Yet, as with so many other issues on the Mojave, the situation may not be as black-and-white as heated antagonists maintain. Pogo was right. Sorting the complexities, once again we find too many people and too little desert at their root.

Dave Morafka remembers well the day the ravens attacked. The biologist had built an enclosure to study young desert tortoises at Fort Irwin, an army base in Southern California. Raven populations were skyrocketing in the Mojave Desert, and shells from tortoise hatchlings were appearing under raven nests. But whether the ravens were a serious problem for the declining tortoises was still under debate.

In May 1991, eight months into the study, the black birds swooped out of the sky and ended the argument. In little more than a week, they killed 18 of 24 hatchlings inside the study site and 8 more that ranged nearby, pecking through their soft young shells and feasting on their flesh.

Morafka, a biologist at California State University-Dominguez Hills, was horrified. "Once they discovered us, the result was quick, thorough and devastating," he says.

In the Southwest, the lives of the common raven and the tortoise are intertwining in a deadly way. Over the past 30 years, raven numbers in the Mojave Desert have risen more than 1,000 percent as people have introduced sources of food and water to this harsh environment. During the same period, tortoise numbers have dropped more than 90 percent in some areas. Ravens are not the only reason for the tortoise's decline, but the quick-witted birds are a significant and growing threat. Ravens have caused more than 50 percent of juvenile desert tortoise deaths in some areas, according to biologist Kristin Berry of the U.S. Geological Survey in Riverside, California.

Biologists worry that, in places where tortoise numbers are already reduced by disease, habitat destruction and other problems, raven predation may drive these populations out of existence. "Normally if a predator eats a prey into oblivion, its own numbers decline," says Morafka. "But raven populations are subsidized by urban irrigation and garbage and can afford to hunt something to extinction."

The desert tortoise is one of four species of gopher tortoise native to North America, and its ancestors have been around for perhaps 80 million years. The creatures are found today in arid parts of California, Nevada, Arizona, Utah and northern Mexico. The lumbering reptiles are among the longest lived of all animals, surviving perhaps a century or longer.

To persist in such a harsh environment, desert tortoises may spend more than 90 percent of their time underground. They hibernate in burrows for several months in the winter, and spend days or weeks at a time below ground during hot summer months.

Much of the reptiles' water intake comes from moisture in the grasses and wildflowers they consume in the spring. "Eating to drink," Morafka calls it. Tortoises store water in their bladders against drier seasons ahead. During very dry times they may give off waste as a white paste rather than a watery urine. Adult tortoises may survive a year or more without access to water.

Although desert tortoises are well-adapted to their arid surroundings, human-induced changes have proven problematic for the reptiles. Urban development and off-road vehicle traffic have destroyed much of their habitat and led to road kills. Cattle grazing has reduced the amount of food available for the tortoises in some areas. In recent years, a respiratory disease similar to some types of human pneumonia has also ravaged tortoise populations.

In 1973, Berry took state officials out for a 6-mile ride through what is now the protected Desert Tortoise Natural Area at the west edge of the Mojave Desert in California. "Every place we looked we saw tortoises," says the geological survey biologist. "We saw as many as 8 tortoises at one time, 50 for the whole day. Of course those days are gone." In the last 10 years, the tortoise population in this 38-square-mile area has declined 88 percent.

There are currently anywhere from 93,000 to several hundred thousand desert tortoises, biologists estimate. In 1990, desert tortoises in the Mojave Desert (which stretches over parts of California, Nevada, Utah and Arizona) were formally listed by the U.S. Fish and Wildlife Service as a threatened species.

The human-abetted ascent of common ravens is now the chief threat to young tortoises in some areas. The reptiles' shells do not become hard enough to protect them from predators until about 5 to 7 years of age. "Up until then, they're just soft little morsels, almost like walking raviolis," says Morafka.

*From Michael Tennesen. "Fatal Attraction." *National Wildlife* 37.3 (April–May 1999): 36–37. Reprinted by permission of the author.

The Jitters: Still Shaking
(1999)

Every time there's an earthquake on the Mojave, there's a run on the local U-Haul dealerships. No wonder real estate values are low. Some people can't take the suspense of waiting for the next quake that will chill them to zero at the bone as pictures crash from the walls, houses hop off their foundations, and trains leap off their tracks.

Note the nervousness in the following piece. The unsettling reality: Edna Brush Perkins may have praised the desert in *The White Heart of Mojave* (1922) as "solid and everlasting," as a restful landscape for a human to behold. That, however, is only the deception of momentary appearances. For all its dryness and apparent stolidity, the Mojave is a fluid place. When the last earthquake hit, the earth hadn't yet stopped shaking from the one before.

L UDLOW, Calif. A magnitude 7.0 earthquake struck the Mojave Desert northwest of Twentynine Palms early Saturday, knocking an Amtrak passenger train off its tracks and damaging two highway bridges, but otherwise causing remarkably little harm and no deaths.

Four people on Amtrak's Southwest Chief from Chicago to Los Angeles were injured, none seriously, when the temblor—the fourth strongest in Southern California this century—rocked the region at 2:46 a.m. More than 250,000 customers throughout Southern California lost power, but in most cases service was restored almost immediately.

Centered beneath a Marine base, the quake swayed high-rise hotels in Las Vegas and jolted millions of people awake throughout the Southland, stirring unwelcome memories of the 1994 Northridge quake.

Although the Hector Mine earthquake, as it was dubbed by the U.S. Geological Survey, was three times stronger than the 6.7 Northridge quake, it caused only a tiny fraction of the damage because it was centered far from heavily populated areas.

"The damage could have been catastrophic, but was minimal," said Mayor Richard Riordan. "It's a good opportunity, however, for everybody to take note that we live in earthquake country. We can never be too prepared for the next one."

Saturday's earthquake, named after a desert mineral mining site, was the fourth of magnitude 7 or greater recorded across the globe in the past two months. Earthquakes in western Turkey and Taiwan occurred in heavily populated areas and left nearly 20,000 people dead. Twenty people died in the third, a 7.5 temblor that struck a mostly rural region in the Mexican state of Oaxaca.

The Hector Mine earthquake hit hardest in an area more highly populated by rattlesnakes than people, and most of its energy was spent harmlessly.

But for those nearest the epicenter, it was a terrifying experience.

"Let me put it to you this way," said Juan Tirado, who lives in a trailer in Ludlow, a hamlet of about 40 people along Interstate 40 between Barstow and Needles. "The first thing I tried to do was jump up and get to my daughter—but I couldn't.

"I got as far as her bedroom door but then I couldn't move another step, we were shaking so hard. I was holding on to the walls but couldn't move. It was like I was in a bottle and someone was shaking it back and forth."

*From Tom Gorman and Mitchell Landsberg. "7.0 Earthquake in Mojave Desert Rocks Southland." *Los Angeles Times* (October 17, 1999): A: 1, 32. Reprinted by permission of the *Los Angeles Times*.

Yucca Mountain: The World's Most Dangerous Poison

(2000)

Imagine someone suggesting he or she create a substance so dangerous that a few pounds of it turned loose would kill everyone on earth. Furthermore, it would be impossible to get rid of, remaining deadly for tens of thousands of years. Such an idea would seem mad. Except that it's now a fait accompli. Humanity is saddled with tons of the stuff, our legacy from spent plutonium and uranium byproducts. The only real question now is, What to do with it?

Why, truck it to a remote site out on the Mojave Desert and, as with some unforgivable sin, bury it as deep as you can. Perhaps that's the best we can do. Not much more than two centuries old, our nation has created a poison that will haunt humanity years longer than any civilization has ever existed. That Indians are protesting the violation of one of their sacred sites is a fetching ploy for our sympathies, one that sells newspapers; with our post-modern mindsets, we are charmed by such existing quaintness. That the violation should take place on the Mojave piques our righteousness as well. That a high-tech society should consider part of nature a useless backyard good only for a dumping ground puts us on the side of the angels. Beyond such emotions, however, is a deeper and more telling truth. Now we are all Indians living in a world without backyards.

ARMARGOSA VALLEY, Nev. If the desert were a city, the ground near the Yucca Mountain ridge would be the lonely part of town where you hope the car doesn't break down. Less than 30 minutes on a winding, pitted road from Interstate 95, the Yucca flats are a different world, scorched and scarred. From here, trucks racing through the hard dirt of the highway, deafening at close range, sound like buzzing bees, and dusky brown rabbits browsing around the spotty brush look like kings of the world.

For members of the Western Shoshone Nation, a desire to protect the jack rabbits and the scrub brush, stubborn survivors of a thousand nuclear blasts, only partly explains why they believe this pockmarked landscape should be spared from becoming the dumping ground for the world's most dangerous poison.

To the Western Shoshone, Yucca Mountain itself, slated to become the home for all eternity to 77,000 tons of highly lethal nuclear waste from across the United States, is sacred. The land, 100 miles northwest of Las Vegas by the Nevada Test Site—the proving ground for the atomic bomb—is part of what was once a vast territory the Western Shoshones roamed, and still claim as their own.

"We don't really say we `own' the land, because we have always been taught to respect Mother Earth as a living thing," said Raymond Yowell, chief of the Western Shoshone National Council, the traditional governing body of his people.

"Traditionally," Mr. Yowell said, "our people would travel through here, camp, forage for pine nuts, maybe hunt deer and rabbits. We took only what we needed, always thankfully. We consider ourselves the land's caretakers."

Mr. Yowell lead the fourth annual spring gathering earlier this month at Yucca Mountain. The social gathering was also a strategy session for Western Shoshones and other Indians to discuss ways to stop the government from making the mountain a nuclear dump.

For more than 20 years, scientists have debated whether Yucca Mountain is the best place to bury the deadly radioactive waste. A 5.4-mile, U-shaped tunnel was bored into the side of the mountain at a cost of $80 million to allow access for tests. If it wins Congressional approval, the Energy Department will construct a honeycomb of 35 miles of additional tunnels to house the waste.

About 50 men, women and children were camped out at the base of the mountain ridge. They danced before dinner and greeted the sun at dawn. In between, they talked about the dangers of spent plutonium and uranium byproducts.

*From Evelyn Nieves. "A Land's `Caretakers' Oppose Nuclear-Dump Plan." *New York Times*, April 23, 2000. 1:12. Reprinted by permission of the *New York Times*.

✺

Giant Rock:
The F.B.I. and Space Visitors
(2000)

At night, some people insist, aliens from Other Worlds swoop down on the Mojave and commune with their waiting human friends.

The Mojave is a land of True Believers, and one of its most famous sites for mysterious happenings looks just like a giant, misshapen rock egg standing on end—but one seven stories tall, fallen onto the desert sands.

The crowds of thousands no longer gather at Giant Rock, but within the nearby Integratron, a white dome constructed according to spiritual dimensions, the faithful come to float in sky chairs and be rejuvenated, according to a brochure, by "the pure harmonics of quartz crystal singing bowls."

Naturam expellas furca, tamen usque recurret.

By the way, on February 21, 2000, Giant Rock mysteriously split, to everyone's surprise revealing inside. . . . But that's another story.

✺

GIANT ROCK has been a place of legendary significance since a hermit miner by the name of Frank Critzer met his maker there in July of 1942.

According to most accounts of the story, Critzer was a German immigrant who in the 1920s worked on the fishing fleets out of Santa Monica. When a doctor recommended he move to a drier climate to relieve lung problems, Critzer decided to try his hand at prospecting. Prior to embarking on his journey to the desert, he took his old Essex to a garage owned by Glenn Paine. George Van Tassel, Paine's nephew, was also there and the two decided to grubstake Critzer's venture.

A year had gone by before the pair heard any word from the miner. Van Tassel later said he and his uncle drove out to visit Critzer on the claim he had filed and found him living in a cave dug from underneath Giant Rock.

The miner had shown the men several bottles full of gold and paperwork detailing ideas for inventions that included a near-completed formula for plastics, an as-yet-unknown and undeveloped substance.

Over the next 20 years, Critzer helped Charlie Reche build and pipe water to his house. He graded the roads leading to Giant Rock and scraped out an airport runway, complete with windsock, on the dry lake bed nearby. When pilots began spotting the runway and landing, Critzer soon had a business of servicing and repairing aircraft.

It was the landing strip that first brought Critzer and his activities to the attention of immigration officers and later the FBI.

Suspicions the airstrip was used by pilots whose planes carried cargos of illegal aliens caused Critzer to be the subject of federal surveillance activities. Allegations were also made accusing the German immigrant of drug smuggling and spying. To top it all off, Critzer was also named the suspect in several burglary cases that had occurred in the region; gasoline and dynamite had been stolen from businesses in Banning, Garnet and Twentynine Palms.

Critzer kept a short wave radio, guns and ammunition and a supply of dynamite stored in his home under the rock, but none of these items were unusual possessions for anyone living in the desert during that time, especially when the remoteness of the area and the fact he was, after all, a miner were taken into consideration.

But with the United States now involved in World War II, the man with the German accent and his activities were thought to be too peculiar.

Several deputies from Riverside County came to pay Critzer a visit in response to fingers pointed at him regarding the stolen gasoline and dynamite. The action was performed in apparent ignorance of jurisdictional boundaries and while neglecting to pay the professional courtesy of notifying local authorities.

There are several variations of the story of exactly what happened at Giant Rock that day; some say Critzer declared he would not be taken from his home under the rock and when deputies entered the cave, he blew himself to smithereens. Others say when Critzer refused to come out, one of the deputies tossed in a canister of tear gas which detonated the ammunition and most of the dynamite.

In 1947, George Van Tassel moved with his wife and three daughters to the remote desert site where he had visited his friend Critzer. During the previous 27 years, Van Tassel had been employed by Lockheed as a flight test engineer, as well as by the legendary Howard Hughes whose eccentricities included an obsession with the physics of flight and its inherent possibilities.

According to stories about the aeronautic engineer, weekly meditation sessions began at Giant Rock in 1953 which, Van Tassel claimed, eventually led to UFO contacts. He later founded the scientific/philosophical organization known as the Ministry of Universal Wisdom "for the purpose of research into the unseen truths of life."

The same year the weekly meetings began also saw the first of what would become an annual event attended by upwards of 10,000 people who came to hear Van Tassel and other noted speakers, as well as with hopes of sighting a UFO—and maybe even the universal explorers inside.

During those early years of the conventions, this tiny spot on the edge of the Mojave Desert was not the only place believed to attract Martians, Venusians and others from as far as the Persies cluster; there was quite a flap across the entire nation concerning UFO phenomena.

Archaeologist George Hunt Williamson was among the notable speakers who lent credibility to the concept that Earth was visited frequently by extraterrestrial beings.

The last UFO convention at Giant Rock took place in the early 1970s when the crowds began to shrink and fights became common.

Ray Pessa, a resident here since boyhood, said he recalls the end of the notorious gatherings ordered by authorities when a fight resulted in a fatal stabbing.

Most of Pessa's memories regarding the UFO conventions are fond ones.

"I remember Van Tassel had some pretty interesting people come out there to speak," he said. "They were scientists and some of them were pretty high up in their field, pretty well respected.

"Everybody would be walking around and talking about going on the spaceships and how they talked to the aliens—and there were a whole lot of people at some of these things," Pessa said, showing surprise to this day at the event's popularity.

"I was maybe around 10 years old when we went to the first one; I went probably four times," he recalled. "It was a lot of fun."

Pessa grinned as one particularly vivid memory appeared in his mind's eye.

"People would dress up—there was these guys, three or four of them, who painted themselves green all over and ran around naked. It actually took awhile for anyone to notice!"

*From Michele Pinney. "From Outer Space to Giant Rock." *Hi-Desert Star* [Yucca Valley, California], August 2, 2000: A: 6. Reprinted by permission of the *Hi-Desert Star*.

Bigfoot on the Mojave
(2001)

Every region of the country needs its Yeti, its Sasquatch, its Bigfoot. If we hold anything in common with humanity, we are, after all, dreaming animals. Our children deserve the right to colorful (if sometimes frightening) nighttime imaginings, and we the possibility, while listening keenly as we lie awake far off in the desert in our sleeping bags, of hearing the pained, otherworldly howl of a lost soul.

All the more appropriate out in the Mojave, land of so many lost souls, that, resembling some of the more human residents of the region, Yucca Man wanders about in his sad state, hairy, unwashed, smelling like a barn.

I think that, in the panic that can creep up and overwhelm one camped alone late at night far out in the land of weird Joshua trees, once I saw Yucca Man. Starting awake for no apparent reason, I saw a huge, monstrous lunatic towering over me, his scraggly arms clawing at the air like those of the damned.

Yet I prefer, when thinking about the Mojave, a different version I heard of this unfortunate creature: that, despite his life of torture, sometimes he runs on his huge, splayed feet willy-nilly over the moonlit lava landscape shouting "Wahooo! Wahooo!"—out of the sheer exuberance of being alive.

❧

IF YOU'RE NEW TO PALM SPRINGS, you will want to be apprized of the few hazards that exist in this otherwise halcyon land. First, don't drive your golf cart into the washes during a heavy rain, in case of a flash flood. Don't leave one of those cardboard sunshades unfolded in your car; it may take flight when you open the windows in transit.

Oh, and, beware of Yucca Man.

Greg Mendoza, owner of Superior Automotive in Twentynine Palms, was hiking in the Indian Cove region of Joshua Tree National Park a decade ago when he came upon a set of massive footprints. The human-like toes were big and splayed, suggesting a powerful and mysterious hominid that used its toes for grip.

The find seemed to be evidence of stories Mendoza had heard since he was a child, stories of a woolly monster-man living in the park. As the tale goes, human parents gave birth to a beastly baby and decided to drive him out to the weird-looking territory of Joshua Tree, far from the reach of tabloid reporters.

The couple dropped the infant off and sped away, assuming whatever demons the baby was incubating would never survive to cause trouble. But the shaggy outcast managed to thrive, with the help of a surrogate coyote family.

When the wild child grew into Yucca Man, park visitors began to report sightings of strange footprints, along with glimpses of a huge, hairy man with an awful barnyard stench. (One local skeptic, a woman, says: "There are plenty of unshaven, unwashed, overweight men living in the 'Morongo Triangle' who fit this description.")

Though most of the reports came from Joshua Tree, Yucca Man apparently has been sighted everywhere from Idyllwild to Borrego Springs, Palm Springs to Desert Hot Springs. Don't assume your country club is safe.

Yucca Man ambulates with a rolling, slump-shouldered gait, but he isn't half-bear, or a descendent of giant apes, like his cousins the Yeti and Sasquatch. Because his skin is tender like yours and mine, he appears scarred and crosshatched due to thousands of encounters with sharp granite and cholla spikes.

His reported hangout is the Wonderland of Rocks area of Joshua Tree, a confusing maze full of perfect hiding places. Even experienced hikers tend to get lost there. When a cave containing half-eaten bones was found in the Wonderland of Rocks a few years ago, some people assumed it had to be Yucca Man's den.

Greg Mendoza has done his part to increase Yucca Man's renown; he regularly tells the story to groups of visiting foreign exchange students— who then take tales of Yucca Man back home to Germany and France. Yet, despite all the free PR work, Mendoza admits he doesn't exactly believe in the Yucca dude. "I've always liked a good scary story," he says.

If you want to talk to a believer, that would be Joan Jackson, a former volunteer at Joshua Tree National Park. Jackson was on duty at a park entrance station on two different occasions in the late 1980s, when panicked visitors reported sighting "a furry-type character with a terrible odor."

A man and his son made the first sighting in Indian Cove, says Jackson, who has lived in the area for more than 50 years. The second sighting involved a park employee, who was able to watch the creature through binoculars as it investigated the water tank in Black Rock Canyon.

The official word: Park Superintendent Ernie Quintana says he's not aware of these sightings and adds there is no secret file on Yucca Man tucked away in park headquarters. Because he grew up in the area, Quintana has heard of Yucca Man, of course. But with a "just the facts" tone he insists: "I don't lend any weight to it at all. It's just a bit of local charm along the lines of Big Foot and the Loch Ness Monster."

But Joan Jackson says she will never forget the faces of those who reported the sightings: "They were really shook." Clearly, they had seen firsthand something they couldn't explain. "They believe it. They believe what they saw," Jackson says. "I personally believe it too. When I'm out hiking, I keep my eyes open."

*From Ann Japenga. "Yucca Man." *Palm Springs Life* 43.9 (May 2001): 46. Copyright © Ann Japenga. Reprinted by permission of the author.

About the Editor

P ETER WILD was born in Northampton, Massachusetts, in 1940. He received B.A. and M.A. degrees in English from the University of Arizona and completed an M.F.A. in creative writing at the University of California, Irvine. He is one of the foremost poets of the American West, has published numerous articles in such publications as the *New York Times, Sierra, Smithsonian,* and *Western American Literature*, and is the author and editor of more than forty books, among them *The Opal Desert: Explorations of Fantasy and Reality in the American Southwest* (Texas, 1999), *Daggett: Life in a Mojave Frontier Town* (Johns Hopkins, 1997), *The Desert Reader: Descriptions of America's Arid Regions* (Utah, 1991), *The Sauaro Forest* (Northland, 1986), and *Chihuahua* (Doubleday, 1976). He was nominated for the Pulitzer Prize in 1973 and in 1991 received first prize in poetry from the *New Mexico Humanities Review*. Wild has taught at the University of Arizona since 1971, and he became full professor of English in 1979. He resides in Tucson.

CENTER FOR AMERICAN PLACES

The Center for American Places is a tax-exempt 501(c)(3) nonprofit organization, founded in 1990, whose educational mission is to enhance the public's understanding of, appreciation for, and affection for the natural and built environment. Underpinning this mission is the belief that books provide an indispensible foundation for comprehending–and caring for–the places where we live, work, and explore. Books live. Books endure. Books make a difference. Books are gifts to civilization.

With offices in New Mexico and Virginia, Center editors bring to publication 20–25 books per year under the Center's own imprint or in association with publishing partners. The Center is also engaged in numerous other programs that emphasize the interpretation of *landscape* and *place* through art, literature, scholarship, field research, and exhibitions. The Center's Cotton Mather Library in Arthur, Nebraska, its Martha A. Strawn Photographic Library in Davidson, North Carolina, and a ten-acre reserve along the Santa Fe River in Florida are available as retreats upon request. The Center is also affiliated with the Rocky Mountain Land Library in Colorado.

The Center strives every day to make a difference through books, research, and education. For more information, please send inquiries to P.O. Box 23225, Santa Fe, NM 87502, U.S.A., or visit the Center's Website (www.americanplaces.org).

ABOUT THE BOOK:

The text for *True Tales of the Mojave Desert: From Talking Rocks to Yucca Man* was set in Stempel Garamond with Gill Sans display. The paper for the text is acid-free 140 gsm Wood Free and for the gallery 157 gsm Gloss. The book was printed in Hong Kong through Global Ink, Inc.

FOR THE CENTER FOR AMERICAN PLACES:

George F. Thompson, president and publisher
Randall B. Jones, associate editorial director
Lauren A. Marcum and Kendall B. McGhee, editorial assistants
Judith Rudnicki, of Skyboat Road Company, Inc., manuscript editor
David Skolkin, book designer and art director
David Keck, of Global Ink, Inc., production coordinator